"This is a book by
awakening being - who brir
those with troubled hearts
become what he calls myo
shining with simple faith." ,
"there is no reason not to be loving, compassionate and wise."
Instead of our living within fear and the narrow specificity of
hate, David Brazier presents us with a way to grasp and
experience the vastness of love."

~ Rev. Saigyo Terrance Keenan, author of *St. Nadie in
Winter: Zen Encounters with Loneliness*

"Engaged Buddhism is one of the movements that is key to the
interdependent transformation of consciousness and society on
which the survival of our species and the development of an
enlightened society depends. David Brazier is an important
agent and catalyzer of that movement. Let us profit from his
contribution to the transformation in question."

~ Elías Capriles, author of *The Beyond Mind Papers:
Transpersonal and Metatranspersonal Theory*

Things blowing into
our lives are all blessings /

DB

"David Brazier is a lucid and brilliant writer. This book offers a generous selection of poignant observations about our lives, guiding us as a friend would to live with greater vibrancy, wholeness, and humility. Filled with profound and practical gems of wisdom, Brazier shows how the path toward liberation involves fully embracing our humanness rather than futilely trying to transcend it. Reading this book will help you feel more comfortable with your humanity in a way that will further genuine spiritual growth. One of the clearest books I've seen on the importance of integrating our humanity with our spiritual practice."

~ John Amodeo, author of *Dancing with Fire: A Mindful Way to Loving Relationships* and *Love & Betrayal*

"In this book David Brazier shows an extra-ordinary, even mysterious, ability to re-discover both the meanings of Buddhist teachings and the inner drivers of our feelings and demeanours. He gently takes the reader by hand on a fascinating voyage, supported by a secure knowledge base and a close intimacy with human experience. Reading *Not Everything is Impermanent* is a challenge to common mind-sets and emotional dispositions concerning the Sacred, spirituality, love and many other aspects of our inner life. The end of the voyage culminates with the sensation of a refreshment of heart and mind, tempting the reader to start the voyage again as a lonely traveller who has had wonderful experiences with a long-eyed guide."

~ Massimo Tomassini, Mindfulness Trainer at the Pundarika centre

Not Everything is Impermanent

Zen Therapy & Amidist Teachings
of David Brazier

For Julius, good friend

Namo Amida Bu

David Brazier

Dharmavidya

Woodsmoke Press

Not Everything is Impermanent
ISBN 978-0-9571584-4-3

Published by Woodsmoke Press 2013
Copyright © 2013 David Brazier

Cover painting by Maitrisimha Leo Kouwenhoven

Woodsmoke Press
37 Clerkenwell Crescent
Malvern
WR14 2TX

kaspa@woodsmokepress.com
www.woodsmokepress.com

CONTENTS

PART ONE: BETWEEN HEAVEN & EARTH

PART TWO: LOVE & LIBERATION

PART THREE: ENGAGEMENT WITH CULTURE

PART FOUR: BODHISATTVA PATH

Acknowledgements

This book is the product of many years of reflection and study. The full list of people to acknowledge would, therefore, run into thousands. It would certainly include my mother who taught me poetry and unconditional love and my father who taught me resilience and common sense, my many spiritual teachers and especially, in chronological order, Nai Boonman, Chogyam Trungpa, Kennett Roshi, Thich Nhat Hanh, and Gisho Saiko among others, my philosopher friend Mary Midgley, those who taught me social work and psychotherapy, especially Marigold McLaren, Anne Trembath, Jenny Biancardi, Carl Rogers, Elaine Sachnoff, and John McLeod, many people in the world of humanistic and transpersonal psychology, those who have recently joined me in establishing the Instituto Terapia Zen Internacional, my close disciples with whom I have shared this journey amongst whom it would be invidious to select some and omit others, all my lovely students in many parts of the world whose questions and experiences have challenged and inspired me so often, innumerable companions, sangha members and friends in the Dharma in many parts of the world. The idea for this book arose out of the efforts of Shantikara Acquaro and Mat Osmond to gather together my teachings and of Satya Robyn and Kaspalita Thompson to turn them into a book. I am grateful to them all and to many many more.

Dharmavidya David Brazier
April, 2013

This book is dedicated to the memory of Gisho Saiko
Sensei and the job he asked me to do

Not Everything is Impermanent

Zen Therapy & Amidist Teachings
of David Brazier

PART ONE: BETWEEN HEAVEN & EARTH

The Path is the Goal

The goal is not how to escape from suffering, but how to live in an honourable way.

Some years ago I wrote a book called The Feeling Buddha. It has been, along with Zen Therapy, one of my two most popular books. In The Feeling Buddha I proposed a new way to interpret the basic teaching of Buddha that is traditionally called the Four Noble Truths. The classic interpretation is that Buddha taught that all suffering arises from desire, that desire can be overcome and that the path leading to the end of desire is that called the Noble Eightfold Path, namely right view, right thought, right speech, right action, right livelihood, right effort, right mindfulness, and right meditation.

My suggestion was that Buddha was not overly concerned about ending all suffering. Buddha seems to accept that some suffering is part of life. However, when we suffer, feelings are aroused and these often lead us to act unwisely. I suggested that Buddha was very much concerned to help us avoid acting unwisely. Furthermore, the Eightfold Path cannot really be a path to something else because it is itself a description of the perfect life, it is the goal.

If we take this view then we can completely reframe the four noble truths and read them in the following way:

1. Life inevitably involves affliction; 2. With affliction come powerful feelings that can lead us astray; 3. We do however have choice in this matter and 4. If we choose wisely we shall find ourselves upon the Eightfold Path. I also noted that the word that is commonly translated as "right" in relation to the eightfold path can also be rendered "wholehearted". So choosing wisely when in situations of difficulty results in a wholehearted way of life. Many people have found this re-interpretation useful and inspiring.

The Eightfold Path is what Buddha discovered. He did not get to enlightenment by following it, he found it by getting enlightened. The Eightfold Path is a description of the lives of enlightened people, lives that are wholehearted. It is a description of a noble life and a noble life is not one that shrinks before suffering. To avoid suffering is hardly a nobler goal than the life described in the Eightfold Path. A means to a spiritual end can hardly be something that is itself more noble than the end. That would amount to saying that if you live a perfect life you may succeed in arriving at a mediocre end, which hardly makes any sense.

No, I think that the basic message is that if you handle the afflictions that inevitably occur in a wise and compassionate manner, you will find yourself to be on a path of spiritual fulfilment, free of inner conflict. Doesn't that make sense?

As I say, many have found this message a valuable gateway. It is realistic. I do not think that it is possible to eliminate all suffering, nor do I think it is possible to eliminate all desire, nor do I think that doing either of these things would be a good idea even if they were possible.

Of course, I cannot know for sure whether my interpretation is right. Buddha is not around for us to ask him what exactly he did mean. Nonetheless, I think that my interpretation is in keeping with other things he said and with the general tenor of his teaching. Buddha was not the sort of chap to run away from a bit of hardship and he was passionate about people learning to live their lives in a noble manner. I am too.

So it is my intention to keep developing the philosophy proposed in *The Feeling Buddha*. If it is what Buddha intended, all well and good. If I am mistaken in that regard then Buddha and I perhaps part company. I'm fairly confident, however, that I am right, at least in the broad outline of what I have suggested. Nonetheless, it is also part of the noble life to go on and on learning, so, who knows, I might still be persuaded that there is an even deeper interpretation just waiting to be uncovered.

In fact I have added a few nuances since I wrote the book. I discovered, by attending a conference of language scholars, that "Four Truths for Noble Ones" might well be a better rendering than "Four Noble Truths". This change, I realised, actually adds strength to my original argument. If these are four truths for noble ones then the first one, which is affliction, *dukkha*, is a truth for noble ones, which suggests that becoming a noble one is not actually a matter of getting rid of dukkha as the traditional commentaries suggest. This is just common sense, isn't it? Isn't nobility about taking affliction in a certain way, rather than avoiding it?

I also realised that since etymologically duk-kha means a dark space, it makes sense to think what we mean when we say, metaphorically, that we are in a dark place.

We mean that we are in a place where we are gloomy, where our thoughts might let us down, where we might do something that is less than noble. Buddha was certainly capable of seeing life as a venture in which there are spiritual dangers. If we take dukkha to mean those times when we are in spiritual danger, then we can certainly see the second and third truths as how we get out of that danger, or how we transform that gloomy dangerous place into one of wholeheartedness. All in all, therefore, I am still inclined to think that the re-interpretation offered in *The Feeling Buddha* is a good way to construe the Buddha's meaning and that the goal is not how to escape from suffering, but how to live in an honourable way.

4

To Enter One Must Become Foolish

The most perfect thing is on the verge of disaster and the most sullied can be the most fertile.

There is cause and there is effect, but we seldom see them clearly. Reliance upon cause and effect liberates, yet requires deep faith when the false prosper and the good must retire. One extreme is to become angry about the bad things in the world and do one's work drawing on that angry energy. Another extreme is to become cynical and feel that there is no point in doing anything. Neither of these is noble.

I was discussing recently a variety of problems to do with ecology. There can be little doubt that humans are doing a good deal of damage to the natural world and the consequences can be extremely serious. This is an instance of cause and effect. "Doesn't it make you angry?" my friend asked. I realised that it doesn't. I can see that humans are in many ways a blight and that I am one of them, but getting angry is not going to change this. "Whether we are in heaven or in hell, our duty is always much the same," I said.

I guess that we become angry when we take something personally and when our identity and values are at stake. In situations of this kind I can see, to more or less the same extent as others can, what needs doing, but it does not touch my personal being in a way that would make me angry, because I know that I am as much a culprit as anybody else.

In order to cultivate the sublime we have to encounter the truth of our selves, which is at first deeply troubling. We are not the perfect beings that we would like to think we are. Even when we discern some way in which we could improve we are often very weak willed in bringing the change into effect. We easily persuade ourselves in the short run to do what we have already decided is, in the longer run, bad for us or others. Actually, we are more likely to succumb if we just think that it is bad for ourselves and somewhat more likely to make the change for the sake of others, but either way we are far from perfect.

It is the function of the mind to perceive the universe in each annoying grain of sand. Only by working with their irritating nature are pearls made. Our lives pivot around crucial intuitions without which we would not be the spiritual beings that we are, but one must soften the glare of wary consciousness to appreciate them. The attempt to deny them only stunts the mind and inhibits its true activity. It is not that we are restored to wholeness, it is that by perceiving our brokenness truly we open the doors to a realm in which broken creatures such as ourselves are the inheritors of heaven and earth. When the ego lies in fragments, indescribable marvels parade before us.

Nor is common knowledge much of a guide. What everybody thinks wise is foolish. What everybody thinks beautiful is trivial art. What everybody assumes to be so is a good place to start asking penetrating questions. The urge to fit in is the source of deception and the urge to stand out, of hypocrisy. Few can be true to the truth and those who do find it risky to utter a word. The teacher seldom gives lectures, but if you can walk in your own moccasins a mile with him you will see the open sky. He has a gentle will. He has a relaxed mind. He can fight a battle if he has to, but does not relish it.

He can cut cane to make a house and dance for joy, yet grieves for the canes he cuts. When young Siddhartha saw the body of Mother Earth cut open by the plough and its denizens devoured by birds he took his first step to true enlightenment.

There is truth beyond human affairs that can yet be the reliable foundation for them. There are paths in what seems wilderness where one can learn ancestral songs. To enter one must become foolish and a bit of a child. Pay the rent and do not make a show of strangeness, but even while rendering unto Caesar turn your mind to God and call a holy name.

The sublime is an inexhaustible source encompassing terror and ecstasy when necessary, yet it is at home in silence and stillness, having no sharp edges. It does not jump out but blends in and most never notice it. There is nowhere where you are beyond its comfort, yet it is also, in a sense, ruthless. Truth is true whether we like it or not. The world is not the projection of our mind, we are the projection of its.

The description of spirituality requires a vehicle or language, a system of concepts and ideas, but these always fall short. Hence simplicity seems complex and straight-forwardness paradoxical. Words can make a map, they are not the territory. Not even a map, they are signposts and some of the destinations may be remote. Other signs might also serve. Signs are, however, useful, though the maps we draw from them are perforce sketchy. If you are alone in a strange city a map is handy, but it is much easier to accompany a local.

The collection of gleanings that I have accumulated over the years has come to be called by the makeshift term, Zen Therapy. It is located somewhere between the two East Asian systems called Amidism and Taoism and the Western ones called psychology and philosophy. It is the cultivation of wholeness. It is a way of liberation through truth, truth which is often difficult and uncomfortable, and is certainly not simply a matter of living to a formula. Rather it is an art drawn from nature who knows better than we do, yet not only from the nature that is close at hand, but Great Nature that is the profound backdrop to all the activity of our mind.

Amidism is the intuition of compassion at work in the world and of the renewal that lies beyond all endings, Tao the intuition of wisdom interwoven with the fabric of things, functioning through the interplay of opposites, Zen a path of personal cultivation rooted in silence and stillness, and Therapy a form of spiritual accompaniment. Since shamans in earliest times began to journey beyond the limited self, ever new paths of cultivation have been emerging. We too shall find new ways. Zen Therapy is not, nor will it ever be, a finished system. It is an ever growing synergism of methods that draw their efficacy from the intuition of a wholeness that transcends the ego. It has many gates.

This book is a collection of essays. The collection has been revised, but not so completely as to eliminate the disparate origins of its parts. They hint at a path of spiritual cultivation that transcends particular religions, that must be explored by each for him or herself, but which does not require that such exploration be a lonely and unaided stumbling in the total dark. We can learn from our forebears and do well to honour them and we can help one another. Such helping, together with its obstacles and disappointments, is itself one way of understanding the nature of the path.

The limited capacity of human understanding is not just a restriction on what we can say, it is also a foundational principle. This is a description of a practical approach to spiritual cultivation from the perspective of the ordinary person, living in this wonderful world, yet beset with all the worries, limitations, pressures, responsibilities and irrationality that most of us have. It is not a presentation from the perspective of absolute truth or ultimate accomplishment. It is not a counsel of perfection and it is not intended to make anybody feel guilty for not being enlightened. One of its fundamental messages is that it is our very misdemeanours that are the seeds for future growth.

Many people are allergic to the idea of religion because they associate it with restriction and the imposition of a sense of guilt. In my view that is the corruption of true religion. True religion would be a re-linking to the source of spirit. It is actually the secular world that makes unreasonable demands upon us and drives us to distraction. It is the place of true religion to provide a refuge where our natural energy may be restored, rekindled, and ultimately resublimated into what is truly sublime, or, at least, into the best approximation that we are capable of at whatever level of spiritual development we happen to be at the time.

This way of cultivation is for people like you and I. All systems of spirituality are made by people, for people and they have the same limitations and faults that people have, but they can indicate a life oriented to something beyond these limitations, not so much as a goal to be attained, as a dimension of reality to be appreciated and related to through all the vicissitudes of real life, as a reliable refuge.

I will talk of Spirit. This is again hardly definable, but the spiritual sense is the general term for the intuition that we have of a greater, meaningful whole. There are levels: we can speak of the spirit in which an act is performed or of the spirit of our times or of ultimate spirit that is like the pole star of all human endeavour. If you are allergic to spiritual language, this is not a book for you. Here the divine is on every page and the greater dimensions of things open in all directions.

I will talk of Buddhism, but this is not Buddhism as opposed to other religions so much as Buddhism as a waking up to universal truths. The essential insights of Buddha and Jesus seem to me to have been pretty much the same. We are not required to imitate either of them, but to each of us individually and all of us collectively find our own way, yet when we do so I strongly suspect that we shall find ourselves in agreement with them on essentials.

As sentient beings we do not just intuit the Whole in the abstract, though that is important, we also experience ourselves in relation to it and this relationship is personal. There are both abstract and personal dimensions to the spiritual sense and both are important. When we contemplate, we may contemplate either or both. When we accompany, we do so within a sense of a greater spiritual whole that seems vast, yet also with a sense of help being intimately close at hand.

This is not really a path with a goal or end. Cultivation continues. The goal is to be on the path. Eternity is reflected in each moment, the ultimate in each particular, but the wholesome life is appreciative of change and realises that the most perfect thing is on the verge of disaster and the most sullied can be the most fertile. All things have a tendency to change into their opposites and those who understand this cultivate in a way that holds to the middle without rejecting the extremes totally.

An Honourable Life

People do not generally make supreme efforts on their own behalf. They do it for others.

So the question that then comes up is, what do we mean by a noble or honourable life? Here the conclusions that I have arrived at suggest that a number of qualities are crucially important. I would like to highlight honesty, selflessness, humility and gratitude. I would like to say a little about each of these.

First, however, I would like to say that the Buddha also has a list. Actually, he has many lists, but the best known one is love, compassion, sympathy and equanimity. Now in this I do not disagree with him at all. I think these two lists are simply two different ways of saying the same thing. At the core of all is love. Nobility is to have the courage of love. Love and compassion naturally go together, one being to wish others good things and the other being to wish them relief from bad things. These together constitute sympathy, but sympathy needs to be stabilised by equanimity which is the resilience to take the rough with the smooth. Although a noble person always strives for the best, he or she has to cope with the fact that the best cannot always be attained. Bad things still happen.

Here in this world we all try to love, but love always runs into difficulties and sometimes we are defeated by them. It takes courage to love again and to go on loving in the face of defeat, rejection or betrayal. Nonetheless, that is what nobility requires.

So this takes me back to my own list of key qualities. Firstly honesty. It seems to me that it is exceedingly difficult for us to be deeply honest. We have such depths of complicated motivations that we do not know ourselves very well. When we look closely we find all kinds of contradictions in our make-up. Also, we feel under a continual social pressure. Nobody really wants us to be totally honest. They actually want us to be supportive, sensitive, and conformist, but not honest. So in order to live in society we do well to dissemble about all manner of things. While we become very skilled at playing the social game, our spiritual life asks us to nonetheless preserve some space where we can be as completely honest as we are capable of being. This is an area where we can help one another. We all need a confidante or confessor who will listen and not judge us. Such wise counsellors are few and far between, even among those who have been trained in counselling or psychotherapy or pastoral care. Creating safe spaces where deeper honesty is possible is one of the things that a spiritual community should always work on.

Secondly, selflessness. To be truly selfless is even more difficult than to be truly honest. Of course, there are innumerable social situations where we do put others before ourselves in practical ways and this is good. This is part of the development of civilisation. True selflessness, however, goes much deeper than good manners. The noble person does the right thing whether it serves their own personal interests or not. For the truly honourable person it does not really matter whether they are in heaven or in hell, they still act in the same spirit. In an important sense, we are always in heaven and always also in hell. There is, however, also a deeper understanding. The truly noble person actually never acts against his own interests because he sees deeply enough to know that "the right thing" is never at odd with his ultimate spiritual well-being. This is what living a spiritual life implies.

Then thirdly, humility. This is the saving grace of all graces. Humility begins, perhaps, with the realisation that we are not always completely honest and certainly not always selfless. We are human and humans are rather cunning, destructive animals. We can also be timid, ashamed, anxious, and querulous, not to mention our propensities toward greed, slander, envy and jealousy. One could go on and make a long list. Of course, the noble person does overcome some of these foibles, but desire does not lie down and die until we do and there is no likelihood that we shall eliminate all sin this side of the grave.

So if perfection is not attainable, what is the noble life that Buddha is talking about? I do not think that we should imagine that there is a state or status that we can reach in which greed, hate and delusion will never arise. Rather, I think the Buddha is talking about how to handle the situation when they do. When things go wrong, that is the time when enlightenment is possible. It is exactly when primitive feelings bubble up that we have at hand the energy to take a further step toward spiritual liberation. Each time we do so we over-turn a thousand years of bad karma at least.

How can we do so? Paradoxically, not really by our own power. What lifts us at such times is whatever inspires us. It comes like a voice out of the future. We shall only change our ways in order to create a better future for those or that which we love. We shall not do it for ourselves. Self-help books can reiterate that "You are worth it", "Take care of yourself", "Do it for yourself" and so on endlessly, but people do not generally make supreme efforts on their own behalf. They do it for others, or for something other, and they do it for the future. Ensuring the better future of others is what we mean by love.

Noble ones are those who live their love and, in the process, learn what they need to learn and overcome whatever it is in themselves that they have to overcome. In this they are certainly helped. When one looks at a noble person, one might think of them as self-reliant, but they themselves do not feel like that. They themselves are likely to be much more conscious of all the help they have received. Some of this help seems to be the work of providence, the experiences they have confronted in life, and some of it has come through encounters with, or the examples provided by, other people. Nobility starts with gratitude for all this. That is what supports a humble attitude which then erodes self-centredness. So the honourable life is one that is constantly evolving between the poles of gratitude and honesty.

Here to Strive

The middle path is not simply the avoidance of the extremes, but rather a way of encompassing them.

"Decay is inherent in all compounded things. Strive on with diligence." These were the last words of Buddha. The image of Buddhism has gone through quite a lot of change over the years. Nowadays people don't tend to associate Buddhism with striving so much as with peace and withdrawal, with being rather than doing. Whatever would old Shakyamuni think of that?

Buddha pointed out that things are impermanent and you might take it from that that he was suggesting that it is futile wasting effort on things that are not going to last. However, the original moral was probably just the opposite. Buddha put a new spin on the idea of karma, remember. Karma had been taken to mean that you are what you are because of what you did in your last life so there is nothing you can do about it. This logic underpinned the caste system and it still does. This was a story about how nothing changes. Buddha came along and said that actually karma is about change; that it is about the fact that if you want to do something about the caste system or anything else that you think is less than honourable, then you can. Striving would be pointless if things were permanent. Impermanence gives the possibility of freedom and emancipation and makes striving worthwhile.

It was this message that made Buddhism popular with the socially mobile classes of merchants, tradesmen and warriors, and it was the fact that such people travelled that took Buddhism all over Asia. It is this message that still makes Buddhism a beacon of hope for millions of Dalits in India, the poor who seek release. As far as Buddha was concerned a person is not what they were born as, a person is what they do. A noble person is one who acts nobly. A base person is one who acts basely. Buddha was pretty down to earth.

Peace is blessed, but mere quietude does not serve forever. When we are having a stressful time we crave for peace. In that peace the many different voices in our brain that have been clamouring calm down, the log jam eases. However, this is primarily so that they can now flow more readily. The peace we seek is a respite, not a destination. It is an aid to more effective forward movement. Life is struggle and it should be. A day without striving would be a wasted day, but stress overload is a common problem these days. One of the reasons that we suffer so much from stress nowadays is that in our complex society it is difficult to see the real outcome of our work. Stress is eased by seeing the bigger picture. Another reason, however, is that we do not value striving itself. A certain amount of stress is a good thing. A third reason is that there are real conflicts of interest in this world and sometimes we face invidious choices: to help one person we will harm another, or we face several options all of which involve disadvantages, or there are several good opportunities but no time in which to do them all so some will have to be sacrificed. To cause pain to others will never be noble even though it is often unavoidable and may even serve a higher goal that is noble. Even in the cause of nobility one will sometimes have to do ignoble things.

Buddha saw that if we are lost in action it will sooner or later all start to feel pointless, but if we are lost in higher meanings we shall not be much use to anybody. There is a middle path that is not simply the avoidance of the extremes, but rather a way of encompassing them: being angels as well as animals, rather than suppressing one or the other, recognising the whole truth about ourselves and our world, not just the nice bits or just the horrible ones.

"Here born we clutch at things and then compound delusion by following ideals", says the Chinese poet author of the text Sandokai. Let us therefore reflect upon being here as the kind of creatures that we actually are, living in the midst of these vicissitudes, and let us try to discern some of the constancies that can liberate us and give significance and direction to our deeds. Though we are but waves of short duration, the truth will set us free so long as we act on it. Above all, the truth about ourselves, however unflattering it at first appears, will ultimately free us if we can only take it seriously. Riding our wave and experiencing our undertow, again and again, let us find what it is in our life that really inspires us. We each have a place and a role in a greater whole and we should not give up just because we are not the author of the drama that we are playing our part in.

Two Approaches to Religion

A person of faith is a member of all religions.

Liberation or Convention

I do not think that it is possible for us to have a final and definitive text on spirituality. We should not think of such texts as final or indisputable. We must proceed with sensitivity and intelligence and recognise both our limitations and the paradoxical complexity of the human situation. Spirituality is the human calling toward a sublimity beyond what our human capacity can grasp in words, but it is the journey, not the arrival. Even when one is inspired by the most perfect source, the medium of transmission is still human. People argue about whether the Bible or the Koran or the Bhagavad Gita is the ultimate holy book, but even if these books were inspired by God they were still written by humans, about humans, for humans, in human language and figures of speech, each belonging to a particular point in history. However, just because we have no perfect guidance it does not follow that one should do nothing. We each have to walk our path by the best lights we can find and we may sometimes find them in unlikely places.

Furthermore, we have to do so as the people we are. To live a spiritual life is to rise above our nature while still knowing our nature and respecting it. The human project is to go beyond what we are naturally given. Thought of the sublime can quickly make us ashamed of ourselves, yet it is only we ourselves as we are who can tread this path.

Nature cares little for us as individuals. Nature proceeds by over-production and ruthless selection. We, on the other hand, would have it that every human life is sacred. We would rise to a higher level, beyond cannibalism, beyond slavery, beyond war. We would build civilisation and be civilised, yet we are creatures evolved for fight and flight. We would transform nature into spirit, or raise nature to a spiritual level. Always there is the danger of falling back into our own inchoate depths and this danger is greater when we lose awareness of it. Pride comes before a fall.

The matter is not simple. Take, for instance, the fact that our great and noble civilising project frequently requires us to dissemble. As ordinary people we are accustomed to living in the midst of social conventions that require us to tell half truths and, sometimes, to hide the truth entirely. We do not want to embarrass others, nor to be embarrassed ourselves, so we avoid uncomfortable details. All respectable people are consummate liars and often with the best of intentions.

What should spiritual people do? Ideally, we might think that they should follow social convention in many ordinary situations, yet not deceive themselves. They should have the ability to flout convention if it clashes with higher considerations of love, compassion or wisdom. This is not an easy ideal to sustain consistently. As a result, many people are really attempting the impossible, trying to be always socially approved of, to always act in accord with high principles (which often clash with each other), and not hurt anybody's feelings in the process. We want to be good and we like our goodness to be acknowledged. We may even tend to equate spirituality with morality and see religion as being about inducing or coercing good behaviour. True spirituality, however, is not about conformity, but about making more honest choices.

The way spirituality is written about here, it is about liberation. There are quite different ways to be religious or spiritual and spirituality as liberation is not at all the same thing as spirituality as respectability, for instance. In conventional religion, the religious dogma reifies social realities. I want to explain what this means. Take, for instance, the idea of God as the creator. One way to view God as the creator is to see all creativity as divine. Whatever is new and spontaneous is then God at work. One person may understand God the creator in this way and be inspired, say, to become a creative artist so that he can be a channel for God's creative energy. Such a person may live a quite unconventional life. Another person may take the idea of God the creator as meaning that God created the social order with everybody in their proper place. Since it was created by God, that order must now be regarded as immutable. Nothing must be changed and everybody should know how to perform their role properly in order to glorify God. We can see that these two interpretations of the same spiritual idea – that of God as creator – produce totally different approaches to life. The two sound the same, but actually are poles apart in real meaning and consequence. Of course the converse is also possible. In the domain of spirituality, there can be people who seem to hold extremely different beliefs who nonetheless actually practise in a very similar way.

I want to try to present spirituality here as a path of liberation because it has been so for me. One should be immediately warned, however, that this path is a mixed blessing. What I have found over the years is that I have arrived at a singularly blessed life in which there is much that is enviable, but the path has by no means been straight-forward or easy and the pain involved in again and again honestly assessing one's course, realising that it is heading into yet another dead end, backing up, dismantling much of what one had constructed, and then reassembling the pieces to fit the new configuration, knowing all the time that one may well have to do this again and again, is considerable. The spiritual path can be lonely, self-defeating, and pass through periods of despair. Indeed, I think it must.

Such liberation, operating at a spiritual level, has real social and psychological consequences. It can turn one's life upside down. I have given up careers for ethical reasons, given up my home to save the lives of animals, given up relationships when they were doing more harm than good, and, even more importantly in many ways, I have had to give up my own spiritual achievements in the service of a deeper recognition of human nature. And the process is far from ended.

A spiritually liberated life comes at a price. It enables one to see through social hypocrisy, but that does not endear one to the people who practise it. Let us consider an example.

Mira of Rajasthan

Mira, the ecstatic fifteenth century devotee from Rajasthan, was, as a girl, a renowned beauty. Born in an influential family she married royalty and was all set to become queen when a series of tragedies despatched all her close relatives in a matter of months. This brought her face to face with the reality of impermanence, especially the impermanence of human pretensions. At this point she turned to God and found a guru. The guru was called Ravidas and he was a cobbler, a man of the shudra caste. Mira became devoted to him and learnt the practice of Nam, calling the holy name. From then on her upper class relatives persecuted her incessantly for associating with a lower caste man, but she persevered. The poetry that she uttered has since made her one of the most popular saints of India.

> Love me, O Beloved, I pray;
> within my temple ever stay;
> my countless faults, I beg, don't heed,
> nor my colour, caste or creed.

Mira simplified her life by devotion. Calling the name of God became her sole practice. It unified her motivation and enabled her to see through the vanities of the social system of her time. She experienced spiritual liberation. She no longer cared about status or caste. She didn't even really care which religion she belonged to – she was a person of faith and that meant she was a person of all religions. She lived for God.

What we can immediately see is that spiritual liberation and social liberation have an interesting relationship to one another. Mira, because of her spiritual liberation, saw society differently. She de-reified it. For her relatives the caste system was a reality independent of themselves, as much to be reckoned with as mountains and rivers. For Mira it was merely a man made convention, and a bad one. She saw no reason to conform to it. This resulted in her being persecuted and meeting all kinds of difficulties. She suffered, but her mind and heart remained free.

Perception and Its Concomitant Intuition

Perception of any quality includes the implicit intuition of its converse. As soon as we have a sense of good, we bring in a sense of bad. As soon as we have a sense of poverty, we bring in a sense of riches. And as soon as we see our limited, conditioned and imperfect nature, we bring in a sense of the unlimited, the unconditioned and the perfect. When Mira confronted impermanence, her husband having been cut down in battle, she intuited a greater whole – eternity – within which all loss becomes bearable. When she met local cruelty, she intuited an all-embracing love, compassion and acceptance that made life meaningful.

However, the intuited perfection, although vital to any attempt to make sense of life, is not something that we encounter empirically. What we encounter tends toward it or away from it, but never reaches such a limit. Love is the essence of life and love is not love unless it is unconditional, yet unconditional love does not exist in this world. To worship unconditional love is, nonetheless, a wholesome thing to do. The act of worship expresses deep respect while preserving distance. Preserving distance avoids hubris. To identity oneself with the divine is to invite disaster, yet to deny it is to invite worse.

Opium or Opening

So we are here looking at two diametrically opposite approaches to religion. The conventional approach is to see religion as a support for social structures. Religion is then a limitation and a confinement. Indeed, in such an approach, religion itself, which is a social structure, becomes a form of confinement. If God ordained marriage, the caste system, the "divine right" of kings, the hierarchy of the church, the roles of men and women, slavery, even, then they are unchangeable. This kind of religion cements the social structure and puts progress and reform out of reach of humans. Religion is then the opium of the people. Of course it is easy to see this when we are talking about distant times and distant countries, but we generally fail to see how we are reifying our own culture. Modern, progressive people can be just as rigid in their thinking, just as certain they are right and just as intolerant of those who disagree with them.

The liberationist approach has quite the opposite effect. Mira's love of God gave her the courage to defy criticism and the clarity to see through conventional structures. She didn't pass her life trying to fit in and do what everybody else thought was right. It was perfectly obvious to her that love was more important than convention, devotion than conformity. She adored the divine yet did not inflate her own importance in the process. She was, like Brother Lawrence, more in need of a confessor than a teacher. In the conventional approach religious people seek to feel justified and respectable. At one and the same time, their religion makes them feel important while rendering them incapable of resisting social oppression. Mira, however, was deeply conscious of her own sins and unworthiness yet did not flinch from defying convention. It was not by her own virtue and power that she was able to be strong. Her strength came

25

from her faith in a power beyond herself and beyond human society.

Sailing on a Bigger Ocean

The modern mind has become inoculated against the divine. We think we have become more advanced, but we have actually only stunted our minds.

How Do We Become Small Minded?

Many people today can read of Mira and feel admiration and envy for her faith yet think it impossible for a modern person to believe as she did or to dedicate their life in such a way. The modern mind has become inoculated against the divine. We think we have become more advanced, but we have actually only stunted our minds. To see why most of us are nowadays incapable of expanding our mind in the way that Mira could, I'd like to take you on a philosophical discursion.

We are actually just as capable of Mira's intuition as humans have ever been, but we have, understandably in modern circumstances, become mesmerised by the extremes of materialism, on the one hand, and a rather paradoxical form of dogmatism, that we do not recognise, on the other. The most difficult kind of dogma to refute is the kind that thinks itself free.

We live in a material world. The world may not be just material – it also includes energies and all manner of hidden forces, some detectable obliquely with various instruments and some existing only in the minds of mathematicians. In other words there are "the ten thousand things" as the Chinese call them, although, of course, there are many more than ten thousand. These things exist in the original sense of the word, to ex-ist, which means to stand out or to be out. They are salient. Each thing forms a figure that can catch our attention. When it does so it is what, in the ancient language of India, is called *rupa*.

Rupa originally meant something that one worships. The statue of a god is a rupa. Rupa came to mean any thing that has form that has a power over the mind. So, at a more trivial level, we can see that the smell of chocolate, or of coffee, are rupa for many people. Whatever is holding one's attention at any moment is, for that moment, rupa. The mind has grasped it and it has grasped the mind. They are in a mutual embrace.

We build our lives around rupas. Many of the most important rupas are actually abstract. Our country is an abstraction – a human convention. So is money. So is status. Others are the significant people in our life. Our parents and our children are important rupas. When we lie awake at night worrying about something, our mind is in the grip of one or more of the rupas in our life. Although a person is not an abstraction in quite the same sense as a country, still, a person is not an inanimate entity in the way that a table or a football are.

Living Beings Are Not Just Machines

Modern thinking has been much influenced by the successes of science, though in a rather naive manner. Science has achieved great success by measuring things and finding relationships among the various measurements that have enabled prediction and control of inanimate objects. Control over inanimate objects has proved very useful. However, as we have just seen, what worries people most tends not to be inanimate objects, but people and abstract social conventions.

One of the great anxieties of everybody's life is the unpredictability of one's neighbours. There is, therefore, a hunger to extend the grasp of science to the animate world. Psychology, the attempt to be scientific about people, is one result. Sociology, another. They have, however, perforce, remained imprecise sciences, which is almost a contradiction of terms. Art might be a better word. The attempt to be scientific about people is an attempt to treat persons as if they were inanimate objects. Obviously there are aspects of a person that are inanimate, like the chemical reactions that take place in one's stomach as one digests food, but, basically, a person is not inanimate, so the attempt to gain knowledge by assuming that it is is bound to have limited scope. Nonetheless, many people are now convinced that people are just sophisticated machines that are only self-deluded into thinking that they are alive.

Of course, even the people who think this suffer from the same "delusion" in regard to all their every day dealings with their family and friends. Life in a modern society can make one feel like nothing much more than a cog in a machine, but even the smallest cog in the social mechanism feels as if it is a living being making decisions and having feelings and does not consider him or herself to be a machine at all. Even the most hardened materialist cannot avoid this fundamental intuition in practice. The person next to me is alive and so am I. However, although we all know we are alive, the fact is that much contemporary thinking is shot through with an anti-vitalist way of thinking that, while it is useful in medical science, has proved extremely dangerous in politics, where scientific approaches to the management of people have often become totalitarian and cruel, and somewhat counter-productive in psychotherapy and social administration, where we have come to think that ills can be righted by finding an appropriate procedure for each that can be routinely administered. All this is closely related to a way of thinking that philosophers call positivism.

Positivism

Positivism asserts that nothing is true unless it is either something that can be empirically demonstrated or that is a tautology. A tautology is a correct logical conclusion in which all the truth in the conclusion was already implicit in the axioms. Positivists included tautology because without it one cannot have mathematics. All mathematics is tautologous. Mathematical statements derive from axioms. Euclid built up a system of geometry derived from axioms that he took to be self-evident, such as that the shortest distance between two points is a straight line. Some modern cosmologists have questioned Euclid's assumptions and talk about such things as the "curvature of space" or "worm holes" and other wonderful and fantastic notions that we do not have time to go into here. The point is that if you change the axioms you change the truth value of the whole system. So much for tautology. What about empiricism? By things being demonstrated empirically, positivists mean, firstly, that they are measurable and, secondly, that relationships between these measurements can be demonstrated in a reliable and reproducible way.

Measurement plays a key role in science and in science this is as it should be. The positivistic idea has led to the assertion that only measurable things exist.

The Limits of Science

Most people think that science proves things by evidence. Actually this is not quite right. As the philosopher Karl Popper pointed out science actually only disproves things. What is considered to be scientific "truth" is simply the sum of hypotheses that have not yet been disproved. You cannot prove that something is always the case because an exception might show up tomorrow. This is called the black swan phenomenon – all swans were thought to be white until Australia was discovered, where there are, behold, black swans. So empiricism cannot actually prove a universal law because to do so one would have had to have examined all actual examples, including ones that have not yet occurred, to ensure that there is not and can never be an exception. While science is hugely important and scientific method yields wonderful results that are immensely valuable, science has its limits. It can never prove anything finally and it cannot deal with questions of value either. Science cannot tell us if abortion is right or wrong, for instance. It can only tell us how to proceed best when we have already decided to continue or not continue the pregnancy. Testing poison gases on human subjects would be unethical, but there is no basis for calling it unscientific.

Measurable Things Do Not Exist

Many people nowadays take positivism to be as self-evident as Euclid took his axioms to be. In order to free up our thinking so that we can once again allow our minds to expand in a way that our ancestors found more natural than we do, we have, therefore, to question the dogmatic assertions of positivism. Essentially positivism suffers from three main philosophical problems. The first is as we have just seen, that it cannot cope with value questions. The second is that it fails in terms of formal logic. The assertion that "nothing is true unless it is either empirically demonstrable or a tautology" is not itself empirically demonstrable nor is it a tautology, so on its own criteria it is false. A philosophical assertion cannot stand if it denies itself. We see from this point that this foundational statement by positivists is itself simply an axiom or dogma and so the whole theory is seen to be merely an assertion and not a demonstration.

The third significant problem is to do with the question of measurement. It is not true that measurable things exist. Things that exist are not measurable. All that is measurable are abstract concepts that can be related to real things. We can measure the height of a table and compare it to the height of another table. "Height", however, is an abstraction. Height does not exist, only tables exist, and table-ness cannot be measured. Real things are not measurable. Real things simply are. We encounter them and bump into them sometimes, or use them, or eat them, or build other things with them, and for some of these purposes measurements derived from them are handy, but we cannot and do not measure the things themselves. However many measurements you take of a table you still do not have the table itself. If we can digest the fact that measurable things do not exist, but are actually conceptual abstractions useful for some purposes that nonetheless leave the real things to be what they are in themselves, we start to get a very different feel for the life that we inhabit and in which we have our living being. We also see science more accurately as a system of extremely useful abstractions. We also no longer need a two part definition such as empirical and tautologous since mathematics is also an extremely useful system of abstraction. Science and mathematics together constitute the philosophy of measurable abstractions. Measurable abstractions, however, are not the sum total of existence. There are also non-measurable abstractions and there are, very significantly, real things.

We Cannot Help Intuitions of Wholeness

There is, however, a further and crucially important point. We have been talking about things existing, or ex-ist-ing. The mind and the object grasp one another. The mind does try to get some kind of intuitive measure of the object. Abstraction is a natural function of the mind. When we see a person we are at some level processing the consideration, "What kind of person is that?" This is both useful and dehumanising. We try to reduce the other to a category about which we can say generalised things. Our minds reduce unique others to abstract concepts so that we can use past knowledge and so that we can measure. All well and good. However, the object, in ex-ist-ing, stands out from something, from a background. The very fact of grasping implies a wholeness beyond. The table exists in the context of the room, the room in the context of the building, the building of the city, the city of the world, the world of the cosmos, the cosmos of a mystery beyond our capacity to grasp.

Implicit wholeness is an unavoidable intuition, yet, this wholeness - the background - is also, and *a fortiori*, unmeasurable. If we see the thing before us as a spacial object, then it stands out from the whole of space. We cannot say that "the whole of space" does not exist. Yet the whole of space is not measurable. This also defeats the proposition of positivism. Positivism does not allow for the infinite. If something stands out as an event in time, it has a duration – a durée as the French philosopher Henri Bergson calls it – and this stands forth from the infinity of time, or eternity. The modernist way of thinking flinches from admitting eternity, which cannot be measurable, yet we cannot say that eternity does not exist. Eternity is. Yet no matter how many finite durations we add together they do not add up to eternity.

Again, space and time for all their infinite ultimacy also "stand out". What do they stand out from? We cannot say. The ultimate background is unnamable. As it says in the Taoist classic,

> The unnamable is the origin of heaven and earth
> Naming is the mother of the ten thousand things

Yet, being the creatures that we are, we cannot help attributing names to the unnamable. In the contemporary age we have access to many great spiritual traditions and in each of them we find names for the unnamable. This is good. It shows that this vital intuition is not just the clever invention or property of one group of people. It is a universal phenomenon. Humans intuit the infinite from the finite, the ultimate from the proximate, the sublime from the ordinary. We are spiritual beings through and through and we do not need to limit ourselves by cutting off our most important intuitions or building a wall of taboo against thinking of greater things.

The Ultimate is Also in the Proximate

The fact that only unmeasurable things exist means that ordinary things actually partake of exactly the same mystery as ultimate and infinite ones. The table, in and of itself, is as mysterious as infinity, or, we could say, is infinitely mysterious in its own being. It is in this immanent sense that, despite what we said earlier, ultimacy is encountered in the midst of the day to day. This is one meaning of the Buddhist teaching of *shunyata*, the "emptiness" of things. Although we try to catch things in our net of measurement, the real things always slip away through the holes in our system.

Buddhism has many words for the unnameable! It calls it the birthless and also the deathless, for instance. The infinite mystery of ordinary things is the no-birth nature of everyday life. This no-birth nature is what we call the "taste" of spirituality.

Of course, all ordinary things are born and do die. The table will one day be no more. It will have become firewood or compost. You and I will die too. Whether we live longer or the table lives longer, all die in the end. However, in its mystery, the table is not a "table" from its own side.

"Table" is a name we impose upon it. We do so for our practical purposes. Tableness is a function of our own imagination in the service of our needs and desires. So we can also ask, is it true that the table ceases? Does it cease or merely change form? And what is form except superficial appearance?

When we taste no-birth nature, are we tasting the Dharma behind the rupa? We only do so by letting go of the self that imposes "tableness" on "that" and let "that" be what it is, which is something mysterious and amazing. Subjectively this means to stand in awe before the least of things and be touched by their infinite depth, which is also no depth at all, but merely the thus-ness of things as they are, always have been and always will be.

The Meaning of the Life of Honen

In Japan there lived a sage called Honen (1133-1212). When he was a child he was present when his father was assassinated by an enemy. As his father lay dying from an arrow wound he called young Honen to him and said his last words that were to have a huge effect on the life of the boy. Honen's father told him not to seek revenge, as family honour might prescribe, but to seek for a greater truth, the *Dharma*, that might heal the conflicts of this world and save us all from war and strife.

Honen took these words to heart. He was a clever boy and his mother decided to entrust his education to the care of an uncle who was a priest at a local temple. The uncle, however, soon realised that Honen was unusually talented and made for better things, so he sent him to be educated at the great national temple centre of Mount Hiei near to Kyoto, the capital. There are touching statues and depictions in Japan of Honen setting out on his journey, a bit like Dick Whittington, to go to the mountain and we think of his mother seeing him off, perhaps knowing that she was never going to see him again, as she died of illness a couple of years later before his return.

At the mountain young Honen, as Mira would do later in history, learnt the practice of Nam, calling the holy name. The words were, of course, different as this was medieval Japan, but the principle was the same. In Japanese the name was "Amida" which comes from an Indian word that literally means "without measure", *mita* being etymologically close to our word "meter", as in thermometer or speedometer, and the prefix a- being the same as in English in such words as asymmetrical, atypical or amoral.

Honen learnt the importance of invoking the immeasurable. With each grasped thing comes the intuition of a Beyond, of something more vast, more encompassing. In the language of India we can say beyond each rupa lies dharma. Dharma means truth, but with the implication of great or encompassing truth.

Meaning is Derived from Context, not from Constituents

Individual things only make sense in context. The small takes its meaning from the larger whole of which it is a part. A bookcase is a bookcase in the context of a room full of furniture and a life in which books have a place. The meaning of a bookcase cannot be divined from any amount of knowledge of planks, screws and spaces. We do not build up meaning from the parts, we derive meaning from the whole. For our life to have meaning we need to conceive it in the context of a greater whole. This is another reason why a materialist perspective, while it is useful for know-how, can never give meaning to one's life. Once one knows what to do, a materialist analysis may be one way of approaching how to do it, but such an analysis can never tell you what is the right thing to do in the first place. Without the bigger context of meaning humans would not have made books, pyramids, aqueducts or opera. For spirituality to be liberating rather than confining it has to provide ways of thinking about the bigger context within which one's life can be meaningful. One needs what the modern Japanese master Shunryu Suzuki used to call "Big Mind".

Meaning as Motivation

Honen studied for many years on the mountain and made great progress. He became a great scholar. He had read all the holy books there many times and was acknowledged by everybody to be a saint and a most erudite authority. However, he knew that something was still missing. He still had not really quite achieved what his father had bidden him do.

So in the case of Honen we see somebody who acquired a sense of meaning early in life. Interestingly, as with Mira, he got this sense of meaning from an incident involving the death of a person close to his heart. The impermanence of things teaches us about eternity and transcendence. Honen had learnt something. The meaning was, however, not complete. It was, rather, a search. His life was meaningful as a quest. This motivated him to study and acquire wisdom, to learn methods, to discipline his life and to become erudite. All these were inherent benefits, but they were really side effects.

The scriptures certainly provided a larger perspective within which he could make sense of life and find a direction. They said how there was a process of karma, cause and effect. Those who lived good lives would come to good rebirth and those who did otherwise would decline spiritually. One could discern different grades and ranks of beings ascending and falling according to their deeds. This all made sense and, to an extent, it "spoke to his condition", but while it went some way toward satisfying his need, he continued to feel that something more was still necessary.

Beyond the Calculus of Karma

Just as measurement provides a satisfying logic but does not quite represent reality, so the same is true of calculation. The idea of karma provides a calculus of faith and virtue that yields a certain sense of satisfaction. One feels that a certain degree of control is possible. The matter seems to be in one's own hands. If one chooses to sin or chooses to be virtuous there is a commensurate penalty or reward. This speaks to our sense of fairness. It is amazing how many people who think they have given up on religion still have a passionate faith in fairness as though they still believe that God is counting every little deed and entering it in His great ledger.

The reason that this was not sufficiently satisfying for Honen was that he was willing to be more honest with himself than most people are. He saw that he was himself one of the most spiritually privileged people in the country. He lived in the most ideal conditions, a hermitage on the holy mountain. He had the best teachers in the land. He had sufficient material support that he could dedicate himself to religious practice day and night. Yet, when he looked into himself, like Mira, he saw the "countless faults" that karma would not fail to heed. If even he could not live an unconditionally virtuous life, what hope was there for the vast majority of people burdened by the necessity to labour, the pressures of a corrupt society, and absence of spiritual education or opportunity? The calculus of karma might provide a logic for purposes of internalised social control, but it was not going to provide salvation for the masses.

The crisis of faith and understanding that this provoked in Honen was similar to that of Mira. Karma tended to reify the social structure. It did not really liberate. Something less conditional had to be the case if he was to reach the goal that his father had set for him. What was the true meaning of Dharma? What had the capacity to cut through the despair that followed from his introspection?

Honen did not deny the teaching of karma, but he did not find in it a sufficient solution. What impressed him more was his insight into his own limited and imperfect nature. Just as being deeply touched by the experience of impermanence gave an intuition of eternity, so being forcibly struck by his own inability to so control his mind that greed, hate and delusion were truly eliminated, brought with it another important intuition. It had to be the case that, in some way that we cannot fully understand, we are loved as we are. It could not be the case that a person is only saved spiritually by reaching a state of spiritual or moral perfection because such a state does not exist. It was when Honen realised this, not just as information, but through direct knowledge of his own state, that the intuition of all-acceptance came to him.

Love Thy Neighbour

This is the condition of all truly religious or spiritual persons. They are liberated by an intuitive sense that we are loved as we are. This does not mean that how we are is good or that we ourselves have perfect acceptance. Quite the converse. We are awash with human frailties. We are readily moved to envy, jealousy, lust, pride, panic, greed and all manner of other faults. As a spiritual person one may strive to reduce these tendencies, but one cannot, even if one has all the advantages that Honen had, eliminate them. Discovering this is a foundation for true compassion. This is because compassion is best regarded not so much as a refined virtue handed down from on high by spiritually superior beings – though it can be that – but, for most of us, as fellow-feeling. Compassion is the sense that arises when one sees that one's neighbour is in the same boat as oneself and one is, oneself, in the same boat as the neighbour.

This is the basic meaning of love thy neighbour as thyself. It does not mean, as some modern interpreters have suggested, first I must love myself before I can love my neighbour. No. It means that to love one's neighbour is to see the neighbour as being not unlike oneself in having similar tendencies to fear, dismay, awe, smugness and all the other great range of emotions that humans are blessed and cursed with. To love one's neighbour is to be a spiritual being. It is to be a kind of therapist, not in the professional sense of accepting money for psychological vice, but in the more basic sense of being somebody who accompanies others through the spiritual journey of life.

The Journey of Love

Everybody is on their spiritual journey. This is true whether they like it or not. Along this journey are many obstacles. The journey is a journey of learning about love. Our basic need and drive is to love, but the attempt to love by creatures such as ourselves, in a world such as this one, is bound to run into innumerable hazards and setbacks. The lessons of life are not about how to love – we can't help doing that – but about how to love again or how to go on loving when we have met with rejection, defeat, loss and failure, as we all do, and how to help one another to do so; how to help our neighbour to do so when she, in her own way, has fallen into essentially the same kind of troubles that we and everybody else is prone to.

It was a similar realisation of the common human lot that led Sigmund Freud much later to write in his book called *On Psychoanalysis* "Psycho-analysis has demonstrated that there is no fundamental difference, but only one of degree, between the mental life of normal people, of neurotics and of psychotics. A normal person has to pass through the same repressions and has to struggle with the same substitutive structures."

The Nature of Sin

When we meet these obstacles we are inclined to seek solace in short term comforts. What are called sins are all really just short term comforts. Alcohol is a short term comfort. Adultery is a short term comfort. Gluttony is a short term comfort. Theft, rape, even murder, they are all ways of seeking immediate solutions that have longer term deleterious consequences. Now we all know what it feels like to be in a serious fix in life and to see there possibilities for such short term comfort. Only some of us have killed another human being, or raped one, or stolen something, or told lies or... well, actually even this isn't true. I am very doubtful if there is anybody who reads these words who has not told a lie ever in their life, and there is probably nobody who has not taken something that was not rightfully theirs, and everybody who has paid taxes is at least implicated in the killing of other human beings somewhere else in the world. Humans, as well as being angels of a kind, are also highly destructive animals.

The Reward of Virtue

Spirituality can be seen as an attempt at moral progress, both collectively and individually, and individually in relation to the collective. The spiritual person has a direct loyalty to spirit and so acts in a pro-social way even when no social inducement or coercion is in view. Some people see spirituality as something that is a private matter and that is a half truth as spirituality does involve the individual in taking responsibility for their own life, but this does not imply a cutting off. The liberated person is not liberated in a way that flouts the common good. Liberation comes through a process of deepening empathy that liberates one from the greater excesses of egotism so the liberated person, while being in a condition that renders them less conventional and less predictable, nonetheless naturally does act consistently in a pro-social manner, and, indeed, does so even when society is in disarray, whereas the less spiritual person may only be social when in pursuit of the approval of others.

We take on moral precepts and try to live according to them. Whether they are the ten commandments, the injunctions of the Koran, the rules of a Buddhist monk, or just the resolutions that we made at New Year, we struggle to be better and rarely meet with complete success. This effort is not energy misspent. It is a wonderful thing to keep one's life in good order. Sometimes one does not realise until much later just what a good thing it is. Now that I am in my sixties I am immensely grateful that the young person that I used to be never took up smoking tobacco, never took non-medical drugs and only once in life ever tasted spirits. I am amazed, actually. I know that my case is a rare one, but I am certainly grateful. Virtue does bring some rewards.

However, at the same time as yielding a modicum of self-improvement, the struggle with precepts also flushes out our resistance. We learn about the fathomless perversity of human nature. We find out how vulnerable we are and we see how the surging tides of nature continue to flow through the basement of the stilt houses we have constructed in an attempt to keep our feet dry.

The Defeat of Pretension

Spirituality is a progressive learning about one's humanity. When I look back on fifty years of spiritual training what I see is not so much progress in morality as progress in a certain kind of wisdom and by this I do not mean that I have become more God-like, but rather the reverse. The wisdom that seems to have been really important and that I am most grateful for has been the

44

progressive – or rather, by fits and starts – arrival of a sense of my own limitations, fallibility, proneness to short-term temptations, and so on.

When I set out as an enthusiastic young person full of zeal for spiritual training, meditation, self-discipline and the imitation of my betters, I was sure that I was on the way to the elimination of greed, hate and delusion, to the mastery of the mind, to the overcoming of desire, to the end of suffering and the dawning of superlative wisdom that would one day set me upon an invulnerable spiritual pinnacle from which I would be able to dispense compassion to poor souls lost in the whirl of the material world who had not had the good fortune that I had enjoyed in finding a spiritual path. How naive I was! What the spiritual path has done is gradually, layer by layer, to strip off the skins of idealism and moral pretension leaving me more and more spiritually naked – just a human being.

The Greatest Treasure

Honen and Mira both realised their humanity and in so doing opened up in two important ways – to their neighbour and to the divine. They conceptualised these dimensions in totally different ways, but I don't think that that matters. This is not about whether you do or do not believe in a certain conception of divinity or a certain conception of humanity – each person will formulate their own beliefs and these will change with experience, but still, a spiritual life is going to be one that opens up in these ways. By seeing that I am as vulnerable as the next person to lust, affront, smugness, crazy fantasies, and so on, I find it much easier to get on with other people and they do find me easier too. I am a long way short of old Honen, but I do

45

see the general drift of what his path was about. I can see how it was that he could as easily converse with soldiers as with monks, nuns as prostitutes, beggars as prime ministers. I can see that this was, from his own side, at least, much more a matter of having faced the truth of his own nature than it was a result of having put himself into a straight-jacket of conformity to a religious ideal. Others might look at him from the outside and praise his self-restraint, his scholarship, even his saintliness, but from his side it was not in the attempt to imitate such ideals that he had found something of immense worth, or not directly, anyway.

By grasping the essence of the matter, Honen was liberated from many of the narrow channels that we habitually keep ourselves in. He was able, for instance, later in life to have disciples from many different schools of Buddhism. He was the creator of a sect that was so structured that it, for the first time, gave ordinary people access to the treasures of Buddhism, yet at the same time he had so sundered the bounds of sectarianism in his own being that he was able to have disciples from many different Buddhist denominations. This shows the remarkable structure of double negation that one sees in people of this kind. Although seeing beyond worldly structures he was not above using them when doing so served a compassionate purpose. The liberated person negates the worldly condition, but then negates the form of spirituality that would handicap use of the worldly circumstances. Though we may be liberated, we never cease to be human.

What the Heart Knows and the Mind Cannot Grasp

Earlier I talked about the principle of perception according to which there is a salient foreground object and a peripheral, implicitly limitless, background. This is sometimes called the gestalt principle. The gestalt is what stands out, but the gestalt always implies a background. You will, I'm sure, have seen those pictures in which it is ambiguous which is the gestalt and which is the background: is it a picture of a black vase with a white background or two white faces looking at each other with a black background? When we look at such a picture, we sense that whichever we pick out as foreground is finite and whatever we have made background is not. The finite and infinite imply one another. This is basic to the structure of human perception. Without it we cannot make sense of anything.

Spiritual progress requires us – especially we who live in materialist cultures that are fixated on the acquisition and manipulation of finite things – to pay more attention to the background. It is not the gestalt, the rupa, that needs yet more attention. The attention that we are accustomed to putting on the gestalt needs to be tempered by more appreciation of the vast context. There is currently a vogue for a form of spiritual practice called mindfulness, but the crucial question in the matter of mindfulness is, mindful of what? Mindfulness is sometimes taken to be about present state awareness, but one's present state is a gestalt and what is required is that that awareness expand to include the implicit vastness that puts that gestalt in context.

This is not just an abstract matter. It is also a matter of the heart. Honen and Mira were able to face their own condition by seeing it in context. While space is the context of physical objects and eternity is the context of periods of time, love is the context of life. Mira and Honen, each in a completely distinctive manner, intuited the vast love that encompassed their existence. They overcame conceit and egotism not by perfecting themselves, but by seeing themselves in context. Each realised that, if they were loved, then they were loved as the creatures that they were. It could not be the case that they would only be loved if and when they attained to perfection because there are no such perfect people.

We intuit limitless space, but cannot grasp it with our mind. We intuit eternal time – if somebody says that the universe started fifteen billion years ago we immediately think, Well, what happened before that? - but we cannot grasp eternity as empirical experience. In the same way, we intuit unconditional love as the vast context of our ordinary life and the more clearly we see just how ordinary our life is the more clear the intuition, but we can never fully grasp unconditional love, or unconditional anything, for we are creatures of conditions.

This is what spirituality is about in its basic form. It is the effect upon one's life of the intuition of that Beyond, an intuition that comes from perception of the immediate. The more clear the perception the more powerful the intuition and the more powerful the intuition the greater the effect on one's life. Mira's intuition lifted her out of the narrow minded consensus of her time. It only came to her, however, through the shipwreck of her dreams. She was all set to be queen, at the pinnacle of the system that she was later to see as a chimera. Honen climbed the holy mountain, but it was only when he climbed down again

48

that he was able to walk the world with bliss-bestowing hands and, in doing so, he was not conscious of his own saintliness, but simply of having found a context for his own life that he was willing to share with others.

The Conditions and Limits to Intimacy

Spiritual awakening is not a matter of pretending that some unreal ideal is the case, but of waking up to how things actually are.

I have been reading "El Camino del Encuentro" by Jorge Bucay. Learning Spanish is opening up for me a new universe of thought and literature, which is wonderful. I am only a third of the way through this book at the time of writing this, so I could still change my opinion before the end. Reading in a language not one's own slows one down a bit. Nonetheless, so far, I am finding his approach refreshing and stimulating. You know that feeling that you get when you read a book that says clearly things that one has felt intuitively for a long time?

Here I'd like to share just one bit of his philosophy. He is looking at the question of intimacy. What does it take to have an intimate relationship? He is not just talking about couples. Intimacy can occur between friends, between family members, even sometimes in work situations, though in the latter case it is going beyond the requirements of the job. Intimacy is that type of relationship in which one can drop one's defences and be willing to take the risk of being more completely available to the other person and inviting them to reciprocate.

Bucay asserts that there are three necessary conditions for intimacy: *love, attraction* and *trust*. He then goes on to point out that none of these are within the range of one's will. I can choose to respect you, but I cannot choose to love you. I cannot choose to find you attractive. I cannot choose to trust you. Either I do find you trustworthy or I don't. Either I do find you attractive or I don't. Either I find you loveable or I don't. There is not much I can do about it from my side.

Of course, from your side, you can choose to act in ways that may lead me to find you more loveable, attractive and trustworthy or in ways that will undermine these for me. Similarly, the other way round. I can act in ways that will make it more likely that you will love me, trust me and find me attractive.

Bucay claims that all three are necessary. It is as a three legged table. It cannot stand without all three legs. This all seems to me liberatingly realistic. Injunctions to love everybody, find everybody attractive and trust everyone are not grounded in the real world. Injunctions to live in such a way that more people will love one, trust one and find one attractive, however, do have some grounding in reality.

This implies, of course, that one does not have a right to be loved, that one will not, in fact, be loved by everybody, that one does not actually love every other person, nor trust them, nor find them attractive. This is the real world. Spiritual awakening is not a matter of pretending that some unreal ideal is the case, but of waking up to how things actually are.

In this real world there is every reason to act well. It will, in general, lead to more intimacy and thus to more peak experience. Many people, however, exist in life situations where they think that they should have intimacy with this or that person and that such and such person owes them intimacy, but if the three factors of love, trust and attraction are simply not all there, it will not happen and no amount of pretending or demanding will make it so.

In my book *Love and Its Disappointment* I take it that love is a fundamental part of human existence, but not that one loves everything. In the approach that I used in that book, Bucay's "love" and "attraction" are conflated. I have to agree with him, however, that trust is also a very important variable. One can love a person and find them intensely attractive, but if experience tells you that they are not to be trusted, enduring intimacy is impossible and short term intimacy generally leads to pain and grief. On the other hand, one may have a comrade who is totally trustworthy and one may even share secrets with such a person, but there has to be something more, something in the realm of personal attraction or positive chemistry before one will, in practice, open one's heart to them fully.

Sometimes we proceed as though we think that all human problems can be solved to the point where we shall enjoy intimacy with everybody. This is unreal. It is not true that if we just communicate enough we shall reach such a point. With those whom we find loveable, attractive and trustworthy, yes; with others, no. Furthermore, the "others" are likely to be many. Yet, is this really a problem? Not really. A person needs some intimacy; they do not need intimacy with everybody.

We are Ordinary

From time to time there has to come a reminder that each of us is not the centre of the universe.

A pitfall of many spiritual systems is that the moral imperative that they carry or the remote glory of the goal they advocate has such a huge weight that instead of liberating it oppresses. There has to be a different way to approach an understanding of the relationship between the "two natures", that of ultimacy and that of our empirical selves and our world. That there is, for us, a gulf between the two is only deniable at great cost to our integrity and simply being told to become non-dualistic is all very well but does not address our actual condition. Non-duality is the perception from the side of ultimacy. However, we are not on that side. We are ordinary, soft human beings and if we do not see a gap between out own state and that of ultimate sublimity we are either divinely enlightened or, more likely, falling into conceit.

The nature of ultimacy is not such that a once and for all definition would be possible, even if one were superlatively wise. In any case, wisdom can hardly be considered to be a personal possession. The wise are those who allow themselves to be led by something wiser than themselves and make no personal claim. Zen Therapy, then, is cultivation of a wholesome and healing intuition of a greater and greater context.

Cultivation proceeds via a relationship between oneself as a mortal, limited, fallible being and guiding powers that *must* remain mysterious. We begin with a modest assessment of ourselves. In the evolution of all spiritual systems there is a tendency toward solipsism. As I am here and now and here and now only make sense in reference to me, we come to think that only this here and now, which is me, matters. We start to think that everything else is just projection of our own mind or is unreal. From time to time there has to come a reminder that each of us is not the centre of the universe. Not even all of us together are that. Spirituality is not about not being able to love anything but oneself. Rather it is about gazing in awe before a Whole that is vast and glorious and in the context of which one's own self is a tiny item.

Buddhists associate the guiding powers with Buddhas and bodhisattvas, Christians with angels, Hindus with gods, shamans with spirit guides and many modern people (and old Japanese people) with Nature. Spirituality is not the exclusive property of any one civilisation, tradition or system. It has been a dimension of human life all over the planet throughout history, and without it there would not have been history. On the other hand, adopting a totally smorgasbord approach does not provide one with an adequate frame for building community or sharing practice. First we have to make some choice in order to practise at all, but if we make a good choice then what we choose will be inclusive enough to allow us to incorporate wisdom from many sources.

We are now in a new age. Never before have the riches of the human spiritual tradition as a whole been so available. This is wonderful. Somehow out of all this we have to find a generic approach that does not in the process screen out what the former sages are saying to us

or explain away all the bits of the traditional wisdom
do not fit into contemporary prejudice.

Gankonin

*It matters what we dedicate ourselves to, however
good or bad at fulfilling that dedication we may be.*

The Japanese term *gankonin* means 'vow-light-
person. *"Gan"* means a vow or prayer or deep aspiration.
"Ko" means light. "Nin" means person. A gankonin is one
who cultivates in the light of the vows and prayers of the
spiritual ancestors. The angels have vowed to help us, the
sun shines upon us, the rain waters us, the clay gives rise
to us and whosoever has been a true sage has loved us and
done their best for our sake. We are blessed and grateful.
In the Shinto religion it is said that when one invokes a
kami spirit one should do so in a deeply apologetic
manner.

Too often we are afflicted and imprisoned by our
conceit and the sense of our own power and efficacy. We
act as though we deserve the sunshine, own the earth, have
earned the rain and possess the traditions and civilization
that we have had the good fortune to be born into. This
common mistaken view is called self-power (*jiriki*).
However, cultivation requires a deep and ever growing
appreciation of other-power (*tariki*). The trick is to learn
how to work with other-power. This is a different kind of
virtue. It is not the virtue of adherence to a codified
formula of thought and conduct that rejects three quarters
of human nature. It is the virtue that is already inherent in
the swirling torrent of life's wholeness. When people begin
this spiritual work it is common to hear them ask how to

know what is self-power and what is other-power. They will say, "If I receive some intuition, how am I to know if this is from me or from the other side?" or words to this effect. However, there is actually nothing that is "me" that is not from the other. It is not a matter of sorting the sheep from the goats but of recognising the goat nature of all our sheep... and knowing what goats we are.

When we operate from an other-power perspective we know that we do not have the power to make ourselves into perfect, enlightened beings, but we know that we nonetheless do long for it. The Spirit that has such power will hear and shed light upon us. In this light we shall see more honestly. In paradoxical and ironic ways that we did not anticipate, the truth will gradually set us free and our lives will become instruments of liberation for many beings even though to ourselves the process will remain mysterious. We just go on cultivating in the best light we can see from where we are and trust that as we do so more light will be given.

Another similar Japanese term to gankonin is *myokonin* which is a word used in Japanese Buddhism to refer to people of simple faith. Myo means shining. Whereas early Buddhism developed the ideal of the *arhant* as the person of complete purity and Mahayana Buddhism developed the ideal of the *bodhisattva* as the person of complete altruism, Japanese Buddhism then developed as its ideal the myokonin, the ordinary fallible person who yet shines with simple faith. These three illustrate well different dimensions of the spiritual ideal.

The idea of a "gan", that is, a vow or prayer, is very important. As the gan, so the future of the person. Our core intentions connect us to spiritual nature and this then creates our future. It matters what we dedicate ourselves to, however good or bad at fulfilling that dedication we may be, because this is what will work upon the karmic stream. The cultivator has his heart in the right place and then makes one mistake after another. In this way much is learnt. The worldly person, by contrast, has many hidden agendas that are less than wholesome and is loathe to admit even to himself that he has made a single mistake in his life.

What is the best kind of gan? The best gan is the intention to live fully and to appreciate the richness of life. The worst kind of gan is self-protective. The next worst is combative. The next worst is idealistic. All these are self-serving. The best gan is that which opens the heart and mind to That which is beyond oneself. One who makes such a gan claims no special wisdom personally, but enjoys being fed by the Mother of all things.

A gankonin is somebody who has a naturally arising vow in his heart that commits him or her to the Way through whatever means and manner the powers may indicate; a life apart or in community, of beauty or of service, of ease or suffering, of simple faith, friendship and community. Such unpretentious ways provide true leadership and re-emphasise things of fundamental importance in a meaningful way.

Questions such as "what is my gan?" and "within what gan do I conduct my life?" are of crucial importance to everybody who takes their spiritual cultivation seriously. To ask such questions effectively, however, one needs objectivity in relation to oneself. To discover the scripts that one is playing out in life, the vows that one made as a child that still hold sway, requires a therapy that has radical honesty at its core.

Gan speaks of longing. Although we might say that Buddhists and Taoists meditate whereas theists pray, this kind of distinction is rather artificial. All spiritual people have a longing toward something that lies beyond ordinary understanding and that longing can be regarded as the core of prayer or meditation alike. Equally we have a sense that we receive help from the beyond, and the contemplation of the mysterious source is, likewise, both meditation and prayer. Prayer and meditation are two sides of the same coin. To fulfil our purpose in life we each have to find our own prayers, those we are already living and those that shall become meaningful to us as we go deeper – our primordial gan, which actually has nothing to do with us personally.

Three Core Principles

It is neither realistic nor sensible for us to think that we can live lives in which everything we do is justified, everything we receive is deserved and we remain pure.

I want now to talk about three core principles that are useful as a framework for thinking about cultivation. They put some of the principles that I have introduced so far into a more systematic pattern. They are of general use in helping us to understand how spirituality works everywhere.

The Bombu Paradigm

For the first principle we use the Japanese word, *bombu*. This is the fact that we are ordinary beings. It is the principle that humans are fallible and subject to conditions. We do not have the power within ourselves to attain spiritual perfection, salvation or apotheosis by our own effort or manipulation. In fact such an idea would be a contradiction of terms. It is precisely our self that obstructs us. Any such consummation comes as a grace and not as something attained as a result of deliberate aspiration or practice. This principle is extremely liberating, cutting through all spiritual ambition. More generally, the idea that, through and through, we are "foolish beings of wayward passion" and that this is not disastrous, is generally healthy, liberating us from unrealistic expectations of ourselves and others. It is neither realistic nor sensible for us to think that we can live lives in which everything we do is justified, everything we receive is deserved and we remain pure. The good and bad in this world are too inextricably intertwined for such puritanism to work. Although spirituality is certainly about over-coming the ego, there is no reason to think that the ego can over-come itself. The ego will be overcome by truth that is outside of itself. Some may wish to call this a greater Self, but the danger of renewed solipsism in such a way of thinking is so huge that I prefer to avoid it. I am simply a bombu being trying to penetrate this mystery called spirituality in my own little way, like the seeker in the well-known mystical book called *The Cloud of Unknowing*.

The Trikaya Framework

The second principle is that it helps to divide the domain of spiritual experience into three provinces, called three *kayas*, firstly, the absolute or ultimate, secondly, the sublime, and thirdly, the transformational. While the ultimate is beyond our ken, nonetheless there is a natural human instinct to venerate it in some form or other. We might name it Nature, or Tao, or Brahma, or, nowadays, even Evolution. We need some way to talk about the greater order of things, not just particular things, the wholeness of which things are parts and that makes everything meaningful, without, on the one hand, falling into the conceit of thinking we know what we do not know, a conceit that is commonly, now, called dogmatism, or, on the other, denying to ourselves the ability to talk about the matters of highest and final concern, a denial that is called nihilism. The trikaya principle aims to provide us with a middle path, a system to aid dialogue that avoids dogmatism on the one hand and nihilism on the other.

a) The first kaya: The Ultimate

We have already said that ultimacy is intuited rather than measured. In fact it is exactly the counterpart to measurement. Our mind grasps some bit of reality and, as it were, cuts it off, but, in doing so, must intuit the whole from which that thing has been extracted, a whole that is not measurable. We must find a way to be in touch with the things themselves, not merely with our abstractions. This all important intuition is to step from the conditioned to the unconditioned, from mortality to immortality, from measured time to eternity, from limitation to infinity, from ordinary love to perfect love, and so on. This step is hugely important to our spiritual health and should not be lost or let out of sight. However, in this form, although we can put words to it in the manner that I have just done and can speak of the Unconditional, the Unborn, the Deathless, etc., the way that we experience it is almost always indirect. We experience the Formless through forms. This is why we need a second level concept.

b) The second kaya: The Sublime

The history of spirituality is the story of how Spirit has appeared to many people in many forms and, through those forms, has touched their lives. This appearance in form is the second kaya. The Spirit appears in dreams, visions, visitations, synchronicities and symbols. It responds to the needs of the seeker. These forms are not totally abstract and known only to the intuition, but are experienced with the heart, mind, feelings and body, issuing in cries, tears, visions, and transports of delight or dejection that are accessible through a devotional life and come unbidden to those who are open to them. We can call this the activity of angels. Such appearances, whether to mystics, sufis, shamans, or hermits, are the occurrences that renew spirituality and are the root of all tradition. Cultivation is a matter of opening ourselves to such revelation whether it comes to us directly or indirectly.

c) The third kaya: The Transformational

Then, finally, transformational nature is the fact that saints, spiritual masters, bodhisattvas, and other great beings do appear in human form in this world. Also ordinary beings like ourselves do manifest varying degrees of spirituality in the midst of ordinary life: the Spirit appears in practical ways in our midst; it infiltrates our lives and we are helped. The example that we give to one another spreads or erodes faith and morale in any community, irrespective of its belief framework. This is a universal phenomenon and a highly significant part of being human. We are all vulnerable to spirit in this way.

This trikaya idea makes it easier for us to talk about spiritual experience. It allows us to acknowledge our intuition of the ultimate without our needing to define or understand it further while, at the same time, making space for us to talk about our spiritual experience as we find it without the need either to attribute ultimate or dogmatic significance to it on the one hand or to dismiss it as not meeting scientific criteria on the other. Furthermore, it acknowledges that our spiritual life is fed by real life encounters, especially those with persons who have themselves lived deeply spiritual lives. It addresses the universality of spirituality in human experience without requiring us to discuss it in inappropriately argumentative ways. The reality of spirituality is not a function of names and definition, but of experience and such experience has these three distinguishable levels irrespective of creed.

The Necessity of Practice

Then, finally, we have a third essential, which is the principle of practice. We need to do something that speaks or enacts our spiritual sense. This sense includes both alienation and awe. It may encompass a wide range of emotions from longing to satisfaction, shame to exultation, sadness to joy and so on. There is not just one right way to feel in relation to greater truth. Living fully brings all manner of feelings, high, low and in between of many colours and textures. In fact, a spiritual life is a more alive life and therefore a more colourful one emotionally. There is an important distinction here between spirituality and morality. Spirituality is not a matter of putting oneself into a straight-jacket, but of liberation. Nonetheless, spirituality does need concrete expression. Practice may be divided into concentrated and extensive.

Concentrated Practice

Concentrated practice generally takes place in a designated place and may involve a variety of ritual forms. We may dedicate a space as a magic circle within which we shall enter into a different state of consciousness. We may make there an altar and place upon it things that symbolise our spiritual path and ideals. We may have ritual ways of behaving. The main forms of practice generally are meditation, prayer, and singing or chanting, combined into forms of ritual that enact important and uplifting meanings. Practice may be routine or spontaneous, calming or ecstatic, peaceful or energetic. I do not intend to write about this extensively here, but rather want simply to emphasise that such practice is important and that to exclude it from our lives is to lose a whole dimension of our being. As human beings we have a capacity to enter into spiritual states, to reach sacred realms and experience inner transformations. These require an appropriate set of ambient conditions and there is a skill involved in creating them.

Extensive Practice

At the same time there is a value in carrying what one gains through concentrated practice into one's daily life. If, through concentrated practice of meditation one acquires a certain degree of inner calm, then it is good to practise such calm in the midst of all the tasks of one's day. What we find and encounter in our concentrated practice needs to accompany us into daily life. And, similarly, what we learn by our encounters with the miscellaneous circumstances of life will accompany us into our formal practice.

Again, as always, there are pitfalls. A common one is the idea of "my" practice. Spirituality is supposed to be a liberation from ego, but it is amazing how much ego investment some people can have in their practice. Practice is not, therefore, in itself, a *method* of liberation, it is a *celebration* of liberation, and often it is a collective celebration, and it is a language of liberation. The term

64

ritual is sometimes used disparagingly to refer to just going through the motions of something time and again, but living ritual is an immensely powerful force in our lives.

Practice has a receptive and an expressive aspect. The primary form of receptive practice is contemplation, and that of expressive practice is prayer. In contemplation we enter into silence and stillness and receive grace. In prayer, through calling, with mantras, recitation of text, or spontaneous utterance, we express our longing. In Japanese, the commonest form of Buddhist prayer is called *nembutsu*, literally meaning the mental impulse toward the Buddha as saviour. It often is expressed in a single line prayer that varies with languages, but in the English speaking world now often has the form "Namo Amida Bu" - "I call to Amida Buddha", "Amida" meaning measureless, "Buddha" meaning awakened. This prayer, therefore, has a universal significance. The implication is that the spiritual life is the crying out of this limited, vulnerable, fallible being that I am toward That which I intuit to be beyond this relative, transient world, and, in addition to this crying out - this longing of the heart - it is an opening to, and contemplation of, what comes into our lives from that ultimate spiritual source, from the Unborn, the Unconditioned. Christians have a similar practice called the Jesus Prayer, the words of which are, "Lord Jesus Christ have mercy upon me a sinner." Essentially this is the same prayer. The Beyond is here identified with Jesus Christ and this prayer is the calling out of a fallible being – a sinner – toward that Beyond. This is, therefore, the general form of spirituality in religions. Buddhists call it "taking refuge". We observe limitation. Doing so, we cannot help intuiting the unlimited. Bringing these two into intimate relation is the key to cultivation. When we do so we experience being part of something much greater than self. This liberation uplifts us and makes us want to express our communion with the Beyond. That the Beyond is clothed in the names of particular sages is natural. To think that that gives any particular group an exclusive ownership of spirituality, however, is not.

Where Miracles Happen

When we are in touch with the numinous, we are led by spiritual powers wiser and kinder than ourselves.

The ordinary nature of ourselves, the graduated (trikaya) contemplation of the Beyond and the practice of calling make up a complete system of spirituality. This is how we clothe what I take to be a universal archetype of the Way. Some conceptualise the Beyond in abstract form and some in personal form. Ultimately this difference is purely style – the Ultimate is beyond form and any God who is truly God can take whatever form He, She or It fancies – it is not up to us. The Unborn appears to us in whatever form works. As it says in the Tao Te Ching, "the space between Heaven and Earth is the gateway to all miracles".

These transformations are personal. They change us. They come to us like intuitive messages. Throughout history humans have recognised these messages and their powerful effect and so talk of angels, spirit guides or wisdom beings. We can thus think of the spiritual life in an abstract dimension in order to satisfy our intellect or in a personal one in order to satisfy our heart. They are just two languages. We shall never adequately encapsulate that life in words, but we can experience its real effects in our life. Our appreciation of our finite all-too-seen world and our infinite, mostly unseen one grows, expands, deepens and works in, on and all around us. Something happens. A mystery unfolds. A Life that is more than ordinary occurs in the midst of our ordinariness and we give ourselves to it.

This Life is love in myriad forms, myriad because true love is not easily attained and has a million applications.

The spiritual life is the evolving community of those touched by love, in which there is a strong sense of common purpose yet a great diversity of activity, in which a simple understanding provides a common, enduring anchor yet wherein new development is always possible. When we are at least intermittently in touch with the numinous, we are led by spiritual powers wiser and kinder than ourselves. We can rejoice in them. Feeling ourselves liberated from our small concerns by participation in something much greater and feeling ourselves blessed by this participation, we feel gratitude. Feeling gratitude we become more generous. We become a channel for meanings that we ourselves cannot grasp fully. Being uplifted, our being shines and we help one another.

Zen Therapy

Every observation is accompanied by an intuition, every presence by an absence, every discovery by a denial.

Zen means contemplation. Therapy means spiritual accompaniment and assistance. Zen therapy is the application of the wisdom of the ancients and of the various paths of contemplative practice and spiritual accompaniment to the healthy growth of communities and individuals in a modern context. It draws on many spiritual traditions, Buddhist, Taoist, shamanistic and the mystical traditions of India, the Middle East and medieval Europe.

Zen Therapy is an investigation into the truth of life. As such it is a way to live one's life deeply and fully, liberated from unnecessary or compulsive complications. However, we should not think that life has one simple solution or a state of perfect health that can be easily reached. Life is continuing cultivation because it is itself dynamic. As soon as we arrive at simplicity we complicate it. As soon as we find happiness we become discontent with it. It is our nature to negate and to strive to go beyond. One koan gives way to another.

Satisfaction deepens and confidence grows not through success in reaching a stable state but through realising that it is possible to live a dynamic life more and more fully. By doing so one is fulfilling a higher purpose even without knowing it and when the time comes one will look back down the years free from regret.

We have here a philosophy of simplicity, straight-forwardness and fullness of life through engagement with reality in all its beauty and ugliness, opportunity and dismay, superficial colour and profound meaning. What the ancients taught is the way to vibrancy of life. We can profit from their wisdom recorded alike in the *Abhidharma* literature of India, the Taoist classics of China, the holy books of the Middle East and the lore of tribal peoples. We should not, however, be deceived by the word simplicity into thinking that such is necessarily a minimalist lifestyle. The simplicity is in the investment of one's love in what is most worthy, but the ramifications of doing so may lead one on a long and complex journey. This is like the hero in the fairy tale who has a single love in view but who must conquer many obstacles.

Reality is more than meets the eye. Humans are gifted with more than just observation. Every observation is accompanied by an intuition, every presence by an absence, every discovery by a denial, or at least a doubt. All perception is relative and partial and we have an inbuilt tendency to recreate the whole from the part and the absolute from the relative. Sometimes perception is mistaken and sometimes intuition is mistaken, but their constant functioning is how we make this life meaningful in a world of beauty and suffering, life, death, opportunity and affliction. The Zen Therapist is always listening for what is not said, what is missing but implied, the wholeness needed to complement the fragment that has mesmerised the seeker.

This is more a matter of intuition than cleverness. The unconscious plays the most vital part. The spiritual cultivator learns to be guided by it. Conscious awareness is only the tip of the iceberg. Even more important is learning to be guided by hidden forces. This is something one can develop. The tight clinging to the bright light of consciousness must be relaxed so that the angels can play their part. If we let conscious control relax, we will be channels for a greater wisdom. Not only that but we shall free up the conscious mind for its real task, which is to understand the truth about our life and to apply the guidance that we receive. We are here to find something out. We find ourselves here drawn into particular situations that hold us with a mysterious power. Some of this power is due to the fact that there is something in the particular situation that we need to know, but have not yet fathomed. When we know it, that type of situation will loosen its hold and our spiritual pilgrimage will move on. In this sense, the spiritual quest is a constant progress from one holy shrine to another. We make offerings to myriad Buddhas. When we can see each situation that we find ourselves in as a holy space in which there is an important spiritual learning for us to discover our life takes on a different colouring and we start to find the divine in every corner of our existence.

This is a path of encounter. It is not simply that a seeker comes to a guide because the seeker needs something that the guide has. The seeker also serves a purpose in the life of the guide. People do not come together by accident. There is always a hidden significance in this meeting.

Zen is contemplation and so has a lot to do with perception and attention. It is not, however, a matter of getting control over them in a restrictive sense, so much as appreciating them as doors to something more than what

71

most people ordinarily perceive. The Zen therapist does not only hear what is presented, he or she perceives the presented as a fragment of a greater whole. Perceiving in this way is also to perceive that we ourselves, in our ordinary being, are only fragments. We do not like to think so, however. We want safety. The ego holds on for fear of the ever present possibility of falling. Although we see spirituality as a matter of transcending and going beyond the ego, it is worth pausing long enough to have some compassion for the ego in its thankless task. We create an ego in order to deal with reality and keep it at bay for fear that we might fall back into chaos and madness. We learn to be stoical or cynical and seek some measure of stability in a world where nothing seems ultimately reliable. To rise into a spiritual life requires faith, but faith may be difficult to sustain in the face of defeat, loss, failure and betrayal.

Our lot is not immune to the influence of others. Ideally, a completely spiritual life would make one so, but we are not in that ideal state. The fully realised person would be so free from ego that they would continue to act for the benefit of all sentient beings no matter what constellation of coercion and inducement they faced, but in practice we have our limits. Nonetheless, this limitation does also means that our salvation is bound up in that of others.

To liberate others, however, has a double significance: on the one hand to help them break free of their own limitations, on the other to liberate them from ourselves. When we vow "Innumerable are sentient beings, I vow to save them all" what we must first save them from is ourselves. In order to maintain the ego's cherished semblance of stability we have to hold others in a kind of

72

psychological captivity. To free ourself from the onerous guard duty that we have thus imposed upon ourselves, we have to set them free. The role of the therapist is often to safeguard those others so that we do not feel too much panic when we let them go.

Our self-story entails enmeshment with others. As we come to understand the true situation we move from enmeshment to respect. There is a simultaneous liberation for self and other. The stronger the sense of self, the weaker the real esteem for what is other, whether empirical or transcendental. Ultimately this would culminate in madness, the condition in which reality is most alien. Conversely, esteem and appreciation of what is other can function in a restorative manner, drawing energy away from the self project into a greater vibrancy of life.

We do not live here alone, yet aloneness can have a great value when it acts as a door to wholeness. Relationship and aloneness can work together to liberate or to enslave us. In Zen Therapy aloneness and relationship are employed to free us from co-dependency and addictive patterns, toward deepening respect for and esteem of what is other. This begins with those others – those non-selves – that are the particular obsessions of our life and moves ultimately to the great other that is the complement to all our limited notions. This progress leads to an increasing richness of participation in ever expanding dimensions of life.

The fact that empirical sensory cognition is always accompanied by a complementary intuitive construction of missing wholeness is what gives rise to human spirituality. As the hidden part of the yin-yang of experience comes to be more and more valued, life takes on a fuller and fuller sense of wholeness and holiness.

Inner Peace

Because we are lost in our own inner war that just goes round and round in circles, we need some intervention external to ourselves.

We cling to the ego because a small minded life can seem safer. The strongest fear is that of being overwhelmed from within by our own feelings. We fear the world for its capacity to present in ways that may provoke just such a capsize. The ego exists to negotiate the world and when possible seduce or coerce it into collusions that will avert just such presentations. To do this we have to be good story-tellers. Ultimately these stories are the lies we live by, but they can nonetheless have an element of touching charm.

Spirituality may be a way of allying ourselves to a bigger story that it not just our own. We may give our lives in the service of a greater spirit. Sometimes the spirit in question is a worthy one and sometimes not. This is the stuff of history. Sometimes spirituality is a liberation, sometimes merely an alibi.

To put the whole thing another way, a person builds an ego in an effort at self-defence and then builds a super-ego to keep the ego in check. These two are then at war and this war consumes much of the person's psychic energy. The person tries to solve his or her life problems by increasing the strength of each and applying more pressure from one side or the other. The solution, however, lies in a completely different direction, in finding a truth that allow this war to die away and the primal energy of the person to once again flow in a less inhibited manner. This requires humility.

Liberated people have no pre-planned script, take life as it comes, and appreciate what it brings. Their baseline is not a state of control but a place of silence and stillness from which reality can be contemplated in its fullness and reached out to in a vigorous and appreciative manner when appropriate. They love life.

Classically, Zen practice is a matter of intense introspection punctuated by decisive encounters with a spiritual guide. The master accompanies the disciple and the disciple tries to accompany the master. The style and traditions of ancient East Asia do not work so well in the modern world, but the principle remains a good one.

Everybody, knowingly or unknowingly, is working on their koan – their inner war – but the koan cannot be solved alone. This is because all koans are to do with the nature of love and love is a game that cannot be played as solitaire. A person is not a rock. A person's life flows. That flow may have become dammed, occasionally over-flowing in destructive out-bursts. Taking the dam down is not something that a person can generally do unaided. Spiritual accompaniment is indispensable. Nonetheless, this fact does not negate the importance of aloneness and personal application. The two complement each other.

Because we are lost in our own inner war that just goes round and round in circles, we need some intervention external to ourselves. Accompaniment catalyses liberation. Yet it can only do so when the conditions are right and the creation of such conditions does involve extensive heart-searching by the individual. In the practice of therapeutic relationship there are two immediate domains of otherness for the client: the otherness that is their world and the otherness that is the therapist. Beyond this there is a greater, all-encompassing otherness, that gives depth and meaning. All these encounters are potential areas for the arising of panic. The task of the therapist is to be with the client in such a way that this panic does not reach unmanageable proportions. Some therapies do so by allying themselves with the ego. Some by allying with the super-ego. Spirituality, however, does not rest with these defensive strategies but seeks entrustment to a love that transcends all understanding.

The love that we receive from a human other is conditional and bounded, yet it is the gateway to our intuition of a love that is unconditional and unbounded. The therapist may attempt to have "unconditional positive regard" but does not succeed. Nonetheless, the sincere attempt yields fruit when it gives rise to a deeper and more encompassing sense of holding power that continues to pervade the life of the client, whether they have words for it or not, even when the therapist is absent.

The spiritual master is barely aware of even being a therapist even though he or she may function as one for other cultivators. The master simply is living his life. This in itself can be enough to trigger the collapse of delusive structures in those with whom he or she relates directly. This is not due to any special knowledge. It is simply the effect of non-manipulation.

Discerning the Shadow

We build our own prison to house those we want to keep under control and then find that we are the only real in-mate.

If Zen means contemplation and therapy means accompaniment, then Zen Therapy is contemplative accompaniment and accompaniment in one's contemplation. Contemplation broadly has two objects, a yin and a yang. The yang is the evidence of life and the yin is the container of life. The zen therapist thus needs the ability to facilitate an enquiry in detail that does not lose sight of the whole; or, to put it in more spiritual language, an examination of bombu nature in full awareness of Amida's grace.

Zen therapy can utilise any methodology. It is not a technique. It is an ethos. It is a way of usually gentle, occasionally startling, yet rigorous accompaniment. Within the context of unconditional acceptance, its style is challenging, paradoxical and alive to life's intrinsic irony, to the spaces as well as the substance, to what has not been said as much as to what has. If something is certain we generally do not waste breath saying it. To take what the client says at face value, therefore, rarely does justice to the truth of their being.

The client arrives early and smiles. The therapist is welcoming and kind but is already wondering about the aspect of the client that wants to be late and miserable, about the hatred or aggression behind the smile and the fear and rebellion behind the conformity. "So..." "I don't know where to start..." The therapist feels the invitation to direct the client and sees the trap already being laid. The therapist makes an open-handed gesture that says, this is your space.

This is a not atypical beginning to a therapeutic session. The client may now launch into a story or may persist in manoeuvring in relation to the therapist by saying something such as "I'm not sure if this is going to do any good." Accompaniment means deep respect and this means not taking responsibility for the other. It is scrupulously non-manipulative. Perhaps the therapist replies, "You are debating with yourself if it is worth coming?"

The client is a bundle of different voices and the therapist does not expect consistency. The client is a crowd. Client: "No, I'm sure it is what I need." The therapist inwardly registers that this is probably a lie, or at least that there will be another voice in the client secretly saying the direct opposite and replies, "So, it's hard to know what is needed." Client: "No, no, I'm sure this is right; my doctor said it would do me good." "Your doctor said; and what do you say?"

The basic question is always, "What is true?" Some theories of therapy say that the therapist must always stay within the client's frame of reference, but the client has many frames, does not know what they are himself, and will, in any case, always resent being framed and try to break out. There is always a bigger frame and loosely we may say that it is the goal of therapy that the client start to experience life in a bigger frame; certainly to explore new ones.

Sooner or later the client gets to his story. "I still live with my mother and I know she needs me, but I also need to get away..." The therapist knows that she is going to sometimes be seen as the mother. The smile and the early arrival already make sense. The likelihood of missed appointments in the future alternating with self-castigation hovers. "Tell me about your mother."

At this point many therapies would have prescribed "How does that feel for you?" but it should be pretty obvious already what the answer to that question is and the figure that fills the client's mind, the all-potent seeming power object, is mother. Contemplation is worship and at this moment the deity is the mother. Beyond this deity there lies a greater divine space that will eventually liberate the client, but let's not try to run before we can walk.

The client is likely now to utter some generalisations, stereotypical remarks or to give a rather biased account. The therapist listens, sensing what feels true, what hollow, and looks for a way to get closer to the truth of the mother. "What does she think about you coming to see me?" "Oh, she doesn't know." "So you already get away from her in some respects." "Well, yes, she doesn't know half my life." "And if she did...?" The client wants to be known by mother and also wants to get free, instead of which he is unknown and tied, or, at least, that is the story that he has bought into, a story that is not true.

Everybody's life is full of stories. All are fabrications, some woven by oneself and some by others. It will always be so. There is no story-less nirvana this side of the grave. Yet some stories can be more enabling and some more dysfunctional and every story is built around a denial. Were it not so there would be no point in the telling. We build our own prison to house those we want to keep under control and then find that we are the only real in-mate, or, rather, we do not find out because we are unwilling to let ourselves know the truth. Outside there is a bigger world and a brighter sun shining, but even if the door of our prison is occasionally left open the brightness outside may take some getting used to.

As the client contemplates the evidence a different mother starts to appear and life starts to show different possibilities. The therapist is not in the least shocked by the fact that most of what the client says is untrue - it's always so. People are bombu. That's what makes them loveable.

Dharma is Therapy, Therapy is Dharma

If therapy is not a spiritual quest it is not fulfilling its potential and if spiritual cultivation fails to address real human suffering it is not worthy of the name.

Being a client and being a disciple seem like very different paths. The client attends, perhaps once or twice per week or month whereas the disciple lives the whole of life in an intense relationship to the guru. Yet, in much therapy, the client lives in just such an intense relation to the therapist and in much Dharma practice the disciple only actually sees the master occasionally.

Some Dharma practitioners think that Dharma practice is superior because it has a higher aim in view in the complete liberation of the person. However, therapy ultimately has the same goal and, in any case, neither Dharma nor therapy achieve such an outcome very often! For most people who practise Dharma, their Dharma practice is a therapy. It serves to improve their mental health, to insure them against panic, stress and craziness and to give them poise, clarity and grace. And, although what brings a person into therapy is generally some dysfunction in their life, they are at least implicitly, and often explicitly, really seeking the meaning of life and a sense of ultimate fulfilment.

A spiritual teacher is a kind of therapist of souls and the therapist occupies a sacred place in the life of the client, at least as long as the therapy continues. Of course, there are different kinds of teachers and different kinds of therapists, but the fundamental of the human quest for liberation remain the same whatever the modality of practice. If therapy is not a spiritual quest it is not fulfilling its potential and if spiritual cultivation fails to address real human suffering it is not worthy of the name.

The logic of therapy and of spirituality are not separate. Though organised into different disciplines the overlap is extremely large and each can learn from the other.

Working with a Dharma Teacher

As long as I live in gratitude to my precious teachers I will not go far wrong, even though my mistakes still be many.

While attending the Conference of Buddhist Teachers at Garrison in the state of New York, it was quite apparent how "Dharma Teacher" can mean different things to different people. Polarising it, there is the educator (of students) who teaches a classroom on a topic and there is the guide (of disciples) who catalyses spiritual maturity. The former may work contractually in an educational institution or be more freelance. The latter might be connected with a religious institution, but not necessarily. Certainly it is not as a function of any such role that the latter has the effect that she or he does.

These two are different in kind, not merely in degree. It is not, for instance, the case that one is more or less hierarchical than the other - either can be done in a more or less authoritarian or democratic style. In the transmission of the Dharma these two roles play different parts. Some of us at the conference occupied only one of these roles - one or the other - and some, like myself, both. The Dharma is not something that can be learnt academically. Academic learning can supplement it but not substitute for direct involvement with a spiritual guide. Learning Dharma as an academic subject is interesting, but it is not at all the same thing as taking up spiritual cultivation.

Educators transmit a culture, an "ism", whereas what is transmitted by a spiritual guide is beyond culture. One of the difficulties for seekers arises from the human tendency to mistake the medium for the message, the culture for the light. The light, however, is universal and transcends social settings. A liberated person is liberated. Whatever enculturation they have is not of the essence.

In the modern West people make a lot of affiliation, but really this is just the delusion of sectarianism. Spiritual training has nothing to do with membership. A trainee might say "I'm Hindu because my teacher happened to be a Hindu", or "I'm Taoist" in the same way, but sometimes the disciple is Hindu because he comes from a Hindu family even though his teacher is Buddhist or vice versa.

What then is cultivated? Open-heartedness: openness to other-power. This is not primarily about nurturant emotion so much as realism and gratitude. Realism means finding out what you are and what this world is. It is as if the universe has put us here to find something out. The koan is the spiritual problem that the person has that prevents them entrusting themselves, prevents them fully understanding, and keeps them locked in a particular pattern of attachment or addiction. We can say that it is what stops a person from fully living their life and induces them into collusive relationships that support others in not living their lives either. It manifests in pride, greed and aversion and is blind to the bigger picture.

While the koan is unresolved we will tend, following self-power, to drift into situations that are particularly suited to bring us up against it again and again until we have found out what we needed to understand. When we have done so the fascination of that type of situation will automatically fade and we will find ourselves doing something else. When we see this process happening, see the universe teaching us in this way, we feel gratitude.

In this modern age of credentials, training courses and qualifications, people may ask "What course should I follow in order to get my spiritual training?" or "How will I get my spiritual training certificate?" but this kind of cultivation does not work in that sort of way. It is not a social game. It is about discovering the "person of no rank" as Zen Master Lin Chi famously said. Social games are all about rank and status. Spiritual liberation sees through them. Society is organised vertically. Spirituality is horizontal.

Everybody has koans so the koan process is happening in everybody's life whether they are aware of it or not, but cultivation can be deliberately under-taken through a relationship with a master or spiritual guide. It is a bit like coaching and a bit like apprenticeship, but it has no standard form or syllabus. The master will watch the disciple and discern the latter's spiritual need and will seek to arrange the conditions that will assist the disciple to progress. Sometimes this is by facilitation and sometimes by sharpening the edge of the dilemma. Often it is by setting roles or tasks for the disciple to complete.

The disciple tends to assume that cultivation is about moral improvement and about making the right decisions and will tend to come to the master with questions of the "What is right?" or "What ought I to do?" variety. However, this misses the point and the implicit moral imperative is a koan in its own right. There is here a subtle attempt to shift responsibility onto the teacher or onto a formula or set of rules. Truth is not what should be, but what is. Cultivation is about being willing to face the truth and act wholeheartedly in each situation. In a hypothetical ethical dilemma there can, in principle, only be one correct moral solution, but in a real life invidious situation there may be any number of wholehearted responses. The spiritual guide is not trying to see if the disciple can discern the correct moral solution so much as trying to see what style of half-heartedness the disciple is given to.

The guide will gradually come to see the type of game that the disciple is playing and will disrupt it in various ways. Or he will disrupt it without even knowing that he has done so simply by the force of the fact that he does not play into it in the way that other social actors generally do. The koan generally functions as an invitation to collusion and the person who is free does not fall into such collusion.

The disciple will, by fits and starts, come to see the extent of their own sense of self-importance and will come to know their own greed, hatred, pride, envy and so on intimately and directly. As long as the disciple hangs onto a self-centred agenda, even one that is couched as moral improvement, he or she will only be willing to see a small bit of the truth about themselves. The super-ego has a plan to put right every fault and so achieve immaculacy. This seemingly high-minded scheme is really just a form of conceit which stands in the way, making the person incapable of seeing the whole truth about themselves or undertaking any meaningful spiritual analysis.

Service to the teacher may also be a valuable mode of cultivation. Disciples will observe the teacher's needs and do whatever they can to care for the teacher and assist his or her work. In the course of this relationship a reliable trust will develop. The two people involved will become aware of each other deeply in all their humanity. Through this love a transformation will come about. This transformation has much to do with the emergence and growth of faith. The disciple will see the master's clay feet. Actually the master does not just have clay feet, he has clay all over. He is somebody who can live his life as it is without having to have a self-perfection project running. Because he does so he is able to live in a wholehearted way and to appreciate the grace that incessantly falls into our lives. Being filled with gratitude, he does generally live a more moral life than most people do, but this comes naturally from his outlook, not from following a set of rules or trying to present himself in a certain way. The master is also quite capable of doing things that will shock those who are attached to moral propriety. He is just living his life. What the disciple learns from him is freedom, not a formula.

The disciple absorbs something crucial from being within the field of influence of the teacher as the teacher asks the disciple to do things or take things on, things that challenge or stretch the disciple in some way. However, ultimately, what the disciple is learning is negative. It is not an accumulation, it is the undoing of obstacles. The things that the disciple is given to do may require some particular talent or quality. They may demand endurance, intelligence, patience, courage or the taking of responsibility, but these are incidental. First and foremost they require faith and willingness. In one sense, we can say that it is over-coming the blocks to these that is the real training, but this way of thinking tends to reintroduce the moral imperative into the trainee's mind. It is more accurate to say that cultivation is just finding out the truth and acting accordingly.

It is in the nature of relationships that they are not all the same. In the course of a life one might only have one teacher or one might have several, but if so then each relationship will be different and what one learns will be different. What I learnt from Kennett Roshi, from Thich Nhat Hanh, and from Saiko Sensei was not the same, but in each case it edged me toward being a more fully-functioning person and demolished some aspects of my rigidity.

Although there are various spiritual systems, training can never really be standardised and too much system can be counter-productive. Even here I must not say too much or it will serve as an immunisation rather than an encouragement. The arhats enlightened by Shakyamuni Buddha were all very different characters. The masters recorded in the Denkoroku each had a different koan to overcome. Although the truth is simple, the ways of avoiding it are infinitely varied and the means of training must be similarly diverse as well as being affected by the available resources. One of the most important resources in this respect is the sangha. It is through life in a community that so many of the facets of one's koan are brought to light. However, living in community without discipleship can easily result in a fixity of role and attachment to a particular identity and functional pattern. One task of the teacher is to disrupt such stereotyping. This is one of the reasons that sanghas are not always efficient organisations in the worldly sense.

I remember being at a large Buddhist monastery and talking to one of the gardeners. I admired the garden and talked about the composting system. He pointed out that some of the system was not working very well at the moment and I asked why that might be. "Well, every time that somebody starts to be competent, Rinpoche sends them on the three year retreat," he replied.

There is an almost endless amount that one could say about spiritual cultivation, its features and pitfalls. It is a kind of therapy, though not a self-indulgent or ruminative one, but rather one that involves facing life more honestly and directly. Although a person may become a disciple because there is something about the teacher that they admire, an important step comes at the point where the disciple experiences a softening of heart and realises that whatever accomplishments the teacher may have, in the end he or she is simply human with all that that implies. At this point the disciple stops trying to get something and it is just at that point that they do get something - though not what they expected.

So cultivation is not a course or programme. It is a matter of following the Way in close co-operation with somebody who has him or herself been a disciple and walked that path for a good while before one. Nobody can be a master who has not been a disciple and discovered the humbling truth about his or her humanity. False humility is exceedingly common and socially required, of course, but real humility is exceedingly rare. Masters, disciples or whatever, we are all human beings with the same vulnerabilities. Cultivation is not a path toward invulnerability, but one towards reality and the acceptance thereof in a manner that actualises our potential for love in a wise way. The spiritual relationship is itself a most exquisite example of such love; tender, caring, non-possessive and liberating, it demands all and freely offers "the one thing needful".

We are all disciples and as long as I live in gratitude to my precious teachers I will not go far wrong, even though my mistakes still be many. It is this reflected light that one can transmit. Although this mirror is cracked in every way, in its facets you still can see God.

Lovely in Its Beginning, Lovely in Its Progress and Lovely in Its Consummation

An enlightened teacher does not produce clones. He or she empowers each to fulfil their spiritual destiny.

The newly enlightened Buddha was travelling to go to see five ascetics with whom he had practised prior to his enlightenment. On the way he met two merchants. They were converted to his message and became the first Buddhists and lay followers. He taught them to take refuge in the Buddha and the Dharma (there being no sangha at that time). Then he arrived at the place where the five ascetics were and they, remembering that he had abandoned them, resolved not to honour him, but when he appeared his new bearing was such as to tell them that some great change had occurred in him and he instructed them in the proper way to treat a teacher. They became his disciples. As the necessary conditions for transmitting teaching were then established, he taught them the four truths for noble ones. Konndinya was enlightened. A short time after, he taught them the teaching of non-self and all became arhats. So he continued and when he had sixty arhats he sent them forth for the spiritual welfare of the world. They went singly or in small groups and spread the Dharma, lovely in its beginning, lovely in its progress and lovely in its consummation.

This simple progression tells us the essence of the Buddha's Dharma. First take refuge and thus put the Dharma at the centre of your life. Then treat the teacher appropriately and become a disciple. Then understand the four truths and so learn how to redirect the energy of your life, unhooking from objects of obsession and so releasing yourself to be on a path of wholeheartedness. Then understand non-self, appreciate other-power, and so become one who naturally liberates others. This order is important. Many Western practitioners try to do it all the other way around and get stuck because their attempt to themselves be something – a great master, or whatever – is itself a conceit and so there is no basis upon which a spiritual life can grow, no matter what forms and tokens one surrounds oneself with.

Thus they went forth and did so in many different ways. An enlightened teacher does not produce clones. He or she empowers each to fulfil their spiritual destiny. Some lived in groups and some were hermits, some travelled and some established communities, some built hospitals and animal sanctuaries and some wrote poems, some danced and some renounced dancing, some were ascetic and some married, some were arhats and some bodhisattvas. All were bombu. All discerned the truth of their lives and gave up their conceit. By doing so they helped others to do so. It was just as the ocean might flow into any number of coves, bays, basins or the open main, yet everywhere it has the taste of salt. Such is the life of faith.

To take refuge is to enter into a relationship with what is beyond the ordinary that opens us to truth and love beyond our personal limited selves.

Faith is Willingness to Die

My beliefs have changed, but my faith is the same.

A good litmus test of spiritual progress is to ask oneself how willing one would be to die. We are not willing to die if we are full of regrets, nor if we are enmeshed and unwilling to let others have their freedom. To give others freedom is another way of saying to have faith. Faith is not attachment to beliefs. Faith is willingness to live, to let live, and to die. Faith is to not sell out. In the course of a vibrant life, one's beliefs may have changed a number of times because what one believes is based upon the experience that one has had. Experience is never a last word - it goes on. Indeed, the whole purpose of our life is to find out what we did not know and so a life in which a person's beliefs have always remained the same may well have missed the point. If one has developed this free flowing faith while living one will die well. Faith is the courage and willingness that comes from openness to a higher purpose in all things. Lack of faith is a deadness of being, "as if dead already" - a deadness in the midst of life. Faith is willingness to live this life as it is, this life that involves many changes including the ultimate change which is to die.

We may say live fully in each moment, but that, of course, is an ideal and we can go astray chasing ideals too - life is, in any case, more than just this moment - but it can be a useful ideal, like a star to navigate by, always distant, but still informative and mysterious. But the idea of willingness to die is also a precious touchstone. If it is life, then life; if it is death, then death.

> Since life and death are both the same
> I give myself to the infinite light

As my life continues to unfold I find that my formulations of belief have changed, but my faith is the same light. It is the same light that enveloped me when I was a child and it has sustained me year after year. It is the faith that mysteriously, I am given all that I need yet that there is always something more to discover; that there is a benign providence yet I must also play my part. My circumstantial life has seen successes and failures; achievements and mistakes, triumphs and defeats. Things in this life turn into their opposites, there is a kind of irony built into the way things work out, yet within this irony lies a wisdom. This is the Tao or Other-power which is the natural basis of spirituality. We cannot always grasp it, but we can rely upon it.

PART TWO: LOVE & LIBERATION

Other-Power Liberates

Time is short, opportunity limited.

Spiritual salvation is liberation. There might seem to be a certain paradox in the idea that a follower is free, or that a committed person is thereby liberated, therefore one has to understand these terms in a more than superficial way. Freedom is always freedom from some form of coercion or bias. The coercion or bias that rules one's life may be internal in the form of neurosis, ego or super-ego, the fear of being overwhelmed by compulsively arising passions or confusion or one's own internalised conflicts; or it may be external in the form of living in an oppressive state or being enslaved or compromised by one's position in an organisation or social relationship. Some people are more concerned about one, some about the other, but both kinds of liberation are worthwhile goals to strive for.

While knowing that they are free, a liberated person may nonetheless experience a kind of necessity. Such a person may feel "I could not have stood by and done nothing to help" or "As soon as the situation became clear I knew what I had to do." Although there is a sort of necessity, it is not the sort that compromises their spiritual freedom, since spiritual freedom means freedom from self-centred greed, hate and delusion. A liberated person tends to be loving, compassionate and wise simply because they have no particular reason not to be and seeing into their own condition renders fellow-feeling for others natural. Such a person may appear to have great courage, perseverance, finesse, skill, dedication and so on, and, in one sense, this is correct, but the person him or herself does not experience it this way. Like Mira or Honen, they just rely on other-power.

The ordinary person tries to rely upon self-power and so is often unable to act because outcomes cannot be guaranteed. If I think it is me alone doing the act then the prospect of failure is grievous. If I rely on the Tao, then if things turn out differently from how I intended it is simply another learning situation.

Reliance upon other-power thus brings surprises, but also equanimity. Things are seen in terms of a greater reality. It implies that in certain circumstances a person, although realizing "Oh, so they are going to kill me if I don't do something unworthy," nonetheless is not so abashed by such a realisation that she or he becomes then willing to betray their awareness of what is loving and good. Buddha asked his disciples whether they would give up their commitment if they were going to be cut in half with a two handed saw because of it, and we know that Jesus himself went to the cross. To be willing, in the extreme, to suffer for the sake of what is good and true is a test of the meaningfulness of one's faith. To think that spirituality is just about "happiness" in any ordinary sense of the word is inadequate. Was Jesus happy to be crucified? Was Martin Luther King happy to be assassinated? Was Buddha happy when Devadatta betrayed him? They were not happy about these things, but they approached them in a noble manner because they saw them in a much bigger context than the average person would.

Although Taoism, Christianity and Buddhism were all founded upon a similar understanding of the liberating effect of other-power, in later centuries all three religions fell under the spell of various forms of sophistry. In Christianity this perversion often took the form of substituting loyalty to the institution for loyalty to the values that it originally represented. This is why many Westerners, especially in countries with a Protestant heritage, are highly suspicious of institutions. In Eastern religions the perversion often took the form of a reinterpretation that made the doctrine passive. It was said that equanimity implies non-action. Wisdom was seen as non-discrimination and if one is completely non-discriminating then "there can be no coming and going." While this notion has a deep meaning, it could also be taken as a manifesto for passivity, in which case it effectively depotentiates the whole movement. In modern times we have seen moves to try to restore a concern for social engagement in Buddhism and attempts to get Christianity to be less hierarchical and institutional. There can also be degeneration into magical superstition of various kinds. All religions, like all human creations, decay and are constantly in need of renewal.

Similar sophistry can occur in our individual lives. It springs from the agendas of the ego and super-ego, which is to say, from self-power. Thus private freedom has been seen by many as the freedom to pursue a selfish agenda and in the world of politics and economics one has even seen such slogans as "freedom and democracy" used as the rationale for invading other countries. Again, all too often one meets people who say "I believe in living a more spiritual life, but one has to make money, etc." This is like the person who could not come to follow Jesus because he had to bury his dead relative to whom the Christ remarks "Leave the dead to bury their dead."

Spiritual masters tell us that time is short, opportunity limited. Whether they talk about an impending judgement or about the rarity of precious human rebirth, the implication is the same, namely, that nobody is saved by prevarication. Neither Jesus nor Gotama nor even Lao Tzu taught a message that was so much in the mind that no change of life was necessary - quite the contrary.

Three Signs of Being

Truth (Dharma, Tao) is in no way dependent upon the internal operations of the mind that perceives it.

I have been asked about the formula in Buddhist teaching that is commonly called the Three Signs of Being. The full text, in Sanskrit, is:

Sarva samskara anitya
Sarva samskara dukkha
Sarva dharma anatma

This is a key text in Buddhism - a core statement of the doctrine. What does it mean?

Commonly it is quoted as meaning "everything is impermanent, everything is suffering, everything lacks self (or everything has non-self nature)". While conveying some truth, I think this interpretation misses an important point. The three sentences are not parallel in this way. Looking more carefully we can see that there is an intended contrast in the text between the first two and the third. In my understanding, therefore, a more correct rendering is, "All our attitudes are ephemeral; all our attitudes are (spiritually) dangerous; reality lies not in self but in what is other". This, then, is a text about other-power and objectivity. It comes right at the core of what Buddha taught.

Sarva means all. *Samskaras* are things that we construct, particularly mental formations. D.T. Suzuki used to translate the term as "confections", which is etymologically correct and has the right tone of slight disparagement. *Dharma* means real things or reality. *Anitya* means impermanent. *Dukkha* mean afflictive. *Anatma* means non-self. Non-self, of course, means other, or can indicate the whole from which a "self" is abstracted.

So, this formula says that all our own mental formations or confections (the things we cook up in our hearts and minds) are impermanent and dangerous or troublesome, since reality is not self. The implication is that to be in touch with Tao or Dharma is to be in touch with what is free of the colouring imparted by one's personal bias. A sage is just somebody who has woken up and sees what is actually so. This is a call for objectivity and also an indication of the importance of the Whole as against the individual things that we become obsessed by. Truth (Dharma, Tao) is in no way dependent upon the internal operations of the mind that perceives it. If it is true, it is true. When we say such things as "my truth" we are not talking about truth in this sense. I do not mean to rule such grammatical usages out of the language, but truth is not self, self is a make-shift construction. This point is often lost in contemporary, popular spiritual discourse. To see the self is to intuit the whole. To intuit the whole is to forget the self. To see oneself truly is to be rendered silent, still and full of contrite awe. Yet we cannot rest there for long without being deeply disturbed and this healthy disturbance projects us forward into new self-building which will soon be disrupted again. Life is dynamic and involves such a dialectic. The self is temporary and makeshift, but we go on creating it and recreating it. The best way is not to give up, but to realise that this is an endless process that is rendered worthwhile not by the perfection of the self we create but by our relation to something greater that is always beyond.

Now, the idea of non-self has commonly been built up in Buddhist circles beyond its basic meaning. Non-self is taken to be an ontological principle concerning the emptiness (_shunyata_) of dharmas, taken to be things in general. This is fine and in no way in contradiction to the above so long as we understand that emptiness means empty of the spin that our ego puts upon things. It becomes problematic when it leads to ideas that deny any place to objectivity. The world is not just a projection of my mind. When we reach that level, religious philosophy is verging on a justification of madness and the only saving grace is that none of the philosophers who take such a stance really believe what they are saying sufficiently to act upon it, or if they did then we can find them in their local institution for the insane.

In Buddhism we also have the teachings of dependent origination and conditional arising. These imply that none of our mental states stands independently. Everything that is self is conditional and liable to change as conditions change. This teaching fills out the above teaching. Of course, here too there is a temptation to extend the idea beyond its original application and turn it into an ontological principle. In this case one asserts that nothing in the world arises except in dependence upon (ephemeral) conditions. I do not have any particular objection to this extension as a philosophical move, but Shakyamuni seems never to have made this move himself. He consistently used these teachings, to the best of my knowledge, solely to elucidate the deluded mind and not as a way of designating the qualities of material objects.

This threefold formula, *sarva samskara anitya, sarva samskara dukkha, sarva dharma anatma*, in effect, says, live your life, live it without complications that you concoct in your own head that are only troublesome, dangerous and do not last; live your life in relation to what is real and important, live your life in the constantly renewing intuition of wholeness: not atma, the fragment, but anatma, the whole.

We do not have to make this intuition of wholeness into something abstruse or esoteric. It is something we all experience. It is something we can use to put our own worries and obsessions into context. It moves us from small mindedness to a much more expansive perspective. It is a key to liberation. We must embrace our partiality, but do so without losing sight of the whole.

Not Everything is Impermanent

Unless there is an encounter with the numinous there is no spiritual healing.

In the text called the Udana, which is a collection of Buddha's most important utterances, there is the core passage that says "There is an unborn, uncreated... the deathless... nirvana... If there were not... then there would be no liberation." According to the text it was this passage that made his disciples really excited "until the hair on the backs of their necks stood on end." This is the key intuition. Between the Born and the Unborn we have our life of spirit.

Buddhism, the Way of Awakening, as presented in the West commonly over-looks or de-emphasizes this central aspect of the teaching. Some others over-emphasise it, seeing the absolute as itself the goal, thus negating all meaning in life in this world. The former stance may be called secular Buddhism and the latter extinctionist Buddhism. What I am speaking for here is a liberationist awakening that frees us from both these common forms of nihilism.

Some Buddhist apologists like to present the idea that Buddhism teaches that "everything is impermanent" when the fact is that Buddhism teaches liberation from taking refuge in impermanent things. There is no classical Buddhist school that teaches otherwise. Different schools have different methodologies and different styles of presentation, but they do not differ on this fundamental point. There is a danger, therefore, that, perhaps in an effort to square Buddhism with reductionist, secular, atheistic scientism on the one hand and popular romantic spiritual ideas of innerness on the other, Western apologists will distort the whole Buddhist message to such a degree that it is not really Dharma any more, just one of the kinds of extreme that Buddha eschewed.

When the sage said that sarva samskara anitya ("all samskaras are impermanent") he was making a contrast with sarva dharma anatma ("all dharma is not self"). To enter the unborn one must leave the self - one must abandon self-power – and one must leave the impermanent. To be at one with what the Buddhas are at one with one must abandon identification with the transient conceits (samskaras) of one's own fancy and put one's faith in something more reliable. Buddhism offers all manner of different methods to help a person understand this point intellectually, experientially, symbolically, literally, metaphorically, analogically, progressively, suddenly, etc. etc. but unless it is acted upon the whole thing is merely academic. As C.G. Jung says, unless there is an encounter with the numinous there is no spiritual healing. The same truth is found in all major mystical systems from Rumi to Francis, Lao Tzu to Krishna.

To illustrate this with a popular item, there is a commonly quoted Zen phrase to the effect that "If you meet a Buddha on the road, kill him." This is commonly taken to mean that if you think anything outside of yourself is Buddha you should get rid of that idea as soon as possible. In fact, the true meaning is surely almost the direct opposite: If you, on your path, ever think that you yourself are Buddha, kill that idea. In Buddhism it is conceit that is the prime target for annihilation. In the

Pratyutpanna Samadhi Sutra the whole practice is precisely to see Buddhas everywhere you look. In the practice of that samadhi everything that is not self becomes Buddha. This is another way of expressing the basic notion that it is from the particular that one intuits the universal. The degree of our enlightenment is in proportion to the esteem in which we hold our world and that esteem derives from our intuition of its transcendent dimension.

The Five Orders or Laws of the Universe

For people to encounter the sublime there has to be a medium in which an encounter can occur.

The idea of five orders (*niyama*) comes from ancient India. They are:

- *utu-niyama:* the inanimate domain, the seasons, the weather
- *bija-niyama*: the vegetative life domain
- *chitta-niyama*: the involuntary mental domain
- *karma-niyama*: the domain of intentional action
- *dharma-niyama*: the spiritual domain, ultimate truth, Tao

We can think of these in a secular manner or in a spiritual way. The former suggests the different domains of human knowledge (physics/meteorology, botany/biology, sociology/anthropology, psychology/ethics, metaphysics /religion) and the possibility of a hierarchy of needs or functions, as, for instance, in the psychology of Abraham Maslow. From that perspective the spiritual life is built upon the other levels as foundation. This teaching also elucidates how one's karma does not encompass everything that happens - there are other laws also in operation.

From the point of view of the person established upon a spiritual path, however, the order is reversed. The dharma-niyama becomes fundamental and the pre-condition for all the others. According as we are embedded in Dharma, so flow our volitional actions. According as our actions, so form our habits. According to our habits, so our basic life state remains healthy and wholesome or otherwise. Ultimately, the way we are in our physical world is a function of how, whether and to what extent one is established in Dharma. In other words, there are two directions of thought. In the secular approach, complex wholes are agglomerations of parts and the whole owes its life, form and purpose to its parts. From the spiritual perspective it is the other way. The parts derive their form and function from the whole. One approach is mechanical, the other is to do with meaning. Each has its proper place.

We can also say that the spiritual cultivator is a kind of artist. Art expresses truth and beauty through a medium. Utu-, bija-, chitta-, and karma- are the layers of medium through which the creative activity of the Tao expresses itself. Tao is the sublime. The person of Tao is an artist always sculpting the spirit in whatever comes to hand.

For people to encounter the sublime there has to be a medium in which an encounter can occur. Thus artefacts may come into being in any of these domains - an object, an architecture, a way of life, an act, a word: all or any of these can be a spiritual trigger. The Dharma-farer naturally gives rise to such artefacts and they in turn have the capacity to trigger those who are ripe for it into spiritual experience.

Thus, we can say, that the Spirit takes form in the world through the enduring or ephemeral artefacts generated by those who entrust themselves to it. This is not something contrived or manipulated. It is simply a result of investigating the truth of our lives. The basic principle set out here applies whatever particular form the expression of the spiritual life takes (love of God, following the Tao, meditation, etc.). If a person has got it, their life is re-ordered in this way. The essential character of this 'it' is a quiet certainty (the "still, small voice", anshin) flowing from spiritual experience.

Typically, the spiritual person functions in each of the realms in a broadly recognisable way:

- *dharma-niyama*: the practitioner experiences times of deep peace, full of love and devotion. Whatever arises becomes grist to the mill of spiritual transcendence.
- *karma-niyama*: the practitioner both goes forth to help all beings and also contributes to the creation of 'Dharma realms' where the spiritual life reaches a particular intensity. They do good gratuitously simply acting in ways that are intrinsically worthwhile.
- *chitta-niyama*: the practitioner's old habits and compulsions drop away through the power of devotion and are replaced by inner stillness and good-heartedness that adapts benignly to all situations.
- *bija-niyama*: the practitioner is full of life, content in the blessedness of being alive, and experiences moments full of wonderment at the natural world around about. She or he is always planting good seeds.
- *utu-niyama*: the practitioner is continually engaged in creating beauty, order, cleanliness and indications

of the spiritual domain (dharma-lakshana) and delights in the progress of the seasons, the sunshine and the storms that nature sends.

So through an understanding of this notion of level or order, we can gain an understanding of the kind of reversal that turning to a spiritual path brings about in our lives. At the same time, the energy that powers such a life is the same nature that we all have. The objectively saintly person is one who has deeply confronted their own flawed nature.

Unconditional Love

In my nature are the same hormones, the same weaknesses, the same propensity to distraction, the same appetites, as everybody else has.

When I was young I was fascinated by the ideal of unconditional love. I fell in love and I tried to be totally devoted. At that time I was working in an office with a group of young men. They had stories to tell about the women they had been out with and they flirted with the women in the typing pool, but I closed my ears. I had no interest in anything but being a perfect partner, completely loyal to my woman. The woman in question, however, was jealous anyway. Although I never so much as glanced at another woman, I still got accused regularly of having unfaithful thoughts. The injustice of this cut me to the quick and in no time she and I would be engaged in grievous arguments. My attempt to be the perfect partner had led me into being just the opposite. Here I was fighting her with all the wit and energy I could muster. So much for unconditional love.

My attempt at self-perfection was a story that I told to myself. I sincerely attempted to live out this story, but doing so was still a self-perfection project that caused many problems both at home where it was attacked and at work where it cut me off and caused uneasiness in my relations with my workmates. When my story was attacked I grew defensive. Of course, she also had self-stories. Part of her story involved getting emotional reactions from me. The easiest way to get an emotional reaction from somebody is to undermine their self-story. Many couples live like this, locked together by their battles over their self-stories, each trying to undermine the other. The story has become so important that it becomes vitally important to defend it and so one engages in the fruitless task of trying to get the other person to buy the story that they have their own vested interest in up-setting. This kind of dysfunctional stability can go on for a long time.

It is many years later. I have, in the meantime, done much spiritual training. I have meditated, prayed, studied, and disciplined myself. I have consulted some of the greatest spiritual teachers alive and lived in communities with the highest ideals. The result has been totally different from what I originally thought that it was going to be.

I thought I would learn to love unconditionally. I didn't. Instead I discovered my vulnerable human nature. I came to realise that my attempt to be perfect was simply a story about myself that I was tenaciously attached to. In my nature are the same hormones, the same weaknesses, the same propensity to distraction, the same appetites, as everybody else has. I have learnt that my love is not unconditional. In fact, in an important sense, I am now less tolerant. There is no need to go on and on participating in situations of emotional self-harm when other options are available. Why would one? Only out of some more deeply seated self-hatred, which is another story.

The reality is that nothing about me or my life is ideal. The stories that I tell myself about myself are never complete or watertight and they all involve some element of self-deception that makes me vulnerable to hurt and to spontaneous reactions that I will later regret. My very attempt to make myself into a perfect being has precisely the opposite effect. It distances me from the other person and makes it difficult to get on with them. Yet it is impossible to live without stories.

It is quite likely that you, the reader, are reading this book with a mostly unconscious motive of finding ways to shore up your self-story. You may be looking for a way to be a better person, but you can, in reality, only be the person that you are. My writing the book is also part of one of my stories to myself. If we did not have such stories we would not do anything, yet every story has the potential to get us into trouble.

My spiritual progress, if we can call it that, has therefore given me a sense of gentle irony about human nature. I have learnt that I am as prone to getting emotionally hurt as the next person. Far from reaching a state of supreme equanimity, I have discovered that such coolness only alienates one from others. I realise now that my original ideal was really to turn myself into a perfectly programmed robot.

What I have discovered that is of supreme importance, however, is that I now have a sense of being one who is loved by the universe. Imperfect, limited and vulnerable as I am, the sun still shines upon me, things do work out, food appears, rain falls, wonderful conversations take place, and the grass grows without any help from me. I grow old and my teeth fall out, but I am more comfortable in my skin than I was and, in consequence, I do not feel so critical of others because we are all in the same boat. I have not learnt great compassion, but I have acquired fellow-feeling. I have not learnt to bestow blessings on the multitude, but I do feel more blessed.

We do not radiate the unconditional love that we read about in holy texts ourselves, but, inadvertently, we often reflect it. All the little loves that make our life what it is are sparks that fly off from a cosmic wheel that is much greater than ourselves. We do live in the midst of an unconditional love that we can never fully comprehend. We can be grateful for that.

Two Practices

It is common to see tranquil abiding as a precursor to insight, but here we do it the other way around.

I'd like to introduce here two practices we call, respectively, *Nei Quan* and *Chih Quan*. *Quan* means enquiry. The Chinese character for quan contains a picture of a heron. The heron is a bird that looks intently. It catches fish by darting its beak into the water. However, it is one of the properties of light that it bends when it crosses the boundary between water and air so when you or I look into water and see a fish, the fish is not exactly where we see it as being. The heron, however, is capable of allowing for this distortion and so catches the fish. This image provides a very good analogy for the work of the seeker looking into the hidden part of the mind. Things are not quite what they seem and things are not quite where we think they are. For those who wish to situate this in terms of Buddhist theory, nei means inwardness, so nei quan is an approach to insight meditation and chi means calm so chi quan is related to what some call tranquil abiding. Both are forms of experiential learning, which is another name for mindfulness.

Nei Quan

Nei Quan is the practice of generating insight by reflecting on the evidence of one's life. In the full classical way of doing the practice one does a complete life review, considering each period of one's life in turn, starting with the first five years and working forward until the most recent past. In each period one considers one's most important relationships, starting with mother. One asks, "What did she do for me in this period? What trouble did my existence cause for her? What did I do in return?" I have recently had several grand-children. When I see the total transformation that their arrival has brought about in the lives of my daughters and daughter-in-law, I know that my own arrival must have caused a similar disruption in the life of my mother. A small child totally monopolises the parent's attention, requires frequent feeding, cleaning, changing, comforting and amusing. The main part of Nei Quan is simply to marshal the evidence. How many hundreds of nappies did my mother have to wash? How many times did she pick me up and put me down in order to attend to my needs? Doing this work of reflection is extremely sobering. We soon see that there is no possible way that we could repay what we received from our parents, let alone from all the others involved in providing the ambiance of our existence. Even if they were not very good parents they still did enough that we survived and that is a considerable amount.

Nei Quan can also be done in a smaller scale way. One can reflect upon the past twenty-four hours, or the period since one last did the exercise and ask similar questions. What have others done for me? What trouble has my existence put them to? What have I done in return? Or one can approach the matter in a different way, perhaps as follows:

First sit down in one's place for reflection and settle one's body. Then become aware of the air that one is breathing. Reflect that "This air is not me; this air is not mine; this air is not myself. I did not make it; I did not earn it; I do not own it. Yet it comes to me freely. It enters my nostrils, goes down into my lungs, and sustains my life. Every minute it saves my life several times over." Then become aware of the floor that one is sitting on. Similar reflections probably apply. Even if I do own the building, I did not create the materials of which it is constructed, I did not do the building work myself, I could not be sitting here if many other people had not done a huge amount of work and if nature had not provided a plentiful supply of materials. Our lives are dependent upon conditions. Nei Quan is an investigation into that dependency. People talk a lot these days about inter-dependency, but Nei Quan shows us how we are just plain dependent in so many ways. The sun shines upon me. This is not inter-dependency. If I die tomorrow the sun will go on shining, but if it stops tomorrow I stop too. I am the dependent one. It is a one-way deal in which I am the beneficiary.

The strength of Nei Quan is that it is based on collecting evidence and teaches us how to be objective. Much of this evidence is physical and practical. When we are new to the exercise it is best to avoid considering psychological or moral factors. Just look at the facts, at what is the case and at what was done. Later, when one has more experience one can start to include psychological factors, but when one does so one needs to have a special kind of objectivity. Feelings and thoughts are also facts. When we consider them it is very easy for us to slide away into justifications and speculative argument. However, it can be useful to look at such questions as "Who did I want to hurt or disadvantage today?" "Whose discomforture did

117

I enjoy?" These kinds of questions can be extremely useful and revealing of aspects of one's own psychology that one may normally be shy of looking at. The aim of the exercise is not so much an effort at moral self-reform as such a programme has all kinds of pitfalls attached to it. Rather it is about gathering the evidence that reveals the true nature of oneself as a human being and thus reveals also what one has in common with others.

Chih Quan

Chih Quan is a different kind of exercise. It is a good idea to do it following on from Nei Quan or it can be done on its own. In Chih Quan we invoke or conjure before our mind our own image of a guardian spiritual being. This may be our God, Amitabha Buddha, an angel, or our guiding spirit. If we cannot get an image it does not matter so long as we have a sense of being in the presence of holiness. Here I will call the spiritual being the _Yidam_, using the Tibetan word.

We should have a deferential or apologetic attitude toward the Yidam, but also feel pleasure in being in its presence. We now mentally make an offering of whatever is in us. This may be the thoughts and feelings left over from having just done the Nei Quan exercise. It may include sensations, images, convictions, insights, situations that we have been thinking about, whatever. We gather all this material together and offer it to the Yidam. We imagine the Yidam receiving it as a happy gift. Even if what we are offering is our resentment and despair or our murderous anger, it does not matter. The Yidam receives it happily. The Yidam has a bigger heart than we do and will know what to do with it and will find a place for it in the greater scheme of things. As we make this offering our mind and heart become clearer. We experience peace and space. We can feel this peace deepening in our body and in our being. This is the blessing bestowed by the Yidam. As soon as we start to feel this peace we allow ourselves to go deeper and deeper into it. We become more and more still and quiet and the peace becomes profound. If the peace is disturbed in any way, either by distractions from the environment or the re-emergence of our thought train, we once again gather these disturbances up and offer them too to the Yidam, once again receiving the blessing of peace and once again feeling ourselves descending into a deep tranquil abiding.

Nei Quan is the practice of generating insight and Chih Quan of generating calm. Together they give us an enhanced experience of the two main dimensions of our spiritual life. Through Nei Quan we find out what kind of bombu being we are. Through Chih Quan we participate in the blessing that is bestowed upon us by spiritual beings, by the Tao, by the cosmos.

In conventional Buddhist practice it is common to see tranquil abiding as a precursor to insight, but here we do it the other way around. First we examine our nature, then we let it go and receive the peace. Thus blessed we can go forth into the world with gratitude.

For those who practise using the nembutsu, Namo Amida Bu, we can see nei quan as an investigation of the meaning of "namo". What sort of a being is it that calls out? And we can see chih quan as an investigation of "Amida Bu". What sort of a peace and blessing is this presence in our life? We can also, if we like, see these two as two basic koans that frame our spiritual life: the investigation of oneself and that of the Other Power.

Three Minds

When we have seen what kind of creatures we are and started to appreciate the love that endlessly descends into our lives irrespective of our own merit then calling becomes an act of gratitude.

In the Contemplation Sutra, an Amidist text from China, there is reference to "three minds". The three minds are sincere mind, deep mind and the longing mind that transfers merit. These correspond, respectively, with the mind of nei quan, the mind of chih quan and the mind of nembutsu or calling.

Sincere Mind

Sincere mind means being free from hypocrisy. This is the mind that is willing to look at oneself as one actually is. It is the willingness to face and admit to one's human nature. People with this first kind of mind are not too certain about themselves. This does not mean that they are ineffective in life - often the reverse - but they know that they have many limitations and so are able to empathise easily with others. They are not full of themselves. They know that their life is caught in a matrix of conditions and that this can bring good and bad alike. Sometimes it results in harm. None of us is innocent or pure. The person of sincere mind does not feel superior. This, therefore, is the mind of nei quan: the mind that looks into how dependent and limited one is and faces the difficulties in one's world. Reflecting on the evidence of one's life and the ways in which it demonstrates one's dependent and limited nature one becomes aware of all that one has to be grateful for. This also allows a degree of simplicity in the midst of complexity. The inner simplicity of living an honest life frees one from having to generate an enforced simplicity in outer circumstance.

Deep Mind

Deep mind means willingness to trust in a deep support underpinning one's existence. There is a little poem by the myokonin Saichi:

> The great ocean is full of delusion;
> It has the seabed to support it.
> Saichi is full of bad karma;
> There is Amida to support it.

This is the mind of *chih quan*: the mind that is willing to give everything into the hands of the angels and enjoy their blessing and is at peace in a condition of complete entrustment. We can see that Saichi makes no pretence at self-justification. Rather it is the sense that even one such as I is supported that makes the experience deep and touching.

The Longing Mind that Transfers Merit

Longing mind is, in Japanese, *eko-hotsu-gan-shin*. This means the mind that reaches out and calls to the Beloved, dedicating all merit to the vow for birth in the Pure Land. It is the mind of faith. It joins the first two minds together. When each incident in life occurs, one says a prayer, invoking the thought of Amida into each incident. In such a single moment one gives up self-power and accepts other-power; one longs to be with that Buddha as one might long to have one's beloved present. The Perfect place to be is wherever the Beloved is. If the Beloved is present here then this place is a Pure Land. So although we do not fully enter the Pure Land in this life, every time that we say the nembutsu that land connects with us. When we have seen what kind of creatures we are and have started to appreciate the love that endlessly descends into our lives irrespective of our own deserts, then calling becomes an acknowledgement and an act of gratitude rather than a technique to accomplish something. At the beginning of spiritual practice, one naturally thinks in terms of self-power and wants to learn techniques to accomplish happiness, salvation, enlightenment or some other goal. As one becomes more experienced one discovers that this has been back to front. By halting steps one renounces spiritual ambition and starts to appreciate the blessings that already cascade into one's life.

Liberation or Extinction?

Is the aim of the exercise that we become fully alive or that we escape from this existence never to return?

Spirituality can be interpreted in a world affirming or a world denying manner. The extinctionist interpretation supports an ascetic tendency in practice. It is common for people to regard spiritual cultivation as a form of privation. Many Buddhists, for instance, think that to be Buddhist is to imitate the Buddha even in his mistakes. Siddhartha Gotama spent five years or so practising austerities before becoming enlightened. People then think that the thing for a Buddhist to do is to become enlightened and that the way to do this is to do what Buddha did and lead an austere life. This completely overlooks the fact that when Buddha became enlightened he said that all the asceticism he had practised was ignoble and worthless. His enlightenment, in fact, incorporated precisely such an insight: neither the pursuit of austerity nor the pursuit of indulgence constitute a wholesome path. It is important to live fully so that the mistakes we make are real mistakes and what we learn from them is real learning. Imitating somebody else's mistakes is not likely to be so enlightening.

True spirituality is liberationist rather than extinctionist. Some see that Siddhartha was enlightened while sitting under a tree and so spend hundreds of hours sitting as if under a tree in the hope of becoming enlightened. I did so myself. What nonsense! If he had been enlightened while eating cherries would we now think that spiritual practice consisted of cherry eating? And what if we can't find the right tree to sit under? This is superstition.

So privileging asceticism is a mistake. Yet the world-denying view remains, and has always been, widespread. Indeed, in the development of the ego elements of stoicism are inevitable. We learn to defer gratification, and we should do so. Yet in the process we make a bargain with God or fate along the lines that we shall be "good" in the expectation of some kind of reward or protection. The enlightening moment inevitably comes when God fails to keep His side of the bargain (which he never entered into in the first place, by the way). The text that most graphically illustrates this theme is the Book of Job. Stoicism is one way that we cut ourselves off from our world, creating a phantasy reality that we feel will keep us sane and make us justified, but which is actually just a scaled down form of madness. When the rude awakening comes we might flip into a truer awakening, but it is more likely that we shall fall into cynicism. Cynicism is the other side of the same coin. It too keeps reality at bay by deriding and devaluing it. The ego is kept in being by an alternating movement between stoicism and cynicism. Yet even these two are superior to the narcissism that we would be liable to fall into without them.

Here is the death poem of Matsuo Basho, generally acknowledged to be one of the greatest haiku poets:

> Sick, on a journey,
> Yet over withered fields
> Dreams wander on.

Is this how we should view life and death? A dream wandering on over fields already withered? A sickness? No doubt Basho is, even at this final point in life, being ironic about himself. Much Buddhism is about sending up the ego. He is saying, here I am this close to death, my life withering away, yet even at this point, my mind is still full of fantasies leading me along. What a fool I am! Or, he is saying, although I am withered and sick, still my spirit is alive and dreams. Poems, of course, can say both at once.

I can certainly relate to the "What a fool I am" sentiment. At a playful level "All is vanity" is a hugely liberating sentiment. Nonetheless, much religion, in practice, takes the fun out of it and makes this negative diagnosis of life into a weighty matter.

Maharaj Neem Karoli Baba, one of the most renowned Hindu gurus of recent Indian history, when he died in 1973, apparently said "Today I am released from Central Gaol forever." On the one hand, one can understand that a dying saint may understand that he is on the way to a better place. On the other hand, is regarding this world as a gaol really the height of spiritual understanding? Is this life essentially to be seen as a penitential sentence? What sort of enlightenment is that?

People may be more or less enlightened in various ways as a result of insights that naturally occur as incidences of grace along the spiritual path, but the aim is not to imitate Siddhartha Gotama's path of struggle nor attain his attainment, but to imitate him in leaving such paths behind and engaging with life. He does not want me to be him, certainly not an imitation, I am sure, he wants me to live my life, to enjoy the fullness thereof and be useful. This means entering into what reality confronts me with in as deeply honest and appreciative a manner as possible.

It is said that one enters the path through the *sangemon*. *Sange* means contrition and *mon* means gate. However, when we say sange, we are not talking about some kind of penitential process but rather about a willingness to live in the condition of deep honesty that melts the heart. When we see into our own addictive patterns, our deeply hidden cruelties, our meanness and dejection, if we are not then defeated by attachment to our idealised self-image, we experience the melting of the ice in our heart. What had been hard and brittle becomes soft and open. Many of the things that I have done in life have been unconventional. Sometimes others have been shocked or hurt. Sometimes their feedback has helped me to identify processes at work in myself that I would have preferred to ignore. Holding to the discipline of looking objectively - being able to say "yes, that is in me"; and, "no, there is not that in me now" - is part of the core of spiritual cultivation. Many, however, think that all that is needed is to conform to a particular outward pattern of life, or to dedicate enough time to a particular ritual or practice.

While it is fairly easy to say what a world denying spirituality looks like, it is more difficult to say what a world affirming one is like. It is easier to describe the extremes than the middle path. The middle path is the line of maximum flow. In a river, the current is slow at the banks and fastest in the middle. The middle is not always at the exact half way point. In life we are here talking about what is most wholehearted: wholehearted outlook, wholehearted thought, wholehearted speech, wholehearted deeds, wholehearted lifestyle, wholehearted effort, wholeheartedly keeping the greatest thing in mind, wholeheartedly entering into the samadhi of love; but what each of these things means in a specific life is something that each must fathom in their own unique case. As a spiritual community we try to help one another to do so and to provide the conditions of kindness and support in which it is possible for each of us to pass through our many transitions amongst good friends. A life affirming spirit is one in which we affirm one another in all our diversity: it is harmony without suffocation.

This world is not "central prison", but nor is it paradise. Things are not perfect as they are, but then nor is this hell. It is as it is. There is always something to do here: always another step, always a need to be "going beyond", reaching the other shore and returning. The truly spiritual person is not just intent on getting out of here, but nor does that person think that there is nothing to be done. Love is an active principle that never rests and never has a final formula. The divine way is never machine-like, but always creative and, therefore, never predictable and though reasonable is not merely reasonable. We can make codes and sutras and books of guidance, but each has to interpret them according to time and place, internal and external conditions, relying on the best guidance that is to hand at the time. All paths can be interpreted in a life affirming way or a life denying way.

There is a basic antithesis between the ideas of extinction and liberation. Is the aim of the exercise that we become fully alive or that we escape from this existence never to return? If the ideal is extinction then it becomes sensible to think of the extinguishing of all passions and, indeed, of all human functioning. Many of the translations of spiritual texts that we have do rest on this assumption. In my studies of Buddhism, I find that the Buddha says to get rid of the skandhas. However, most of the standard translations take the skandhas to be universal attributes of all living human beings - perception, feeling, consciousness, and so on. The only way to get rid of them would be by complete extinction. However, it is also possible to translate these texts differently. The skandhas may well be processes that we would be more alive without - over-reaction, exaggeration, narrow-mindedness and so on. Does *vijnana* mean all types of consciousness or just unwitting narrow-mindedness? Does *samskara* mean all mental formations or just exaggerated, unrealistic ones? Does *samjna* mean all human perception or does it mean being in a state of obsessive entrancement? In each case either is possible as a satisfactory translation, but the sense of the texts changes substantially according to the choice you make. If you make the former choices then the Buddha was talking about how to avoid being reborn in a future life and how to achieve exemption from this world for all eternity. If you take the latter options as more correct, then the Buddha is talking about how to live a vibrant, passionate (in the positive sense) life here and hereafter. Almost all Buddhist texts can be read in either way and as one gains more experience of the Buddhist culture one comes to understand that these two approaches - liberationist and extinctionist - vie with each other in all schools in many different ways.

Interestingly, a similar dichotomy occurred in Western religion in the first few centuries of the Christian era with competition between, on the one side, those who saw this world as the work of the devil and all good things as being elsewhere and, on the other side, those who saw all worlds as mixed and wanted to find the faith to live well in all worlds, this one included, no matter the obstacles that come and go. These differences of philosophy often remain hidden to the casual reader, not least because there have been great thinkers and great saints on both sides. Many seekers adhere to a composite of beliefs, some of which are extinctionist and some of which are liberationist. People are surprisingly good at glossing over their own self-contradictions.

If the liberationist position is a middle way and extinctionism is one extreme, what is the other extreme? The opposite extreme is materialism. Materialism is completely this-worldly and does not allow for a spiritual life at all; consequently it does not satisfy the deepest regions of the human mind and heart. It broadly shares with liberationism a sense that all worlds have good and bad aspects, but it does not really give one any solid basis on which to decide what "good" or "bad" are. The pitfall of materialism is that it leaves one alienated and purposeless.

So beware! Many contemporary translations of spiritual works are shot through with extinctionist assumptions that the unwary reader may fall foul of. Of course, it is possible to practise and to be a decent human being without having an ability to think clearly - but it helps.

Faith in Love that Does Not Fail

Damaging experience can defeat our spiritual life or make it triumph. What makes the difference is often encounter with another loving being.

There is a sutra called *Making Manifest the Land of Bliss*. It is commonly called the *Larger Pureland Sutra*. In it are the vows of a spiritual seeker called Dharmakara. These vows provide a kind of manifesto for a better world that he desires to see come into being. In effect, he says, "There is no point in me having a spiritual life unless doing so brings the following benefits for all beings..." These benefits include an end to prejudice based on colour or other social discriminators, an end to punishment and cruelty, liberation from hellish realms, and respect for all spiritual seekers and practitioners. They speak of a faith in faith, a faith that faith will bring grace and salvation. There is emphasis not just on giving people the ability to perceive and create a better world for themselves, but also the ability to see the truth being taught and implemented by many different groups in many different ways.

Here, therefore, we have an ancient framework within which to work toward the realisation of a spiritually perfect world for the benefit of all sentient beings that includes a recognition that many (and, in a sense, all) of those sentient beings are already working toward the creation of Pure Lands each in its own way. This conception is the complete opposite of exclusive. We recognise the effort that is being made by everyone everywhere and we do not feel that we have an exclusive possession of anything. I am very happy that this canonical text that is so pivotal in East Asian spirituality includes such a strong injunction to revere all those who are on spiritual paths, not just those who are on the path that one has chosen for oneself.

Love is unfolding everywhere in everything that happens. Generally the ways in which it is unfolding are distorted, compromised, or soiled in various ways, but everyone is doing the best they can by their own lights and even the distortions, if we were able to trace them to their deepest roots, are also related to love. The classic analogy is that the sunlight still illumines even when the sky is completely overcast and the sun cannot be seen. The light is still unimpeded, it still gets through. It is we ourselves that make the clouds. We distort our own mind in order to hang onto our story about life and about ourself. These are the clouds.

When we look at ourselves with this in mind we can see the sharp contrasts in our own nature. Or, perhaps, nature is too strong a word. What we are really looking at is our current condition. In the course of even a week of reflection one goes through so many changes of emotion, perception, interpretation and discourse that one can hardly continue to regard oneself as having anything so stable as a nature. We are contingent beings, and yet, in the midst of all the impermanence and vicissitudes, there is still something that does persist, does endure, does provide the continuing thread, which is the whole, of which all these variations are facets. This whole, however, is more than just oneself.

Sometimes we are loving, sometimes we seem not to be able to be so. Sometimes we receive love and sometimes it seems somehow missing from our life. Yet the continuing quest for it, the desire to open the portal through which it flows, remains an insistent driving force. We look at ourselves and see that we are bombu. We are bombu inasmuch as we repeatedly fail to turn on the love tap. However, it is our bombu nature that itself actually makes us loveable. Gradually we learn that in many cases we are actually turning the tap the wrong way. Our perfectionism makes us less rather than more loveable. Our very effort to open it is making it more tightly closed. If we were to stop pushing, the elixir might find it easier to gush forth on its own. Sometimes it takes the innocence of a child to show us where we are going wrong.

Such turning-the-tap-the-wrong-way is a form of hatred, for ourselves or others or both, and it is important to recognise this in ourselves, not in order to berate ourselves, but just for the sake of honesty. It, in turn, is generally driven by our fear, loss, grief or dismay at harm that has already happened or that might yet happen. In life, sometimes we are defeated, robbed, damaged, humiliated or hurt. We feel then offended as if the universe had gone wrong, but nothing has gone wrong. Reality unfolds and we experience its vicissitudes. When we have experienced savage betrayal or cruelty we cannot eradicate the memory and it is hard to trust and love again. We feel discouraged, tearful, shocked, weak, and irresolute. Nonetheless, such experience can sometimes be the foundation of love. Love is the desire that others be benefited and that they be spared from wounding or damaging experience. Experiencing such damage oneself sometimes leads to an angry desire for revenge and sometimes to a compassionate desperation to ensure that others not have to experience what one has experienced.

Pain impresses itself upon the mind forcibly and this is a doorway to both terror and sublimity. The existence of hurt and of love are closely related. Love seeks to create a pure domain where hurt is banished, yet love only actually functions in worlds like this one where hurt is ubiquitous. In fact, spiritual cultivation is to be continually transforming the experience of living in a world such as this one into the path of love. Damaging experience can defeat our spiritual life or make it triumph. What makes the difference is often encounter with another loving being.

What Dharmakara experienced that caused him to give vent to this outflow of great vows was just that. It came as a result of meeting a sage. The sage was called Lokesh-vara-raja. That encounter enabled him suddenly to start turning the tap the other way so that a great surge of love burst forth from him. Encountering the sage constitutes other power, a source of love from beyond our ego. A being that embodies such power is a spiritual master. This completely open encounter with a completely open being transformed him. It was not that Lokeshvararaja gave him some clever formula or secret knowledge. Rather the sage simply showed confidence in Dharmakara: "You yourself must know what to do," he said. Lokeshvararaja was in the flow of the love that is always present, the light that floods the world even though the clouds be ever so thick.

134

Hate is a Gate

If we want to learn to love we have to start by identifying and studying ourselves as destructive demons.

Love is often hidden in its own shadow. To understand love one must first understand one's hate. To understand it one must first see and admit it. Start with the hate. Find it. Do not condemn it. If it is real there is no point in starting a war with reality, you will only lose. Notice the harm you do and trace it to the hate you feel. Who do you hurt? When you are miserable, who are you being angry with and about what? What hurtful words or actions do you enjoy uttering? Who do you enjoy defeating? Who do you want to lose? What superficially positive action that you do actually damages or disadvantages another person? We have all been trained to put a socially acceptable face on our competitiveness so to see our own active or passive aggression is not easy.

As we become more aware of what we are, our stories about ourselves become more difficult to believe. We see a new more honest truth and this is liberating. The real is more liberated than the ideal that we pretend to.

Hate is specific where love is vast. The necessary intuition comes this way round. Say there is a man who watches pornography sometimes, not somebody who is addicted to watching it every day, but occasionally. He finds himself browsing the web looking for a perverse film to watch. Perhaps this man has had some spiritual training, so he stops and thinks, "What am I doing?" with a genuine curiosity. What does he find? He notices the tug-of-war within himself, one part, his dog nature, hot with the pursuit of what he wants, what he feels will give him a release of tension, and another part, his inner policeman, chastising himself for doing it, creating a new tension. Many people try to regulate their lives between the pressure of these two tensions. That is not liberation. Liberation is to let the whole tension war go by returning to a fuller honesty. Neither of these parts is the one that really matters, yet, of the two, the first is closer to his reality than the second. The old dog may not have Buddha nature, but it is onto something.

Beyond both there is something else to be found. He probably finds that sometime during the past twenty-four hours a woman did something that upset him and now he is angry with women in general and wanting to see them humiliated. Now he starts to sees his hate, his wish to harm, humiliate and destroy. This is a really important step. It is vital not to try to wiggle out of it either by moralising to oneself or self-justification. If, at this point, he up-braids himself with some moral injunctions he is fleeing back to the policeman which is actually the most superficial layer and he will probably miss the really important learning that is available in such a moment. Spirituality is not primarily morality; it does not come from the super-ego, it comes from a deeper place that is uncompromisingly true, no matter how good, bad or indifferent truth may be. Seeing the hate in oneself can be a door opener. Yet, what is beyond the door? Can this go further? Yes, it can.

When he looks even more carefully he may well find that what has happened is that the upsetting incident implied a disparagement of him and he has, at some level, taken some of this on. He has allowed the woman to define him. His hate is actually fundamentally directed at this version of himself. After all, what is he actually doing? The pornographic film will be there whether he watches it or not. His present action is not actually going to hurt any woman, it is going to hurt him. It is going to damage his own spirit. He is the one he hates and he hates himself because he allowed the incident to define him. He has been hooked by an identity, in this case a negative one. He took on the story and made it his own. This is a second door opener.

And beyond that door there may be other doors, right back to Adam and Eve. We could call this kind of process spiritual analysis. It can be exceedingly liberating if we do not fall back into pride. Pride is our story about our own perfection which also sometimes appears in the negative – a story about our own hopelessness. Pride feels miserable when we see the truth and then it evaporates. Spirit is not proud; spirit is honest and actually enjoys finding the truth, especially truth that is hard to find.

We have used the example of pornography, but it could have been alcohol or binging on sweets or tobacco or having an argument. All these forms of self-destructive behaviour are manifestations of self-hate growing out of mishandled interactions with others. Our complex world is a lot to cope with. When we have been buffeted by circumstance, we feel that we deserve some relief and we often seek it in ways that are actually harmful to ourselves. This is the basic meaning of the Buddhist teaching of four truths. When we find ourselves doing something of this kind, there is an open gate into a bigger life, a spiritual possibility. Looking at our own compulsiveness toward what seems a death-instinct we may find the life-instinct hidden behind it.

However, it is not that we have to find and open every door one by one. Ideally we find such an inspiration that the whole bundle of trouble falls away at one go. If the man had handled the incident the day before in a different way he would not be at this point now. Yet some reflection and analysis can be useful. The woman who criticises her husband is manifesting hate. The first thing to do is to recognise it. It may be as much hate toward herself as toward him, or it may be hate for men in general, or her father or whatever, but in it there is a story that she has taken on, that she did not have to take on, that has turned her into a self-destructive demon. If we want to learn to love we have to start by identifying and studying ourselves as destructive demons. When one sees what sort of destructive demon one is, then it is possible to get close to some firm ground upon which a spiritual life can be built.

Modern spiritual teachings are often unable to grasp this point and therefore tend to remain superficial, but ancient masters understood it all too well. When modern commentators write about a master like John of the Cross, say, there is a common tendency nowadays to explain away his statements about shame, evil, sin and so on. There is a feeling that the modern reader needs to be cheered up about himself and cannot be expected to stomach anything too realistic. We apparently must only be allowed to think positive thoughts about ourselves. This is a mistake. The shadow of such positive thinking will invade our unconscious mind and paralyse all further spiritual progress. Unless we are willing to be ruthlessly honest the angels will, rightly, consider us not worth talking to. Love and hate are closely related. Most people's hurtful actions are mostly directed toward people they love.

The object of one's love may be wholesome or not; the manner in which one acts out one's love may be skilful or not; one's capacity of heart and mind may be big or small; but, whatever, love and its shadow drive our life and we shall not be destroyed by having the courage to face that shadow; quite the reverse. Even the most negative seeming things are driven by love ultimately. Hitler loved an ideal of Aryanism. That same love could potentially have been put to much better use. He wanted to accomplish his idea of a perfect world. Every lover is trying to do so, just the ideas of what a perfect world is differ. We all seek our idea of the Pure Land, then we punish those who seem to stand in the way. Spirituality is the process of clarifying the love that is at work in our life and directing it toward the most worthy goal, but to find it and untangle it from its currently distorted expressions.

When Siddhartha Gotama's love was self-directed he first lived a life of indulgence until it nauseated him. He then turned to spiritual practices, but these initial practices were tainted by hate. They were self-destructive forms of asceticism. He was too proud to look at what he was doing honestly and so it got more and more extreme. He could not discover what love was really about or what its proper object was. He was still hating himself and hating his family and hating his mother for dying on him when he was born. Hate is distorted love and it was running his life. Then, when he was starving and down and out, Sujata the milk maid took spontaneous pity on him out of the goodness of her heart and he thus learnt the most important lesson. She was not following a plan. She was not applying a principle. She did not use a therapeutic technique. She was not doing something for herself (she probably got into trouble later from her parents for what she did). She was just doing something loving in a simple and immediate way while he had spent his time trying to do something much more complicated. She fed him the milk and he got stronger. It was an act of love. When what had happened sank in he probably felt ashamed. He spent a whole night reflecting on his own greed, lasciviousness, envy, sloth, pride, resentment and other destructive passions that he later referred to as the hand-maidens of Death. He saw their reality, which, symbolically, is that he turned them into celestial flowers. Thus he saw the cycles of the mind, how our very refusal to look at ourselves honestly creates the necessity to invent all manner of self-stories that enslave one. Then, with the dawn, he saw the morning star rise, a beautiful phenomenon that shed its light as a sheer gift even on someone like himself and thus he knew that he was enlightened and all beings are enlightened even without knowing it. We are enlightened in that the light of love and beauty shines upon us however wretched we may be, but mostly we do not see it because our spiritual eyes are closed and they are closed so that we do not see ourselves as we actually are.

Thus he saw that it is possible to cut straight through all the false stories and simply live life. Doing so he felt a great compassion for all those who were trapped as he had been in patterns of conceit and self-deception that issue as contorted thoughts, destructive actions and wasted lives. He did not have this compassion because he had learnt that it was the right way to behave, he had it

140

because it arose naturally from living his life without complicated self-justifying stories. Thereafter his love flowed outward toward others all of its own accord. "After that he was never alone" as it says in the *Denkoroku* - meaning that he was ever ministering in some way to somebody. He did not get "burnt out" or suffer "compassion fatigue" because his love was then genuine, not just part of another self-serving story.

I used to work in social work and many of the people I worked with were doing all manner of compassionate acts, but behind their actions one often found a hatred for the people that they saw as social oppressors. They had not faced their own dimensions of hate and so could not live life in a totally honest way and so their love could not issue forth cleanly. The self-hate buried in their efforts frequently led them to burn out. Buddha, after his big realisation, gives us an example of somebody who was able to go on and on precisely because he was free from self-love and self-hate. By realising the wholeness of things he did not need his old story any more. His perfect world was the reality right in front of him, just as Sujata's had been when she saw him in the gutter and had been moved to pity. His love had been liberated by hers. His whole life became meaningful.

Everybody that he met received love from him. Some were more open to it than others, but he was always open-handed. This does not mean that he was naïve; he became exceedingly wise and skilful in helping people each according to their propensities and potential. It does not mean that he went round agreeing with everybody and sparing their feelings. Many of his dialogues are arguments. Some of his action and instructions cut to the quick.

We each have a life. We each perforce must do something. Even if one is a housebound invalid one's mode of life can be loving or bitter. Even if it is bitter, behind that bitterness somewhere is a reservoir of love. All sages have taught from their own experience: liberate the reservoir of love! Worship it! Let gratitude for it over-flow your being. Don't worry that it might run dry, it won't. It is fed by a "source inexhaustible" that has nothing to do with you. That's the message. Actually, it helps enormously to realise that that source is not oneself: that in and of ourselves we are just weak vulnerable creatures, dependently originated, full of crap, but through us can flow the most amazing grace if we are willing. To become so we need to clarify the truth about ourselves.

Liberation

Going through the world banging a drum for vibrant aliveness, love, fellow feeling, joy, honesty and courage.

"Well, does anything mean anything anyway?" Nowadays one gets asked all sorts of questions that betray a cynical or nihilistic attitude. Although this seems to be particularly characteristic of the modern age which many people align themselves with non-belief, relativism, reductionism and secularism, it is clear that two and a half millennia ago Shakyamuni met with many similar sentiments. People have always been concerned about the meaning of life. They are lost in the particulars and have disallowed their intuition of the whole on grounds of supposed realism or common sense, though, in fact, it is just the opposite. Why does anything exist? Why are we alive? What is life, anyway? These questions, if taken in a practical way (i.e. what does this mean for my life?) lead to spirituality because their solution cannot be accomplished by rationality alone. They require the courage to redeem both one's inherent faith and intuition and one's raw desire and passion. This was the central insight of Kierkegaard, Sartre and other existentialist philosophers. When we let go of pretension, we stand spiritually naked facing the challenge to actually live and love as the beings that we are, in a world such as this one where nothing is totally clean and one cannot make omelettes without breaking eggs. They saw that being authentic is a huge challenge to people. Most prefer to slide along immersed in the common half-truths that oil social intercourse and minimise spiritual demand.

Buddha's wholehearted way is not like that. Yet, nor is it about ending all passion, suffering and struggle - paying off one's karmic debt and saying goodbye to the world, or, at least, I do not believe so. If he had done that we should never have heard of him. Rather he went through the world banging a drum for vibrant aliveness, for love, for fellow feeling, for joy, for honesty and for the courage to rise above setbacks and difficulties. It is important to live and to do so we need to let go of our unnecessary complications.

When one wakes up one may make many mistakes, one may have joy and suffering, one might discover one is not such a nice person after all, one might laugh and cry more, one will find out a lot about life. When we let the light illumine our world it may be like turning over a stone; when the light falls on what was previously in shade all kinds of wiggly creatures may dash about, but at least one is alive and as one examines that life one sees that in all its diversity it is really love and we can have faith in that.

The Taste of Eternity

When one is a disciple one's assessment is vertical.
When one is a Buddha one's assessment is horizontal.

I have been asked to explain the notion of *adhisthana,* its relation to guru-yoga in Tibetan Mahayana Buddhism, and to say whether this is the same or different from Amidism. Adhisthana refers to spiritual support. It is that upon which one can take one's stand. It is a reliable condition as opposed to worldly conditions that are subject to impermanence. Adhisthana is not subject to impermanence because it is not itself dependent upon anything. Hence the notion of *shunyata.* Adhisthana is, therefore, other power (Chinese: *ta-li,* Japanese: *tariki*) and it is the Pure Land (*Jing tu, Jodo*). These are not separate things. In the original Indian language, "other power" is parabala. Bala means "power". *Para* means "other", or, more precisely, "beyond". Buddhism frequently uses the idea of *paramita*, meaning the "other shore". This is all linked up with the teaching of dependent origination. We are dependently originated beings (fragile, vulnerable, fallible, and impermanent), but what can we take refuge in? Certainly not our own ego. We need something from beyond our own limited capacity, something that can help us and give inspiration. Adhisthana is refuge and refuge-power. These are all just different ways of talking about universal love.

In Buddhism, adhisthana is what Buddhas rely upon. Buddhas share it with Buddhas. Since the disciple regards the teacher as a Buddha, for the disciple adhisthana resides with the teacher and, hence, with the lineage of teachers. However, it is also recognised that teachers may have found adhisthana directly from an encounter with a cosmic Buddha such as Amida or by remembering his land or just from deep honesty about life. This would be the case, for instance, with Honen Shonin who, on reading Shan Tao's Commentary, realised what true compassion was.

If, at any time in the vast wanderings of time one has ever chanced upon that land of light then all that is necessary is that one remember. Anything may be sufficient to awaken such a memory. Such remembering is an-amnesia (*smriti*), as Plato says.

Actually, it is my impression that this is quite common. Many people have had spiritual experiences, though they may not have realised their full significance. In my own case, I had powerful spiritual awakenings long before I knew anything about Buddhism. Later, when I met teachers I had more experiences that they recognised and that I recognised as being the same in essence as the earlier ones. Many people have awakening experiences and so enter the path. They are not all signed up members of a religious community. It would be a grave mistake to think that the spiritual treasure that Buddhism points out is the exclusive property of members of the Buddhist club. The exclusivism of some religious groups merely indicates that they do not realise the universality of what they are dealing with. Encounters with adhisthana occur wherever people awaken to spiritual reality. These may get recognised or not, but that does not detract from their significance in the lives of those who take refuge in them, or those who benefit from their transformation. Lineage is a qualification like a pedigree or diploma, but adhisthana is not limited to holders of certification nor do all such have it. The adhisthana that is where Buddha is found is openly available through deep honesty. True lineages are those made up of teachers who rely upon it. However, as soon as one calls sincerely from the heart one is standing on that ground.

This is a bit like one of the founding issues of Protestant Christianity: the assertion that each believer stands naked in confrontation with God with no priest or priestly lineage in between. Of course Buddhism does not go so far. It does not reject priests, because the priest, if true, does dwell in the adhisthana too, but the priest is not the only gate. So guru power is a sub-set of lineage power and lineage power is a sub-set of other power, Spirit power, the power of the beyond. Teachers point it out, support one through one's encounter with it, and are loving friends and fellow disciples of the awakened ones. Devotion to the teacher can be just as powerful in Amidism as in any other branch of Buddhism and some, such as Rennyo, did think it essential, but in Pureland the teacher regards himself simply as another disciple of the Tathagata. It is precisely because he does so that he is in adhisthana.

When one is a disciple one looks up to the Buddhas. One's assessment is vertical. When one is a Buddha one's assessment is horizontal. All equal. Reverence (the cure for egotism) rightly abases itself. Love, however, knows no distinctions of rank. Adhisthana is both universal and particular and it requires the asymmetry of vertical and horizontal. Sometimes one is disciple and sometimes one is Buddha. Adhisthana is the

ground on which Buddhas stand: the stillness and silence
in which a still, small voice can be heard.

> Even the dull stones
> come alive as he passes
> and turn into bread.
> Though I strive to worship him
> he raises me up instead.

Continuous Prayer

Although I am a modern person with modern ideas, teach me how to pray.

Spirituality is continuous prayer. Just pray incessantly. This means that all activities must become prayer. To cook a dinner, to go for a walk, to write a book, to pause in silence, to listen to a friend; all of these things can be prayer, or not be, depending upon one's intention and upon the frame of mind that one holds them in. To pray is to be in the presence, to sit in the presence, to stand up in the presence, to walk in the presence, to lie down in the presence. To acknowledge the Beyond, the whole, the ultimate, the Tao, with one's body, with one's voice and with one's mind.

Prayer has many elements: creating a sacred space, worship (with the body), praise (with the voice), and vision (with the mind); it can be an expression of warmth of heart, of contrition, of asking for protection and inspiration; it can involve making offerings, reflection, or recitation; it can be dwelling in peace and grace, transferring merit or giving thanks. All of these and more are encompassed in a moment of true prayer and sometimes we focus on one or other element individually.

We study our own life flow to make it prayer, see where it is not prayer, pray for it to become prayer. We study the world, its needs and its nature that our prayer may have a universal dimension. This might mean relieving suffering, but more important than being free from suffering is to live a good life. A person who sets out on a noble life does not thereby avoid suffering. They are likely to suffer more, for they will encounter the sufferings of others. They will confront the great grief of the world. They will meet the disappointments of love. All this will become part of their life of prayer and that prayer will set them free.

To create a sacred space can be done formally or informally. Formally, one can have a place of prayer, a practice hall, an altar, a grove in the wood, a hilltop, a cave, a circle drawn in the dust. Informally, one can designate where one is, where one has one's being, as being the place of endless prayer. It is all in how we see it.

To worship is to employ one's body in a manner that honours and adores. I encounter some people who say, "Surely we should not worship," these people being in flight from one or another theistic religion who think that in Buddhism they have found a place where there is no worship, but worship is the most natural thing and worshipping Buddha has been the centrepiece of Buddhist activity from the very beginning. Bodhidharma, the founder of Zen in China, was saying the same thing when he said "When bowing ceases, Buddhism ceases." Here too, however, there is the formal and the informal aspect. Really, Buddhism is just endless bowing. When everything we do is a bow, then we are practising and bowing is prayer.

To praise is to do the same with the voice. When everything we do is a bow it is also a nembutsu. Nembutsu is the basic prayer of Buddhism, the prayer of refuge. To be Buddhist is to take refuge, endlessly. We have times to formally chant together as a group and there is great merit in such harmonious collective worship. There are times when two might pray together, as when visiting a person in hospital, for instance. Then, in a spiritual community, whether Buddhist or not, the saying of the Name will pepper every activity.

Beyond body and speech there is the heart and mind, wherein we keep something of great worth and hold it holy, as a keepsake, like the moon reflected in a puddle. The softening of heart and mind is what we call contrition, the realisation of our bombu nature.

To say that life is prayer is also to make it an offering. We make offerings through our love, our learning and our labour. We give away whatever little merit or credit we have. Endlessly we receive more than we give. Prayer is to ground one's life in gratitude.

How can we support each other in living noble and worthwhile lives? This is something to pray for, more than to be free from hardship. Hardship can ennoble a person and is certainly not always to be avoided. Spiritual life is not a flight from suffering; it is about living a worthwhile life, which is a life in the presence: a life of prayer. Prayer is what transforms ordinary - and often difficult - experience into the path.

Although I am a modern person with modern ideas, teach me how to pray.

Although I have been taught to assert myself, let me worship something greater.

Although I am full of doubts, let me have faith at least sometimes.

Teach me to use my doubt constructively so that faith and doubt co-operate.

Although I have the habit of self-justification, let me see what I freely receive and learn gratitude.

Although I have been taught to think in abstractions, be personal for me, be my Beloved, as I know I must be beloved to all the sages and ancestors.

Prayer is adoration and longing. These are fundamental dimensions of human life. We are inherently incomplete. That is the nature of life. Only in death is there completeness. In life there is longing. This longing may take the form of worldly desire, lust or ambition, or it may take a more spiritual form. Prayer is transformation of base energies into sublime purpose and it manifests as a deeply plaintive emotion that is both sadness and joy all at once. This is the passion of the holy life.

Learning from Death

A spiritual act is unilateral; it is never a trade.

While conducting seminars based on my book *Who Loves Dies Well* there has been much discussion of dying, death, loss and human contingency. A dying person is often in a condition of almost total physical dependence upon carers. At the same time, the dying person is leaving this life and there may well be nothing that the carers can do about that. Further, dying, commonly but not universally, has a liberating effect upon the spirit. The dying person may not even be able to direct the actions of their own bladder, but, at the same time, they have a spiritual independence that seems almost absolute. Actually this is just an extreme or more obvious case of what is true all the time even of the person who is not close to dying. We are all radically dependent as physical beings in a physical world and yet we are absolutely independent (*ekagata*) in as much as we are spiritual beings in a spiritual world.

Strangely, we become independent by realising that we are part of something much greater and actually lacking in a separate power of our own. This true spiritual independence is different from worldly independence. Worldly independence means that a person can pay their way within a particular social system. Spiritual independence means that the person cannot be coerced spiritually by any worldly system. This is what we see in the life of Mira.

The notion of ekagata does not, however, mean that we do not have impact upon one another. Being with a person who is close to dying can be inspiring. Liberation is infectious. Those who are free make others more free, but the truly free never lose any of that freedom to those who are not free. Freedom is like infinity, you cannot add to or subtract from it, whereas non-freedom is finitude where all is a matter of degrees.

It may seem paradoxical that a person gets closer to an appreciation of their spiritual independence as they become more dependent physically, but this seems to be the case. Many people, as they approach death, or even during periods of severe illness, experience some degree of spiritual liberation. This is surely what leads us to believe that the soul is separate from the body. When we are fit and healthy we are less aware of our physical contingency and at such times we are more likely to lose awareness of our spiritual freedom. Great sages have sought to bring us close to our physical dependency - close to death (*Mara*) - in order that we rediscover our spiritual liberation, just as Buddha came close to death in his extreme ascetic practices or Jesus did in the desert. Everything in our life of form (*nama-rupa*) is contingent and yet, at the same time, we are spiritually liberated, participating in the Unborn.

There is much contemporary theorising that suggests that all things are interdependent. Personally I think this is a mistake and a misinterpretation, even though it is well meant. No doubt the intention is to emphasise that we should pull together, be loyal to one another, treat the world with respect, be ecologically conscious, and care for others. All these are good sentiments and positive values, but belief in interdependence is not the only way of arriving at them and the idea of interdependence within the form realm does actually tarnish them by suggesting that we care for others in order to care for ourselves whereas real care regards the other as an end in itself not merely a means to self-benefit. Love is not a means.

No, the correct interpretation is that radical dependency co-exists with absolute spiritual independence. They cannot take my spirit away from me even if they boil me in oil, but everything in the realm of form - even the forms in my head - remains contingent.

The human mind operates in both domains. The freedom that derives from spirit can inform our actions within the world and the attachments that we fall into in the realm of form can occlude our awareness of liberation.

We can be free without knowing it and some people do not know it until they are dying. Spiritual training aims to help us realise things earlier so that we can have the benefit while still having some lifetime left. Imagine a person confined in an area surrounded by a high voltage electric fence. He stays confined within the area and never touches the fence. However, it could be the case that the fence is not turned on. He could be free without realising. He might go a long time confined even though he was actually free.

What is it that enables us to realise that the fence is switched off? It is loss of the fear of death. If the man loses the fear of death, he might touch the fence and discover he is free. This is why near-death experiences not uncommonly have a liberating effect. When a person knows that he or she is dying, they touch the fence and discover that they are free. Spiritual practice is a matter of learning to be free without having to wait until one is on one's death-bed. A spiritually liberated person - one who has faith to touch the wire - can go forth in the world of form in full knowledge of their spiritual liberation. Such a person is a blessing for the world.

Seeing this blessing, some people want to pursue a spiritual path as a means of getting or distributing such blessings, but this is a mistake. Liberation is not something contrived in order to deliver blessings, it is reality itself with no further goal. Blessings are incidental. Awareness of physical and psychological dependency is thus part and parcel of awakening to spiritual independence.

What is termed inter-dependence is the fact that blessings flow in more than one direction, but mostly this is not really inter-dependency, it is dependencies of several kinds that are independent of one another. The dying person is physically dependent. Because the dying person is often spiritually reconciled, there is a spiritual benefit in being in their presence. The carer may receive in spirit and give in physical care. This is a kind of inter-dependence, but it is not really, because neither dependency is done for the sake of the other and either could exist without the other. The sick person could be cared for by people who were untouched spiritually and the person at the bedside who is inspired might not be involved in the physical care.

The value in separating these factors is that it is liberating to deeply realise dependency and liberation itself means an ability to act unilaterally. If everything really were interdependent there could be no liberation. To realise that, in the world of form, one cannot exist without an endless stream of benefits that are not of oneself, that one did not earn, that one has no right to, yet which arrive unilaterally, as does sunshine, is to appraise life in an honest way. Doing so one realises great gratitude. A spiritual act is similarly unilateral; it is never a trade. The spiritual person co-operates with others because it is good to do so, not because they have earned it and still less for any benefit he himself receives. A loyal friend is so because it is good to be so, not because of favours or rewards that might follow. A noble person treats the world with respect because that is the noble thing to do. He trusts his intuition and when he benefits someone or something that is an end in itself, not a means toward a personal benefit. This principle of unilateralism is the basis of liberation.

To the worldly mind it seems risky to act thus because we are not omniscient. We never have full knowledge so may prefer to rely upon common opinion rather than take our life into our own hands. Consequently many people try to live safely and have a dull time. Freedom, on the other hand, is not dull, but it does mean using the whole of one's being, feelings, thought, imagination and so on, in a courageous manner. Most people only fully understand this when they are facing death and many not even then.

The Pure Land is born when people have the faith to touch the wire and realise that they have been free all along. As soon as they do so, however, they assume a responsibility for unilaterally living their existence in a manner that transcends even the boundaries of life itself. A surprising number of people, even after they have touched the wire, prefer to go on living as if they had never made the fateful discovery of their own freedom.

Zen is a Special Kind of Empathy

The particular grief is the great grief; the particular joy is the joy of the universe.

While I was in Korea we had much discussion of spirituality and psychotherapy and especially of Zen, which is the predominant form of Buddhism in that country. Zen is much concerned with a particular kind of sensitivity in how one sees the world. This is Zen mind. So what is that mind and what is the Zen of psychotherapy? I suggest that it is a special kind of empathy. Empathy is the mind that enters into the other and does so by cognising the other's others in an appreciative way. Mind, in Buddhism, is defined as "clear and cognising". In other words, the Zen mind is "no mind". It is the mind that adds no colour from its own side, but is "mirror mind". Mind is always conscious of something and ordinarily our mind is conscious of ordinary experience.

Zen mind is:

- perceiving with freshness, free from prejudice
- perceiving in terms of the whole of space: seeing the particular as a fragment of a much greater whole
- perceiving in terms of the whole of time: seeing dependent things in terms of their origin, sustenance, decay and demise
- perceiving in terms of the whole beyond time and space: seeing dependent things as embedded within a reality that is timeless and all-embracing

- perceiving emptiness: by grounding oneself in silence and stillness, seeing the whole in the part and the part in the whole, and allowing the intuition of absolute reality, the Unborn, to have honour in one's heart.

This mind is the mind of an ordinary person restored to its proper setting, just as if one had walked out of the shadow into the bright light of day. To perceive in this way truly as a human being is not to abstract oneself from ordinary daily life nor to distance oneself from ordinary people. It is the reverse. Each move in the above list involves poignancy. To perceive freshly is sometimes to realise how jaded one's perception had become. To perceive in terms of the whole of space is to see how things depend on their context, how nothing can be taken for granted, how all ordinary beings are fragile and dependent. To perceive in terms of the whole of time is to see that all this that surrounds us now will pass away, the beautiful person before us will become old and wrinkled and then be a corpse and eventually dust. Every moment some part of us is wearing away or wearing out. To perceive the spiritual reality that enfolds us is to know how blind we are most of the time. To have the intuition of emptiness, the real ground of our being, is to feel the "great grief" of this world. Yet, with each grief there also comes the joy of liberation and of a more profound intimacy as the centre of gravity of one's being come closer to the truth.

So, Zen mind is seeing "deeply", as Thich Nhat Hanh says, and seeing deeply may mean having a full and rounded appreciation of what is before one, seeing its dependent origin, its dependent present and its dependent transformation in the future, both appreciating this fragment of the universe that each of us is in all its tiny, yet all-consuming, drama, and through the particular knowing the universal. The particular grief is the great grief; the particular joy is the joy of the universe. The greater cannot be known any other way than through the particular and it is in the depth of our empathy for the singular that we commune with the All. Love is love and to know the smallest particle of earthly love truly is to know the love of God.

When Buddha saw a person he saw that person in the whole trajectory of life: birth, ageing, disease and death, triumph, boredom and disaster, work, leisure and prayer, greed, hate, delusion and liberation. This made him smile, weep, commiserate, celebrate, feel a myriad emotions, laugh and clap his hands. To see another truly is to be touched in one's heart by the frailty, the mystery and the glory.

It includes seeing the transcendent dimension that renders the object into powerful appearance (rupa) in the positive sense, something extremely precious and worthy of worship. Thus when one sees an object one also sees the effort that went into making it, one sees its transience and fragility, one sees it as something precious. When one sees a person, one has a sense of what has gone into making that life, one knows its transience and fragility, and one finds it precious. Yet when what one is seeing is another living being, one is also seeing a mind. To see another mind is to see what that mind is cognising and to see what is precious to that other life. Zen mind, in relation to another, is a special kind of empathy. It is to be mentally alongside that person, seeing what they see, an empathy for their empathy, a love for the love in them. If I see what they see and do so with the Zen eye, then I also feel what they feel deeply in their heart, even deeper than they themselves are, perhaps, willing to be aware of. This is therapy.

Therapy is to open the depth of the heart of the other by standing alongside them, seeing their world through open eyes with an open heart. But I can only do this if I am willing to trust that I will be given those eyes when I entrust myself to that situation. Therapy therefore rests on faith. It is not something done out of my own cleverness. My cleverness just gets in the way. Better to remember that I am just an ordinary being, but when I trust it something greater will operate. Zen mind is like this.

The client appears before me and tells me a little of her world. She opens a small window. I stand beside her and look through that window with her. We are aligned. I see with eyes given to me by powers I do not understand and I feel what is hidden in her heart. The resonance is reciprocal and she learns what is in her heart by sensing it reflected in mine. That mirror is Zen mind. When she knows what is really in her heart, she can live her life truly. She will make her own decisions. I do not know what she will do with what she has found. That's fine. I just know that we are both richer for the moment of transmission that has occurred between us. Sometimes I know what she has found, sometimes not. Sometimes even she does not yet know. What matters is not that I end up with information, but that she end up more liberated than before.

Probably she does not find what she expected to find, some secret about herself or some key principle upon which to base her behaviour, perhaps. When she is enriched in this way, she sees what her others see; she is more open to her world. She expected to be narrowed down to one right thing and found herself opened up to a bigger world. She and I together enquire what those whom only she knows have in their hearts. Now she is enriching them and they her. There is a tiny bit more love than before and that is the elixir that matters.

Zen mind is honest. It is willing to find whatever is there. It is not trying to manipulate a desirable outcome. Maybe what is there is greed, maybe hate, maybe something not very nice, maybe love, maybe courage, whatever. How can we summarise all this? Be humble, be honest, have faith, don't manipulate. This is not a psychological trick. It is not a technique. It is something most true.

Zen mind is contagious. I do not need to ask her what she is feeling for it glistens in her eyes, yet, I know that it is a function of what she perceives in the hearts of others, others that I shall never meet. In this process there is much that I never know. Therapy is not a function of how much the therapist gets to know. It is a function, as Dogen says, of tenderness spreading. The impression is a deep one. It does not necessarily take long.

The Person Who Practises

It is not a gain to him that the other person loses something.

When we meet people who practise we notice that they do not tell lies; they do not cheat; they do not take bribes; they do not pursue simply their own advantage; they do not steal. When we meet people who practise we notice that they do not kill sentient beings; they are not cruel; they are not violent. When we meet people who practise we notice that they speak words of kindness; they rarely become angry; they are patient; they speak well of others. When we meet people who practise we notice that they are helpful and kind; they are happy to co-operate in good work; they are generous and hospitable, and, usually, they have a developed sense of humour. When we meet people who practice we notice that they are adaptable; they have few desires; they are easily pleased; they have peace and contentment irrespective of the circumstances that they find themselves in.

Why are people who practise like that? Because, firstly, they have been honest with themselves and realised that self-importance is nonsense, secondly they have learned to be quiet in their heart so that they can attend to the leadings of spirit, and thirdly they have gathered their faith and centred it upon something wholly worthwhile. They have placed it upon enlightened people; enlightened teachings and real community. These are the things that they treasure and have faith in. These are the things that they believe to be worth working for.

Such people rarely lie, cheat or steal because to them there is no point in doing so. Only in the most invidious of circumstances do such behaviours make any sense. Everybody does things and everybody has reasons for each thing that they do. The person who steals does so in order to get a personal advantage and does not see the loss to the other person as something that matters. To the person who practises, however, firstly that person has few desires and sees that gaining many things is going to be a burden rather than an advantage and secondly that person cares for the other people and so it is not a gain to him that the other person lose something. In fact, he sees that theft simply spoils the world that he loves.

We use the word practice and this has become a standard usage, but originally practice meant something that happened in preparation for the real thing. Spiritual practice, however, is the real thing. It is not a preparation for something else. Indeed, the very essence of it is that it is living the real life. In the modern world we have achieved a great and wonderful development of society. This is amazing and wonderful and keeps people from starvation, illness, and exposure and gives them many opportunities. However, in order to keep this great human machine turning we have to control human activity and to do that we have to classify it into functions and these classifications easily come to seem more real than the reality that they represent. The big spiritual need of the modern person is to somehow cut through this web of artificiality so as to live a more real life so that what they do springs from real conviction and real experience rather than from merely conceptual ideas alienated from the reality. A person who practises lives a real life.

The Zen of Then

A bit of here-and-now is a welcome break, but we should not throw the baby out with the bathwater.

We are all born hedonistic and present oriented and through education we get a wider perspective that takes in the past and the future and this is what makes life meaningful and productive. To make the past and future part of our awareness and to give our life such perspective is an essential part of becoming a mature person. It is spiritual advancement. That people learn how to defer gratification, appreciate history, reflect on past activity and project into the future in an intentional manner is a necessary foundation for the creation of culture and civilisation. That they can help another to relive a past experience or do so themselves is essential to helping a person grow, change and become liberated from past troubles. That we can sit and reminisce or share dreams is also part of what makes social intercourse rich, cultured and rewarding. As Zen Master Dogen says, the essence of spiritual maturity is to understand the relationship between past, present and future, and it is the height of folly to misunderstand or lose faith in the working of cause and effect.

Religions traditionally - and classic Buddhism is no exception - encourage us to value the past and to have a positive view of the future. Indeed, religions enable us to extend our time perspective hugely toward measureless time, eternity even. One of the real values of religion in our lives is that we live not just for now, but with a perspective that is much greater and shades into eternity. Far from seeking to narrow us down, true awakening gives us a capacity to live in the whole expanse of time and to make the past and the future as real as the present. If the past and future do not exist for a person, that is a handicap not a blessing. Without a past, people are anxious. Without a future they are depressed.

In Buddhism we practise mindfulness (smriti). Smriti means remembrance. Buddhism is, first and foremost, the remembrance of Buddha. A Buddhist is somebody who relies upon the memory of that great sage. The knowledge that such a person walked this Earth is a remarkable source of strength. When we are in deep difficulties, this memory will help us. It gives us an example of a person whose faith in the noble life did not falter even when he was face to face with the mass killer Angulimala. Buddha taught a variety of techniques for developing mindfulness. These begin with putting the object of one's remembrance before one and then being infinitely carefully aware of one's every breath and every movement while in that presence. From this comes an awareness of our own uncontrollable senses, emotions, imagination and thoughts. The contrast between what we find in ourselves and what we try to hold before us in memory has a profound effect. Mindfulness, therefore, is a kind of experiential learning about the rising and falling of states. In particular, it is a means of learning about dependent origination. It was his own insight into dependent origination that was the substance of Buddha's enlightenment and he wanted to pass this on to us. Dependent origination is about the relatedness of past, present and future as well as being about how our lives are substantially under the control of forces from beyond the reach of our personal will. The content of Buddha's enlightenment was a realisation that there is more to life than just this here-and-now moment.

The proper Buddhist attitude to time is that of living in the past, the present and the future simultaneously, letting them integrate into a seamless reality. When one sees the origin of deeds and the consequence of deeds at the same time as one sees the possibility of the deed, then one naturally lives an ethical life. When one senses eternity in an hour, one naturally enters samadhi. When one understands the succession of the seasons of life one naturally acquires the wisdom of the enlightened and when one sees the tears and joy that come down through the generations one gains their compassion. Such people are not ethical, contemplative, wise and compassionate because they follow rules, but because they are attuned to what is genuine and to the whole rather than just to one part of reality.

From the Buddhist perspective, non-virtue is not due to the failure to follow the dictates of a divine being; it is due to a failure to understand the three times. It is when we do not see the roots and consequences of what we do that we act unskilfully and harmfully. We do so in avidya (ignorance, non-comprehension). When Jesus is depicted as saying "Forgive them for they know not what they do" he is uttering a truth that is also at the heart of Buddhism. One can forgive others for not knowing what they are doing, but one knows that the universe will be less relenting. The Taoist sages tell us how to live so that we can cooperate with that universe. Appreciating its paradoxical course. Those who pursue only their own benefit end up losing.

We become moral beings by learning the lessons of experience and this means having the ability to vividly relive the past. Our ethical sense is also brought to maturity by increasing our empathy for others and empathy relies heavily upon having an enhanced imaginative capacity that goes well beyond perceiving what is true at this moment. Sometimes in my work of training counsellors I have encountered students who have an acute ability to detect the client's present moment state but who remain ineffective counsellors because they have too short a horizon of comprehension and fail to see how this present state is meaningful in terms of the trajectory of the life.

There are some who advocate living in the here and now as a fundamental principle of the Dharma, but I cannot agree. Awareness of the here and now is an important part of life some of the time, but it is only a part and it is not always appropriate. Of course, one can say that one can take account of the past and future while still living in the present, but if one takes this position one has to ask whether anything remains of the live-in-the-here-and-now principle. For that principle to mean anything one must be able to say what is the alternative: what does it mean to not live in the present moment?

Sometimes I taste an ice-cream and enjoy the flavour. Sometimes I do not notice what is impacting my senses because I am lost in thought about my friend who is suffering in hospital. In the first, I am in the here-and-now. What about the second? If we say that I am still in the here-and-now thinking about my friend then is there any time when any human being is not in the here-and-now and, if not, what is the point of the principle? If, on the other hand, we say that in the second case I am not in the here-and-now, can we also really say that it would be better for me to forget about my friend and just enjoy my ice-cream? Surely not.

The past and the future are at least as real as the present and the far distant is as real as the near at hand. Realising this releases us from solipsism. My being here does not make this place more real than another place and my being in the present moment does not make that moment any more real either. To think so is to be lost in self-importance. To realise this is maturity and to fail to do so is to remain immature. Spirituality is surely not narcissism.

The present is fleeting and many present moments may be of no particular consequence while an event from the past can dominate a whole life. Nor should one see this latter phenomenon in negative terms only. Was not Shakyamuni's life dominated by his enlightenment experience and do we not know of it in some detail because he recounted it on several occasions, evidently enjoying reliving the reminiscence? Spirituality frequently takes the form of reliving, either of personal experience or of collective matters that are ritually celebrated. Indeed, it is a major function of religion to give us this extended perception and appreciation. It also includes rehearsing. It is doubtful if a person is capable of doing anything without fore-living it in their mind. If one does not have a vision of what one intends to do one will probably not do it. This is how the mind works. If we prevent the mind from fore-living we will become ineffective human beings.

The Zen of then is the ability to fully appreciate what is not present with the same vividness as what is. It is the divine eye that sees, hears, smells, tastes and cognises realities that are not forced upon us in the now, but which enrich our existence and make life worth living.

The purpose of meditation is not to shut out or to shut off this capacity, but to expand the mind so as to encompass it more fully and find the whole that is greater still. When we "place our mindfulness before us" we bring something from memory and seek its reality. Mindfulness is to live in the three times together, not to live in one to the exclusion of the other two.

As Thich Nhat Hanh says, it is when one takes a cup in one's hand, to see the potter who made it, the earth from which it sprang and the toil that it has involved, and it is also to see the cup broken, discarded, returning to the earth sometime in the future, its form dissolved. And if, in the reverie of such reflection, one is lost to immediate awareness, as young Siddhartha was when sitting under the rose apple tree, then do not up-braid yourself for that. There are good precedents. It was the remembering of this reverie that triggered his enlightenment experience.

So why has the supposed power of nowness become a popular cause? In our contemporary world, as we never tire of saying, we live in situations of great stress. We have targets and deadlines and these cause us much anxiety and distress. Much contemporary dukkha is decidedly psychological. Our forebears had to wrestle more with strain than stress, with disease, fatigue, long hours of physical work, difficulty in protecting themselves from the elements, malnutrition and so forth. Many people in the world still do. In the sophisticated countries, however, it is performance anxiety and social stigma that threaten. All of these have to do with judgements made of us by others based on assessments they make of our behaviour over a period of time. Retreating into the present moment can be a way of attaining temporary relief. We go back to our "inner child" for a short time and our physical system enjoys some relaxation. The self-critical inner judge switches off. This is undoubtedly a relief. So as a short-term first aid measure, dropping into the here-and-now can be a benefit.

Contemporary civilisation, especially in the Protestant world, has been built on the principle of deferred gratification. When this becomes too much, a bit of here-and-now is a welcome break, but we should not throw the baby out with the bathwater. The last thing that most of the impoverished people that we work with in India need is to live more in the now. They need a vision of the future and to absorb the Buddhist sense that time unfolds in a lawful manner such that actions can be confidently expected to bear results; and they also need an enhanced sense of the "there" so as to feel themselves to be part of an international community and of a more than local movement so that their lives have purpose. Without this their hand-to-mouth existence lacks the possibility of collective liberation and their lot would remain a sorry one.

Here-and-nowness has several aspects. One is not to worry about what is not worth worrying about. This is the idea that "Sufficient unto the day are the evils thereof," and Buddha also says something similar. By concentrating on what is immediately present we can sometimes free ourselves from neurotically worrying about distant things.

Some people, for instance, can get into a sweat thinking about the aeroplane flight they are going to take next week. In this case it is certainly better not to think about it until it happens. On the other hand, when they are in the airplane it might help to distract them from immediate terror to think about something completely other than the here-and-now.

Again here-and-now can imply don't put off to tomorrow what you can do today, which is also often good advice. At this rule of thumb level some aspects of nowness are very handy. However, if one did not live at least a bit in the future and in the past, one would not know what needed doing and one would certainly fail to catch one's flight.

Similarly, by refining the art of here-and-now-ness, an increased awareness of immediate sensual gratification is, up to a point, an enrichment of life. To more fully taste the banana as one eats it, to more appreciatively perceive the depth of colour of the sky above one's head or the feel of a texture that one touches; all these are benefits. Again, to be more in touch with one's body, so long as it does not spill over into hypochondria, is a useful skill and a natural faculty that some people have lost and can usefully restore. So, as I said earlier, the skills associated with being-in-the-here-and-now, at their best, are useful and valuable.

What has gone wrong is that in some quarters the usefulness of these skills has been taken to imply that we have here a complete recipe for life. It is as if finding that a spoon is useful and that one can eat all one's food with it, knives and forks should be discarded. However, the knife of the past and the fork of the future are actually exceedingly important and useful tools and we should not throw them away. Rather we should become as skilful in their use as in using the spoon of the present. And this analogy is quite good because in order to use the knife and fork one does sometimes have to put the spoon down.

We should remember that one of the things that people evidently valued the Buddha for was his ability to perceive the past and the future. "What will become of so-and-so?" They asked him. After a particularly drawn out session of such questions the Buddha tells his disciples that if they just follow the principles he has enunciated they will be able to see for themselves. Dharma is about consequentiality. To understand Dharma is to be able to step back from the blinding glare of the here-and-now and understand the there-and-then, the one-thing-leading-to-another.

The Zen of Two

Subsequent to Shakyamuni, we do not hear much about the ancestors becoming enlightened while meditating. They were almost all enlightened by an interpersonal encounter.

Another area where essentially sound ideas are sometimes carried to a ridiculous extreme is in the obeisance paid to oneness and non-duality. The danger is rather similar, namely, that the doctrine is used as a restriction rather than an expansion of the mind. The human mind functions in a binary fashion. The brain has two hemispheres and they give us two distinct takes on each perception. We work things out by drawing contrasts. At this moment I am writing and the point of writing this is to point out that a certain idea is sometimes taken the wrong way. I am therefore being dualistic. I am distinguishing one view from another. This is useful. Even the idea of non-duality itself is a dualistic idea. It distinguishes dualism from non-dualism. Philosophically, it therefore suffers from the fallacy of being its own refutation. If we were strictly non-dualistic we could never think how to improve anything or even decide which side of the road to drive on.

How has the over-emphasis of non-dualism come about? One reason is experiential and another is historical. Historically, I think the problem is that an idea from Eastern thought has chimed with a different, but analogous idea from Western religious history, one over which a good deal of blood was spilt long ago. When there is a trauma within a culture it does not die with the people who committed or suffered it, but lives on to haunt future generations. Issues of dualism and non-dualism afflicted the early days of Christianity in the West, as well they might. If one has the idea that this world was created by an all-good God it becomes difficult to explain evil in the world and much of the doctrine of theistic religions tends to be taken up with this problem. One way of doing so is to see this world as separate from God. In God's world all is good whereas everything here is bad. This solution was dualism in its most developed form. It is the idea that this is a corrupt world and the best thing to hope for is to get out of it as relatively uncorrupted as possible so as to go to a better place. Such dualism effectively excludes God from this world. This dualistic doctrine was fiercely opposed by the Catholic Church which preferred to see the hand of God at work everywhere and consequently saw all of creation as having potential for both perfection and corruption, this potential being due to God's grace in giving us freedom of will. The Catholics, therefore, opposed dualism, especially that of Gnostics such as the Albigensians. Without going further into the theology or metaphysics we can see that this was a great struggle and left a scar on the history of Western religion. As a result, when a new religion comes along with ideas of non-duality, it is not surprising that they are seized upon and affirmed with alacrity by people who have no conscious idea that what they are doing is actually to re-enact the part of their Catholic forebears by proxy.

Non-duality in Eastern thought, however, is only remotely connected with the question of God's realm being the same as or different from this world. Actually, as an

English word, nondual is a translation of the Indian term *advaita* which is not a Buddhist term at all. It comes from the Hindu Upanishads. However, the idea has penetrated Buddhist philosophy, especially in the Zen, Madhyamaka and Dzogchen schools, where some teachers equate "non-dual awareness" with enlightenment. I wrote in my book *The New Buddhism* about the wide variety of ideas that are claimed to equate with enlightenment. This kind of non-dual awareness is, apparently, a state in which there is no distinction between subject and object.

Here then, we come to the experiential aspect of nondualism. There are times when one walks across a field and looks around at nature in all its diverse profundity and feels deeply at one with it all. One might say to oneself, "This is all perfect, just as it is." Such feelings of completion are certainly spiritual and they can be described as nondual moments. The point about perfection, however, is that as soon as it is experienced it is already passing away. There is an understandable longing to hang on to it. After having had spiritual experiences as a child I spent many years longing to get them back. However, in grammar, the perfect tense is the past tense and that is how it is in our experience. Though such moments are glorious and inspiring, they pass. The goal is not that of remaining forever in such a state, but of living in the dual world, as dual creatures, in an inspired way.

My point here is not so much to analyse the idea of nonduality philosophically as to advise that we guard against taking it as either a universal principle or as a rule of thumb for the conduct of ordinary life since if we do it is liable to lead to solipsism, moral paralysis and intellectual confusion.

Nondual essentially means singular. Now Buddha does advise us to be singular in the sense of what he calls ekagata, which we have already discussed. In practical terms, ekagata means to not be psychologically oppressed by internalised others. This does not mean to treat others as non-existent, it means to recognise that they are other. When we recognise the true otherness of others we can respect them and allow them to live their lives for their own reasons without falling into co-dependency or requiring them to conform to our standards or to be there as props for our own script. Ekagata, far from implying that all is one, actually requires us to recognize multiplicity and difference.

Difference can induce fear because of the risk of conflict. Advocates of oneness are generally actually advocating harmony, which is not really the same thing. To have harmony you have to have two or more. Or they are advocating relationship, but the same logic applies. A relationship takes two. Actually, as a general rule, most problems arising from dualism are most immediately resolved not by a move to oneness, but by a move to recognising pluralism. This is why I much prefer the term wholeness to oneness. Wholeness does not imply a denial of either singularity or multiplicity. It is inclusive rather than exclusive.

Zen is something that happens between two. Shakyamuni was enlightened when he saw the morning star. There was Shakyamuni and the star. A Zen master might have been enlightened hearing a frog jump into a pond. Again, it takes two. We might be told that it is important to meditate because that is how Shakyamuni became enlightened, but in the Denkuroku, which is the history of the masters subsequent to Shakyamuni, we do not hear of them being enlightened while meditating. The ancestors were almost all enlightened by an inter-personal encounter. Usually this was with an enlightened person. The same is true in the Pureland tradition. Some were enlightened by reading written words (Honen) or by the appearance of a celestial (Shinran) but most by meeting another human being in a profound way and even the cases of Shinran and Honen are also really forms of encounter. In the sutras and annals, enlightenment comes mostly through meeting rather than solitude. Solitude plays a part, but enlightenment requires something that will jolt a person out of their old rut and this is not something that one can do for oneself.

Zen is about the relationship between mind and its object. It is a special relationship, a relationship that appreciates the particular in the same instant as appreciating the whole. However the primary characteristic of the whole is its boundlessness, which is none, one and many all at the same time. If we want to say that seeing the frog and oneself in terms of the whole makes them one and so dissolves the distinction between subject and object, we shall not be wrong, and in that sense we can say that it is true that enlightenment is non-dual awareness and that all is one, but this is only one aspect and if we take it as a complete description we limit enlightenment. The dangers of talking in such a way are substantial and as a route toward Zen mind it may well be much better to think in terms of more deeply appreciating the otherness of the other than to try to pretend that one is part of the other or, even worse, that the other is part of oneself. Real nonduality occurs when the other is liberated to be other.

Zen and Pureland

The wise are those who know they are foolish. The foolish are those who think they are wise.

Zen and Amidism or Pureland are two schools of Buddhism that developed in China. My Zen teacher Kennett Roshi used to say that Zen and Pureland were two entrances to the same tunnel. The implication was that if you went in Zen you came out Pureland and vice versa. I studied under her and then later became Pureland. Now I'm interested in the point where they meet. If we make a quick comparison of the salient features of the two systems we get a chart something like this:

Zen	Pureland
Self-power (jiriki / svabala)	Other power (tariki / parabala)
Sudden awakening (satori / samadhi)	Awakening of faith (shinjin / shraddha, prasada)
Nondual	Dual
Buddha nature	Bombu paradigm
Koan	Nembutsu
Silent sitting (Zazen)	Heartfelt calling

Zen and Pureland are both expressions of Mahayana Buddhism, both value the bodhisattva ideal, both value the teacher-disciple relationship, both "practice schools" as distinct from "philosophical schools". In Chinese Buddhism, Zen and Pureland are often practised together, though it is generally more a matter of Pureland practice within a Zen ethos. My own style is rather the other way around. I like the Pureland ethos but also value the Zen practice.

Zen means contemplation. Pureland schools have often practised contemplation. Shan Tao was perhaps the most eminent Pureland master in history and he was known for his contemplative practice. Zen, therefore, is not alien to Pureland. Similarly, chanting is not alien to Zen. Many of the benefits that come from one come equally well from the other. Some people think of Zen practice as hard and Pureland as easy, but our recent Ten Day Chanting Intensive was certainly tough and Zen also has an ideal of effortlessness. These observations show us that some of the supposedly sharp differences tend to melt away when one looks closer.

Sometimes Zen and Pureland are, as it were, looking at opposite ends of the same elephant. The Zen notion of self expands one's self-identity until it is identical with the universe. The Pureland approach on the other hand is to reduce self-esteem until a deep insight into one's foolish nature is obtained. Are these really so different? In one case the ego bursts, in the other it melts. Either operation can be messy. In both cases one is left with a direct encounter with existential reality within wholeness, informed not by self-concern but by mindfulness of a higher purpose.

The human spiritual quest involves searching the gap between what is empirically encountered and what is encountered in intuition. We find ourselves and our world limited, vulnerable and transient. We intuit measurelessness, infinity and eternity. In the gap between observation and intuition occurs all human creativity, science and spiritual development. This is common ground to Zen and Pureland and, indeed to many other spiritual systems. Both bring us face to face with the existential while mindful of the eternal. We experience gratitude, humility, awe and wonder. We have moments of ecstasy and we also have the experience of finding truth in the midst of the mundane – after the ecstasy, the laundry, as Jack Kornfield famously said.

The idea of self-power is that one has within oneself a great potential that can be realised as enlightenment. The idea of other power is that one has no such potential and can only be saved by the intervention of a greater spiritual influence. However, from the position of the practitioner, personal potential is unknown and the experience of striving to realise it from within the frame of one's unenlightened outlook leads to ultimate frustration. Zen is the path of thwarting. Pureland does not assume any such power and so expects that life will be a series of obstacles and fooleries. In accepting his bombu nature the Pureland practitioner may fall into the hands of Amida and be enlightened. Was that a personal potential realised or a gift of grace? Does it matter?

I personally find much that is valuable in both systems for the advancement of the spiritual life. The Zen notion of koan is particularly useful, and, as I see it, the ultimate koan is the nembutsu which is the core of Pureland practice. The nembutsu is the act of refuge, of self-abandon. One recognises one's own foolish limitation and stands before the intuited wonder of the enlightened. One cries out "I can't" and one is turned around in the very moment of one's despair. All koans are about whether this old dog that I am ever had a Buddha nature – or any nature – and what this life can be. If we did not have the intuition we would just be old dogs forever. If we did not have the animal nature our awakening would have no purpose and no vehicle.

Practically speaking I have always used elements of both systems. I have found the frame provided by the three dogmas of Amidism – the trikaya nature of Buddha, the bombu nature of the adherent, and the nembutsu as favoured practice – extremely useful in providing a frame within which an open-minded, open-hearted approach to the practice can flourish. The role of training, koan practice and contemplation of Zen then fit nicely into this frame and provide tangible means to confront our foolish nature and enter into a fuller mindfulness of and gratitude to the Buddhas. Pureland says, "Have faith!" Zen says, "What is faith?" The practitioner says, "Where is my faith? What do I actually trust? What is my deepest intuition and value? Before what am I holding my life? What is the hook that I will not let myself off?" Day in, day out, we say the nembutsu. Day in, day out, we contemplate our own ignorance. The wise are those who know they are foolish. The foolish are those who think they are wise.

We are now in the modern world. The spiritual quest remains as it ever was, but the conditions change. In our hearts we harbour something that will never be content with a wasted life. Each generation must make this encounter afresh.

PART THREE: ENGAGEMENT WITH CULTURE

Liberation in the Midst of the Restrictive Society

Love is never wasted, but things never turn out quite as we expect either.

When I was about twenty years old we lived in what was called the Permissive Society. Notwithstanding the fact that we had entered the nuclear age, it was an era of hope. Many people thought that some of the tight disciplines of earlier eras had been swept away for good. A new age of creativity and love was upon us and the human race would be able to make a great leap forward into a new kind of society. The exploration of outer space was opening up. We all thought that humans would soon be living on other planets. There was an open frontier for humankind physically and intellectually.

The actuality of some of these changes and the anticipated soon coming of others of like kind was a strong motivator and led many people to undertake substantial changes of lifestyle, experimenting with relationships and ways of organising that seemed radical and liberating. It was widely believed that we were entering an age of plenty and that the problem of producing enough to meet the needs of people was all but solved. With ever increasing leisure ahead of us, we needed to find ways to be creative and to get more out of relationships rather than work harder. We were the generation that would make love not war. The reality of the Cold War hung like a shadow behind this scene and served not so much to depress people as to make issues of ideology matter. One had to think which side one was on. Idealism was possible and widespread.

Since then there has been a huge disillusion or swing back. Such advances as occurred during the flowering have mostly been commercialised. Sexual permissiveness has been curbed by fear of AIDS. Ecological disaster now hangs over us as the threat of nuclear war did then, but under this shadow we seem to have become depressed rather than progressive. There has been a sharp decline in optimism. Such idealists as there are are interested in restriction rather than expansion. People live with shorter horizons. Outer space has been forgotten. Rather than working shorter hours, people work more.

Some of this is, perhaps, attributable to the fall of communism. Communism was, on the face of it, an experiment in a more idealistic way of life. The fact that it failed and that the societies that attempted it are now mostly seen as having been brutal, oppressive places, has left us in an "end of history" period in which there seems to be nothing ideal to aspire towards or struggle for. The idea that one might as well make a bit of money and spend it on indulging oneself became a prevailing sentiment until the economic downturn came along and seemed to demonstrate that even that degree of liberation is more than one can realistically have hopes of.

The flowering of the permissive society can also be seen in terms of the dynamics of peace and war. Britain was just recovering from the Second World War. We were the generation of hope born in its aftermath. The war swept away a lot of regulation. In peace time there is a gradual cumulative growth in regulation that progressively strangles society. In the past this effect was periodically reset by the arrival of the next war. Now war is a less proximate possibility and restriction continues to proliferate unchecked.

So now we live in the Restrictive Society. Surveillance cameras in every public place, visa restriction on travel, constant talk of cuts in public services, detention without trial on a scale never seen before in modern times in peacetime, engagement in distant wars that few people understand the rationale for, general distrust of leaders and politicians, and economic turmoil in which rich institutions like banks are subsidized while the poor go to the wall. These things all indicate that we have entered an era of low expectations and repressive realities though it is, overall, a time of relatively less actual warfare. There is even a kind of masochistic relish apparent with political parties competing to say how tough and austere they will be - a bizarre sight really.

What is really happening? Can we see a bigger picture? Is it, perhaps, that, broadly speaking, the cost of wars with guns is now so horrific that economic means have become the agents of struggle? Is humanity struggling to achieve a higher level of social control than ever before, a process that would inevitably involve massive centralization of power which would carry with it a variety of predictable deleterious effects for those who do not share in that power?

Can we get beyond this? If a big process is underway that we cannot prevent, is there a way to achieve a good outcome at the end of it? If we are committed to a difficult flight, can we achieve a soft landing? What must we do?

One message of spirituality is that love is never wasted, but that things never turn out quite as we expect either. Along the way, those who are open learn and those who are not become embittered. Samsara continues to turn and turn, showing the different facets of its paradoxical nature. Can we be a light house in the midst of it? A smiling face is a joy to all no matter what the circumstance. The circumstance in which we live is always both heaven and hell.

My mother thought that the war was the best time of her life. At that time people pulled together. They helped each other spontaneously. They performed acts of heroism. There was love and freedom. Of course, there was also killing and brutality. Is it possible to have the good spirit that appears at such times without having to have a war to create it? Interestingly, Buddha was from the warrior caste and there are a lot of words in his vocabulary that rely upon a military metaphor. An arhat is a foe-destroyer, the foe here being greed, hate and delusion. A bhagavat, now commonly translated as "blessed one" was originally one who enjoys the spoils of victory. Buddha taught a kind of nobility in the midst of struggle. The transformation of his message into the metaphor of endless peace is perhaps similar to the creation of the image of gentle Jesus, meek and mild, which the sage of Nazareth seems not to have been either.

After fifty years without a major war, Europe is in economic turmoil. The new war is being waged with money rather than guns. In some countries, like Greece and Portugal, this is leading small groups of people to attempt completely different lifestyles, just as happened in the period of "flower power" back in the 1950s and 60s. Can such a love and peace revolution occur in less taxed circumstances?

We work to set up and maintain conditions not just for wholesome living but also for creativity. We preserve space for optimism and experiment, for the magic of becoming more fully alive. These are our important concerns as a spiritual community: to be an oasis in the desert for many people and a springboard of creativity for others. The bursting of the consumer boom bubble has led some people to begin to think more deeply and ask what life is about. There is a need to sow the seeds of a new phase of hope. Perhaps a thousand flowers will bloom again.

Culturally Engaged Spirituality

Resisting oppression, assisting the afflicted and demonstrating an alternative.

The expression 'socially engaged Buddhism' was coined by Thich Nhat Hanh and the idea in its modern form derives substantially from Sulak Sivaraksa in Thailand. It has become a widely used term referring to the activism and social work performed by some Buddhists either individually or as a function of their sangha activity. The Amida sangha that I belong to became well known for its commitment to this type of activity, resisting oppression, assisting the afflicted and demonstrating an alternative, in arenas as varied as the Balkans, India, Africa and city centre areas of the UK. All well and good. However, it goes further than this. I would like to float and advance the term Culturally Engaged Spirituality as a relatively more apt description of what we are trying to do here. I understand cultural engagement as including everything that might fall under the rubric of social engagement and more, and all of it with a shift of emphasis.

Spirituality should be culturally engaged, which is more than simply engaged in socially useful or politically implicated actions. It is to be engaged with the spirit and meaning of society, which is constantly evolving. This means being also engaged in the arts and letters and performance, in writing and intellectual culture, and in creating alternative forms of community. We are concerned about the kind of values that underpin society, and especially those that conduce to community; we are concerned to generate the conditions that give rise to creativity; we are interested in friendship, co-operation and synergism, and in unleashing the energy of people who have something to offer, helping them to become both true individuals and contributing members of "rightly resolute groups". We are not just into service delivery - in fact, we are hardly into that at all - we are more interested in how to help people to become creative and in helping people to help other people. Above all we are concerned with finding a way to act that has joy rather than anger as its core feature.

I want to invite us to think about how we can generate the kind of matrix of conditions, both locally and internationally, that nurture creativity of many kinds and that build the flowering of community at a more sublime level. This can include supporting social causes, but it is not limited to it and we need to think carefully just what the Buddhist cause in society is. We should not simply jump onto bandwagons that are only tangentially related to our true values; but nor should we flinch from actions that will bring out the potential in a wide range of people yearning for spiritual liberation in a wide variety of ways, not limited to orthodox religious ones. We should be well placed to bridge cultures and to help generate the meta-culture (and '*metta*' culture) by which the future of our world may be enriched.

Creativity means not knowing in advance what the outcome is going to be. It involves enjoying the journey. It includes struggle, but avoids bitterness. Many Buddhists nowadays are also followers of various progressive or leftist political causes. Some of these are good causes, but we should be careful of not falling into a kind of self-righteousness. We do not actually know how a world without war, poverty, or oppression would be. So far in history, humans have taken war to be the ultimate way to resolve disputes and war is now becoming so destructive that we may actually be, bit by bit, renouncing it. We have also lived with an assumption that nature is never exhausted and that the human struggle would always be to extract as much as possible from nature in order to feed the expansion of the species. This, too, we now realise cannot continue, at least as long as we remain confined to this one inhabitable planet, but we do not know what a society that lives in sustainable harmony with nature would be like. In the process of trying to deal with these two unprecedentedly huge transitions, we are seeing the unfolding of political and economic changes that have all manner of unwanted effects. A new world is dawning but the birth pangs may be severe. How can we act to ensure that the baby is not killed by the contractions? Something in the core of our being must relax and learn to trust as we enter the great unknown and, wherever each of us happens to be situated in the social world, we must each do what we can to foster help and co-operation and reduce threat and fear.

Mysticism and False Dichotomies

If you come here for visions, think first what they may get you into and consider whether you are ready for that.

The spiritual apostle goes forth for the benefit of the many. This does not mean that such people are opposed to the practise of a mystical discipline. Nothing could be further from the truth. I was taught by my Zen Master that "Service to humanity is another name for Zen training". For "Zen" one can read "mysticism", the deeper experiences of the spirit that arise through the discipline of religious prayer, reflection and meditation.

A hallmark of spirituality, as I understand it, is the bringing together of two dimensions of religious life: the socially engaged and the direct seeing into the heart of reality. Tearing these two apart does profound damage to the human spirit. Nonetheless it is common and many people fail to see how the two come together as one. One key to this mystery is provided by a reflection upon the subject of human longing.

King Bimbisara was a friend of the Buddha. He was overthrown by his son Ajatashatru who had been egged on by the Buddha's disaffected cousin Devadatta. The usurper had his father starved to death in a prison. He also imprisoned his mother, Queen Videhi. The Buddha visited Videhi during her incarceration. Queen Videhi said to the Buddha, "What must you and I have done in previous lives to have such awful relatives in this one?" Betrayal is one of the most painful things that can happen to a human being.

When a parent is betrayed by their child or a teacher by their disciple, or *vice versa*, there is a great grief.

We begin with recognition of this grief, which does not just pertain to these two situations but permeates the whole of life one way or another. This recognition is the first noble truth of Buddhism. It is noble to recognise this grief. From this grief springs an equally great longing. Videhi had such a longing. By the power and sincerity of her longing, the Buddha was able to reveal to her a great vista of Buddha–worlds. In other words, she entered into a mystical vision. We call this the vision of the Pure Land.

This longing for better worlds is one of the deepest realities for a human being. It is the substance of spirit. Visions of pure lands are generated. Because visions are generated, humans are inspired to actualise them. Religions come into existence as a result of a mystical inspiration. Buddha getting enlightened, Mohammad hearing the voice of Allah, and Jesus encountering Satan during his forty nights in the wilderness are all examples of this. All three visions were subsequently to have huge effects upon culture and civilisation. The mystical and the social are not two independent processes.

What commonly goes wrong is that the religion is then appropriated and developed by people who do not have access to the vision. This is a bit like the builders not having access to the plans. Something gets built, but it may be only a distant approximation to the original intention.

The plan, however, was not made simply to be worshipped. It was made in order to be implemented. True mysticism gives inspiration for action. After his enlightenment, the Buddha did not retire to a cave or commit suicide. He went forth and for forty more years lived out the inspiration that came from the vision that had come to him. Religion in its true sense is precisely the living out of the vision in the real world. Buddhism later became, in one form or another, a major political ideology in many countries, not simply a private religion.

When people hear the word vision, they are often inclined to think that something escapist or fantastic is being described. The Buddha, however, had his feet on the ground. His mysticism sprang from the hard experience of open–hearted living. He taught his disciples an approach to meditation that began with deep reflection upon their material nature. Meditation upon the earth element was generally the first topic studied in Buddha's meditation class.

The guts of the message is thus that the deepest experience of life is not to be obtained by escaping from concrete reality, but by entering more deeply into it while seeing it in a spiritual context. To train in spirituality means to enter into a deeper and more intimate relationship with concrete reality than most people have even dreamt of. It is the purpose of spiritual training to bring one to this point of intense encounter. Such intense encounter is faith. Faith is to live in direct, intense, intimate encounter with reality. This is more than bitter-sweet, it is simultaneously bliss inspiring and heart breaking. It is to know and feel in one's bones how every moment of life partakes both in the great grief and in the wonder of ever fresh awakening.

It is because most people cannot stand the intensity of such a life that they retreat into the defences of ego and attempt to keep reality at a distance. Ego is the creation of a false, make-believe life, one or two or several removes from reality. In the make-believe world one can live voyeuristically. One can convince oneself that by mentally replicating something one has done the real thing. One can pretend that one's mood and sentiments are profound when they are merely selfish, and so on.

Spiritual training repeatedly turns the trainee back toward reality. It may be the reality of putting your shoes neatly outside the meditation hall. It may be the reality of the cat killing a mouse. It may be the reality that the teacher also farts sometimes. In any case, it is the reality of Quan Shi Yin appearing "on the street, and in the shops". It is the Buddha lifting his foot and stretching out his arm. When the trainee knows in his bones the stretching out of the arm and the lifting of the foot, he or she will be plunged into a spiritual free fall from which there is no possibility of rescuing even a shred of the ego's carefully constructed defence system. This is a fall into a place that is as terrible as it is wonderful. It is the place that Videhi went when, in the full knowledge that her son was, right then, in the process of killing his father, she saw the Pure Land.

Nobody should enter into such training lightly. It is not a hobby. Nor is it a business of building up a successful club or institution. Who can build who has not seen the plans? No wonder the spiritual scene is full of jerry buildings. But do not doubt that there is indeed something very wonderful to be had here, for those with the stomach for it. The word bodhisattva means one who has the courage (*sattva*) of the enlightened (*bo*) vision (*dhi*).

As a sangha, our task is to bring the enlightened vision into the light of day by transforming the vision of the Pure Land into action in the real world. Every person has at least a glimpse of some bit. Each worker on this building site may not have the whole plan, but everybody does have a piece of it. That piece is represented by the love and compassion that he or she does find in his or her own heart. If each of us acts on that, although the individual may not have the whole plan yet, the pieces of the jigsaw will gradually add up. If you take part in the attempt wholeheartedly, each building a bit of the Pure Land where he or she happens to be, one day when you least expect it, the whole pattern will suddenly become clear. That is mysticism as well as engagement. Engagement and vision inspire one another.

Going forth is what makes us realise how much work we have to do upon ourselves. Doing work upon ourselves inspires us to go forth. Mystical experience does not come from chasing after it. It comes as a by–product of carrying out the Buddha's original intention to the best of one's ability. If we do so, the larger picture will in due course dawn upon us. Everybody can have a part in this. Those who wish to do it wholeheartedly, however, should not be lulled into thinking that it is an easy road. The ego is not built for nothing. The ego is a bulwark against individual and collective madness. To build a better world, however, we must do better than just keep madness at bay. The world beyond ego is a much higher proposition.

The primal longing is the *dukkha–samudaya*: that which arises in us as a result of encountering the affliction in the world. This longing is not an imperfection. It is a noble truth. Before we can make the best we must accept the worst. Before we can be our best we must be willing to see our worst. To sustain our faith through dark times we must appreciate the irony and paradox of life. Whatever one attempts will probably not work out as one plans, but love is never wasted – something else will eventuate. Have faith.

Generally, every idealistic venture sooner or later runs to waste in the sands of distraction, ego and oblivion. However, not everything is impermanent. Somehow, mysteriously, the love continues in the world. Generally people stop at what the Buddha called dukkha-samudaya which means that they react to what seems to be wrong and do something, but these reactive ways often carry a bitter flavour. Beyond dukkha-samudaya is something Buddha called *nirodha*, which is a harnessing of that energy by means of a much greater and more all-encompassing faith. This unconditional or universal love is not something we can ever possess or tame, but we can still have faith in it and in doing so we become channels for a process that is bigger than ourselves.

It is this kind of dedication that we call the vow or prayer of the bodhisattva. Though beings be innumerable, one will save them all; though delusions be inexhaustible one will transform them all. In the midst of cruelty, we shall not be cruel. In the midst of avarice we shall not refrain from generosity. In the midst of many vying egos, we shall keep faith in the beyond. We dedicate ourselves to this vow-prayer, knowing that we are incapable of realising it, knowing that we are each as foolish, limited and vulnerable as the next person, but, yet, putting ourselves forward and being willing to be used by a greater spirit. This is what makes a person shine and that reflected light has a transformative effect upon all around.

This vow can take hold of one's life and set one upon the right track (*marga*) even in the midst of one's own ignorance. This track leads to samadhi, the consummate vision. We should not allow such visions to go stale. They were made to lead us back into a total involvement with life. Mysticism is vibrant aliveness and affirmation. If you come here for visions, therefore, think first what they may get you into and consider whether you are ready for that and, correspondingly, if you come here for engaged activism, ask yourself first if you are willing to undergo the religious training that will genuinely ground you in universal compassion.

Metaphysical Memes

It is impossible to think without resort to metaphysical concepts yet it is impossible to achieve any metaphysical concept that is flawless.

The idea of memes is an interesting one. It is an extension of genes, but whereas genes are substantive entities of encoded information that are chemicals incapable of selfishness or other anthropomorphic attributes, memes are a purely speculative concept. That does not mean that it is not a useful concept; the idea that ideas have a life of their own and use us as vehicles is an intriguing way of thinking about things. My philosopher friend Mary Midgley hates the whole idea because it is totally non-specific; you cannot tell where the edges of a meme are. Is there a meme for Catholicism, or just for the Virgin Mary, or the use of the rosary, perhaps, or, you name it. So it seems to be a concept of limited utility, but one that does sometimes help to bump one off one's normal tramlines and that can certainly be useful sometimes. Some proponents of memes, like Susan Blackwell, suggest that it is a scientific way of conceptualising non-self, but what I find most interesting about it is that it is a metaphysical idea that has come from the metaphysics-denying school of new atheism, having been propounded originally by the geneticist Richard Dawkins.

What this seems to me to demonstrate is that when one tries to strip metaphysics out of human culture yet still attempts to be comprehensive in one's explanations both of what happens in human life and supportive of values and human psychological (dare one say, spiritual) growth then one finds that one cannot help using metaphysical categories in one's reasoning. Memes apparently are non-physical, non-measurable, therefore non-empirical and non-scientific, yet Dawkins of all people believes that they have us in their power (as, apparently, do the 'selfish' (sic) genes). So having overthrown God, the new atheists have placed us in the power of a new pantheon of non-empirical beings. Perhaps memes live on a predecessor of Mount Olympus, Mount Scientifico, perhaps.

The correct approach to metaphysics is to say that metaphysics is necessary, but that human formulations of it can never be final. Who among us knows the true nature of a Buddha? Who knows where Shakyamuni is today? Yet we still take refuge in him. We do so on faith. He taught us that while we cannot do without metaphysics, pursuing metaphysical questions too far is just a waste of time, a point that was even more firmly asserted by Nagarjuna who holds a respected place in the lineages of all Mahayana Buddhist schools. We need to pull out the proverbial arrow, not spend our time debating what the name of the fletcher was, but that does not mean that we can ignore the whole business of this life being full of darting arrows. We do need some help. Some things we must try to understand and some have to be taken as good enough.

Each religious approach has a system of metaphysics. It's as well to keep it fairly simple and straight-forward. Some groups try to pretend to do without, but this is a stance only ever achieved by dissimulation and mystification. Some try to *solve* the problem by being "beyond words" but, you may have noticed that the "beyond words" approaches to spirituality are the ones that publish the most books. The correct attitude to non-empirical concepts is to ask if they work. Is this conducive to the good life, to the Dharma-faring? Is it consistent with the high intention of the spiritual ancestors? Does it tend to liberation? If so, use it. Do not think that it is ultimate truth; such is not given to bombu beings of our kind. However, do not throw the baby out with the bathwater or you will quickly find yourself having to invent a new kind of baby and it is unlikely that the baby you invent will be an improvement upon the one that you threw out.

On the other hand, the babies that we have do grow. Metaphysical systems are not as static as people tend to assume. Within the basic vocabulary established, be it memes or gods or buddhas, there is always the possibility of speaking the Dharma or speaking iniquity. Some languages are more suited than others, but it is inevitable that our spiritual life depends upon the skilful means evolved by our forebears and equally inevitable that we must participate in its further evolution, both in thought and in lived life and that generally means becoming part of a community with an established framework of ideas, both metaphysical and practical, as a springboard.

It is important that people engaged in socially relevant action think about what they are doing and in order to think one needs concepts and some of these concepts are going to be metaphysical and it is pointless trying to escape from this. A great deal of nonsense is talked by people who purport to eschew dogma, metaphysics, ritual and religious form yet themselves, unwittingly, are invariably at least no less dogmatic, no less dependent on non-empirical ideas, no less prone to formulaic procedures to preserve their favoured symbolic system, and so are, in reality, just as much examples of *homo religiosus* as those that they try to distinguish themselves from.

There is a middle way. On the one hand it is impossible to think without resort to metaphysical concepts. On the other hand it is impossible to achieve any metaphysical concept that is flawless. It is in their nature that when pushed to a logical conclusion they crumble. In order to advance society we have to think clearly and to think clearly we have to make metaphysical commitments, but, in doing so we run the risk of thinking that we have grounded ourselves in something absolute and ultimate. We ourselves can never be so grounded. We can revere the absolute and the ultimate which we intuit to be flawless from their own side, but from our side we face a different situation. Our situation is existential and we have to live with the limitation thereof without swinging to the nihilistic opposite extreme. Absolutism and nihilism are to be equally avoided. Applying this principle is a constant challenge, one that we frequently fail.

Jesus and Buddha

Let us find the original spirit of Jesus and that of Buddha. Then we shall have the most important thing.

Amidism is the form of Buddhism that is most similar to Christianity in some respects. Or, we could say, Christianity is interestingly similar to Pureland Buddhism. We do not know who taught Jesus his spiritual wisdom and we do not know who the three wise men from the East were, but the best guess could be Buddhists. In all respects in which Jesus departs from Old Testament Judaism, he does sound remarkably Buddhist. Is Christianity a Jewish-Buddhist synthesis?

Amida's light of unconditional love enters this world through many channels. One of the brightest of these channels was the foremost of sages, Gotama Shakyamuni. Another was surely the man Jesus, or Yeshua, from Nazareth. Just as the former spoke the language and culture of India, so Jesus framed the message appropriately for the Jewish culture of his time and place, replacing the "eye for an eye" justice approach of the Old Testament with the compassion-centred "love thy neighbour as thou lovest thyself" one of the New.

I have often said that it does not matter whether Buddhas are gods or not but it certainly matters whether one's god is a Buddha and the God of Jesus was undoubtedly that. The God of Jesus shines the same light of unconditional love that we receive from Amida. Whether this means that Jesus' God and Gotama's Tathagata are one Buddha or two is something we can leave to others to argue about. The point is that the spirit is holy in the same way in both.

The difficulties that have arisen in Christianity over the centuries seem to me to derive from the fact that the Jews understandably identified that god with their traditional "one god" who had originally been their tribal god of war and so was rather intolerant. Jesus was revolutionary in pointing out that the one god that mattered was not tribal, not warlike, and was one who bid us turn the other cheek and go the second mile, love those who use us spitefully and recognise the beam in our own eye. This was revolutionary and this revolution is still not fully appreciated, much contemporary "Christianity" still being set in the "justice" rather than "mercy" mode. The light of unconditional love is not a source of judgement. One may lose out by not regarding it, of course, but that is distressing, not a judgement. It is people who "judge after the flesh" while Jesus and Gotama would say "I judge no man". The original intuition of Buddha and of Jesus appear to me to be identical in spirit.

I have seen some write that they wonder if the fact that they have some affinity for Jesus might be a barrier to them becoming adherents of the Dharma. I would say, rather, that if they know of Jesus and do not feel an affinity for him that would be a barrier, but, whatever, Amida loves all.

Some others say, when they encounter Pureland Buddhism, "But isn't it essentially the same as Christianity?" as though this would be a reason for rejecting it. However, the fact that there are profound similarities seems to me affirmative, not an obstacle. The institutions of religion may become barriers for some people, but the original spirit is most precious. Let us find the original spirit of Jesus and that of Buddha. Then we shall have the most important thing.

Shinjin by Drama

We cannot make ourselves immune to criticism, especially if we live life boldly, but if we entrust ourselves to the nembutsu we can experience a most wonderful assurance.

Having trained in psychodrama and having been involved in ritual and liturgy for many years I am interested in the potential for the use of dramatic means in the path of liberation. Theatre enables a person to experience not being oneself. The inventor of psychodrama, Jacob Moreno, at one stage in his life, organised a small community in Vienna in which one of the rules was that one not allow other residents to know who you really are. Much modern thinking concerns the needs for people to know who they are and to understand each other, deeply knowing who the other is. However, there is a strong current in spiritual thinking that points in exactly the opposite direction. Thinking that one knows who one is or who the other person is can be a source of rigidification that makes us less liberated, not more. Bringing together this dramatic and spiritual thinking led us to the invention of pandramatics.

Pandramatics is not exactly a therapy, not exactly a spiritual method and not just a theatre training technique, but it partakes of all three in various ways. The point of pandramatics is to get out of yourself to the greatest possible degree. The rest is experimentation. This might be by role-playing or by fantasy improvisation or by exercises; by resort to history or fable or "surplus reality".

At a weekend event organised to celebrate the 799th anniversary of the death of Honen Shonin we investigated the figures of Honen and some of his disciples using drama. Two relationships that we looked at particularly were those between Honen and his disciple Zenshin (Shinran) and that between Honen and the samurai Tadatsume.

In the latter enactment, I was cast as the samurai and another sangha member as Honen. Tadatsume's problem is that it seems to be one thing to have faith in the abstract and something quite different to live a real life in the real world where sometimes all options involve hurt and risk humiliation. Sometimes battles are unavoidable and in the one that Tadatsume is going to fight he knows that he will have to act wholeheartedly as a soldier if he is to be honourable, yet may still lose, die or fail his family. He fears that in doing so he will inevitably lose consciousness of his dedication to Amida in the heat of the moment and that that is precisely the time when he is himself most likely to be cut down and die. If we believe that the deciding factor is our state of mind or our awareness of the spiritual dimension and we lose that precisely at the point where our life ends, what will become of us? One might have practised meditation all one's life but still not be able to guarantee one's state of mind at the all important moment. This is a fundamental problem for all forms of self-power spirituality. We simply do not have that degree of self-control, especially when engaged in actions that require us to be in a flow.

We started the enactment and I found myself easily sliding into the perspective of this rough Japanese soldier who was attracted to the nembutsu teaching but also conscious of his worldly duty and of the passion that he had to rouse in himself in order to carry it out. If one transposes the social factors, this is one of the archetypal dilemmas that each of us faces in life one way or another. We are all surrounded by social expectations and we do have to act in situations where there is conflict, rousing sufficient passion to play our part, all the while knowing that we shall be judged by a variety of others who all have different values and different vested interests. The two of us, in our respective roles, re-enacted the drama, improvising as we went along.

When I was deeply into role and was asked by "Honen" what my heart was saying right now, I knew immediately that my heart was what had brought me to him (rather than me bringing it) and so it was always saying the nembutsu even when I was not conscious of it doing so. He then said, "And can you hear the nembutsu, right now?" and this took me down a further level to the realisation that I am accepted completely by the Buddhas, by the universe, even when I am not listening to them. It was a profound moment like ice melting or like being welcomed home into safety after a long journey. Suddenly what was happening was a great deal more than play acting. I underwent a deeply moving experience both mentally and viscerally which, according to the reports from the audience, was visible to everyone present. I felt suddenly completely accepted by the other (Honen), in my own being, and, most profoundly, as though by the universe itself. This experience of acceptance "even as you are" is, of course, the hallmark of shinjin, and it was remarkable to experience in the midst of a drama when one was not even playing oneself, though, of course, the improvisational method does mean that one does invest oneself in the character one is playing. In fact, it is perhaps more likely that one will have such an experience when one is not being oneself.

This kind of drama is quite close to what must have been the origin of the koan method. A koan is a "case study". From the earliest days it has been recognised in Buddhism that there are different characters of people who have correspondingly different spiritual problems. The Buddha did not, therefore, give identically standardised teachings and methods for all. Different people have different spiritual needs. Over the years there developed the koan method. A trainee is told to give particular attention to the story and experience of a particular master from the past. He learns what the spiritual dilemma of that person was pre-awakening and he learns the story of how the person finally broke through his or her difficulty and arrived at awakening. Through identification, the trainee is able to study their own problem, at first vicariously, and then more directly. In some approaches, trainees study a series of cases one after another, each revealing a different facet of the spiritual problem. We might know philosophically that this problem is universally that of over-coming self conceit, but how it manifests is unique to each particular case. Furthermore, koans do not only apply to individuals. Groups, families and societies have their koans. Each involves a particular kind of blindness around which cluster concepts, customs, mores, manners and the supposed certainties of that particular culture. Those who inhabit such a culture tend to be completely blind to the relativity and partiality of their "certainties". Our own culture is no different.

In some ways, the principles illustrated here run completely counter to popular wisdom. In our modern age people have to invent one or more identities that become their passport to participation in the society and hold to them firmly. The mythology of our modern system is built around ideas of choice and personal identity, democracy, capitalism, professionalism, the nation state and so on. All these things seem normal and inevitable, though they would have seemed strange to a person from medieval times and will no doubt seem equally odd to people centuries into the future. A liberated person is able to participate in the system, whatever the system happens to be in a particular place and epoch, but not be overly seduced by it. They need to know that it is as much as it is and nothing more than it is. Drama gives us, individually or collectively, possibilities to explore ways of being that are outside of what we are used to, not only as a way of understanding particular situations better, but also as a means of loosening the hold of conditions altogether.

Life is full of uncertainties and whatever one does one will be variously judged by others. The spiritual path requires that one trust one's heart and trust that the right path will unfold step by step. It is not wholly inner and not wholly outer. It is easy to do good when well motivated and when good is being praised by all, but what about those situations where one's heart says one thing and society says the opposite? Or when one is internally pulled by a variety of conflicting considerations? How liberated are we then? I have many years of spiritual training, but in the step by step detail of life I am as bombu as the next person. To take part in this drama and experience myself as a samurai who has done things far more seriously destructive than anything I have ever contemplated in my real life and still feel completely an acceptance that puts all relative judgements into eclipse was both liberating and shocking. As a spiritual teacher, my wish is that every person that I have dealings with may, one way or another, have such an experience. We cannot make ourselves immune to criticism, especially if we live life boldly, but if we entrust ourselves to the nembutsu we can experience a most wonderful assurance. Experiencing that assurance we can go on living boldly.

It is a fascinating paradox that the self-power approach in which one seeks to be in control of one's life can be paralysing since when one feels that the responsibility lies entirely upon one's own shoulders to get every step right and be always beyond reproach there is actually very little in life that it is safe to do. One is best to retire to a remote mountain and see other people as little as possible. On the other hand, when one trusts in an other power, realising one's ultimate helplessness and dependency, one has the kind of assurance that makes it possible to engage with others, take risks, make changes and continue to act boldly even knowing that whatever one does will bring approval from some and condemnation from others. The other power approach is by no means a soft option, but it can be a profoundly moving one.

Rebecca

Would we go on loving the person whom we discover to have committed a great crime?

Recently I read the novel *Rebecca* by Daphne Du Maurier. It is a very well told story with a compelling narrative. The characters come to life strongly and the plot swings back and forward in a convincing manner that keeps the reader gripped. The book was written in the nineteen thirties and so is a period piece, but the moral content is timeless and provocative. Then, having read the book and been full of admiration for Du Maurier's style and skill as a writer, I watched the Hitchcock film of the same name. The film follows the book quite closely in many details. It takes theatrical licence quite properly, truncating scenes and making certain points more obvious or in a simpler way than is possible in a novel. It is dated to modern eyes, perhaps, but an excellent piece of cinemacraft. The point that is so striking, however, and that makes it worth writing about here is that the film changes one crucial detail that is pivotal to the whole meaning of the story and this change was presumably made because the most challenging aspect of the story, one that did make the book a best seller, would nonetheless have been considered unacceptable to cinema audiences in the mid-twentieth century. This is the following.

The book tells the story of a young woman, an orphan from a humble background, who marries a rich man. Initially she is quite over-awed by her new circumstance and particularly daunted by the fact that his first wife, Rebecca, was a powerful and well regarded figure who died six months before their own marriage. She starts to believe that her husband is still in love with Rebecca even though the latter is dead, having drowned. In due course, however, after we have become enthralled in the love story and the dilemmas of the new bride, it becomes apparent that he does love her and did not love Rebecca - what relief !! - and, in fact, that he killed Rebecca, shot her with a revolver, having gone into a rage when she was taunting and mentally torturing him. The story continues to unfold and the plot revolves around whether he will or will not be found out, brought to court and hanged. Sometimes it looks as though he will, sometimes as if he won't. The whole thing is told completely from within the perspective of the young wife who loves him.

Now the point is that from one third of the way through the book onward the reader knows that he is the murderer and the reader's sympathies remain strongly with him and his young wife. This is the moral dilemma of the book and its challenge, a crime story in which the murderer is the hero. In the film, however, Rebecca dies as a result of an accident in which the man has some responsibility, but we are led to feel that he is innocent really. Presumably cinema audiences cannot cope with a hero who is actually guilty. The formula of films, at least then, was that the hero has to be unassailably a good person. The book, however, brings us into sympathy with a person who is objectively a bad person. Both book and film are executed with great skill and mastery of their medium, but the book is a much greater work of art and also more thought provoking philosophically.

From the perspective of the bombu paradigm, sympathy for the bad person is an important theme. We are all *akunin*; nobody has lived a faultless life, yet we live in a society in which blame and complaint have become highly institutionalized. Can we avoid this circumstance contaminating our life as a religious community? Can we have sympathy for the wrong doer as well as for the victim, or is our actual approach to life still shot through with an attitude of dividing people into acceptable and unacceptable, condoned and condemned? Does the present matter more than the past, or is it the case that once certain things have been done there is no redemption? More personally, we might wish to ask ourselves whether we would, as does the heroine of the book, go on loving the person whom we discover to have committed a great crime.

Again we can also debate the issues from the book itself. When I talked about the book with my philosopher friend Mary Midgely who has also enjoyed it, the question arose whether the murderer should have given himself up or not. This would have probably resulted in him being hanged, and depriving his young wife of her beloved. What do you think? Interesting dilemmas. Moral issues should not be relativistic, but rarely are they clear cut.

Un Prophete

If one is not a saint, is one then open to a process that will turn one into a hell-being inexorably? Is there a middle way?

The French film, *Un Prophete*, directed by Jacques Audiard, won a premier prize at the 2009 Cannes film festival. The central character, Malik El Djebena, is played by Tahar Rahim and the Union Corse boss, Cesar Luciani, by Niels Arestrup.

The actual experience of watching the film was challenging in several ways for me. Firstly, there are scenes of violence that I sometimes preferred to avert my eyes from. I do not want that sort of stuff impressed on my brain's retina and insofar as I did not avert them I found myself haunted over succeeding days by images that I would have preferred not to be harbouring. On the other hand, I do not think that the violence was overdone in the sense that the film deals with a violent topic and does so without exaggeration. In fact, one major strength of the film, along with the quality of the acting which is excellent, is the fact that it does not seem in any way overdone. It rather verges on being a documentary. As such, it is an unflinching yet not extravagant study in the brutalizing effect of the prison system and the making of a criminal mind.

My second challenge came from this documentary nature. Whether the film works for one, I imagine, depends heavily upon whether one can identify with the central figure - I hesitate to say hero. This young man is initially faced with a kill-or-be-killed situation and, having killed and so then being himself under the "protection" of the sponsors of the killing, finds himself on a career track leading to a future as junior henchman to a gang boss. However, by a mixture of running various rackets of his own on the side and of insinuating himself with other criminal factions, he finally plays off his rivals against each other and rises to a position of supremacy. The film ends with a tantalising image of him emerging into a situation where we, the audience, are left, as the film closes, unsure whether this particular triumph will transmorph into him leading a reformed life or descending into a long trail of murder, theft and corruption. The future continues to hang in the balance. This is, therefore, a skilfully constructed plot. I myself found the main character difficult to identify with, but others might feel otherwise. A sub-plot that does add artistry to the work is the continuing influence that the victim of the hero's first murder continues to have on his life, inspiring the element of nobility in him.

The film, therefore, succeeded for me more as a stimulus to consideration of important issues than as entertainment. I recognise and admire, but was not seized, by the art in it. The detail of the plot was difficult to follow, but the general drift of it was apparent even when one had forgotten which particular criminal was working for which particular boss or why he would want to kill a particular other one. There were times when I lost interest in who was hating who now and why.

So, overall, *Un Prophete* is an accurate portrayal of hell. The effects of racism, gang identification, callousness, corruption, greed and hatred are precisely depicted. I found it admirable, but not gripping, but if one did manage to identify more closely than I did with the characters one might find it that too. Certainly the film is an indictment of the prison system and the criminal world and of the racist society that en-frames it and an account of how corruption and degeneration of the human heart occurs, though it does also manage to show that even in the most corrupt soul some element of nobility is still operating and that is the true genius of the film.

One is left with the pivotal questions: In a murder-or-be-killed situation, would one? If one did how would one be afterwards? If, in the course of approach to the crime one formed any degree of human relation with the target, would that change one's course of action or not? How would it affect one afterwards? Is murdering murderers sometimes appropriate/justified/understandable? How much is one's own life actually affected by the impulse to revenge? Or by biding one's time? Is the rise to power of a criminal essentially any different from the rise to power of a politician or industrialist, say? Is the factionalism so well portrayed here - our-people against their-people - also a feature of our own lives? A saint might have behaved differently, but most people are not saints. If one is not a saint, is one then open to a process that will turn one into a hell-being inexorably? Is there a middle way?

Beyond Mindfulness

To assert that only the here and now exists is solipsism and the complete opposite of what spiritual cultivation is about.

On the same visit to London as that in which I saw *Un Prophete*, I visited the National Gallery. I adore some of the paintings there and it does not matter how often one sees them. It is interesting how images become iconic. Will a film like *Un Prophete* become so? If not, what is it that adds that little extra that gives an image power, that makes it truly a power object (rupa)? Is it all in the eye of the beholder? Clearly there is an element of subjectivity, but great art responds to the human condition not just the individual one. It somehow manages to do both. In fact, maybe my problem with *Un Prophete* was exactly that: that it spoke to me more of the general human condition than of my own specifically.

This distinction also plays a part in the important question that is often raised in discussions of spiritual matters, that of the nature of presence. We might say that one is not present when one is day dreaming and many people nowadays extol the cultivation of mindfulness which has come to mean a state of awareness of the immediate here and now. However, the mind is always full of something and, in a sense, present to it, so, is one present to one's day-dream? Why should one object be privileged over another? Is an object of mind to be valued less than an object of the eye or the nose? If so, why? Has mankind not benefited as much from dreams as from tangibles? Are not great spiritual teachings themselves primarily mind objects? Should the mind not object to being thus down-graded?

There are important paradoxes here. If sanity is a matter of cognizing reality rather than fantasy, what is to count as which? Our lives are lived in the service of dreams. Sages dream. They spend their whole career inspiring others with the dream and that is what then lives on. We are spiritual in that we keep such dreams alive. Spirituality is not just fantasy reduction. We might talk of shifting perception from rupa to dharma but in our practice we worship rupas. That is what brings out the best in people. The Dharma itself is a rupa: an inspiring mind-object.

There is also the distinction between the contrived image and the spontaneously arising one. To sit in meditation and contrive an image of a yidam, say the angel Gabriel or Manjushri Bodhisattva, is a well established spiritual procedure which is meritorious. We all also know, however, that it falls way short of having Manjushri spontaneously appear and address one in a vision or vivid dream. If the aim of our spiritual practice is actually to eliminate the possibility of ever having this happen, then something has been turned up-side down.

Many contemporary Buddhists put much store by the *Sati-patthana Sutta*. This title is usually translated as The Sutra on the Setting Up of Mindfulness. It begins as an instruction in painstaking self-consciousness: "When a practitioner reaches out his arm he knows 'I am reaching out an arm'" etc. Some have taken this as the core prescription for the Buddhist life and have taken it that *sati* (*smriti*, in Sanskrit), or mindfulness, is to be defined as this practice of acute self-conscious awareness of the concrete world, of the here-and-now. A substantial industry of writings, courses and procedures supporting the cultivation of this form of self-study has arisen. All this over-looks, however, the fact that this practice of here-and-now concreteness is, in the sutra, merely preliminary. Much of the sutra is given over to the contemplation not of the concrete, but rather of mind-objects. It is the Buddha's vision and doctrine that we are really enjoined to contemplate. To amputate the Buddhist content, as some have done, is to ignore the purpose of the sutra and enshrine a preliminary exercise.

Something has gone wrong in the current understanding of mindfulness. The here and now is only here and now inasmuch as it is when and where I am. To assert that only the here and now exists is solipsism and the complete opposite of what spiritual cultivation is about. On the one hand, the there and then is just as real and significant as the here and now and often more so, and, on the other hand, it is dreams that actually organise and run our lives. Can we not treasure our mind-objects and be engulfed in their mandala to the point where it is no longer oneself doing it? Is spirituality not as much about being carried away as being cool? And is not great art that which has the ability to seize us and carry us away and do so in a manner that leaves us afterwards uplifted or purged? And is it not great because it is memorable?

To be spiritual is to live with one's toes dangling in the pool around the divine fountain, and to occasionally drink or swim there. Our contemporary age is in love with technique and the concrete, but it is the being-in-love itself that matters and there is no technique for that. One day we shall be allowed to dream dreams again.

A Funeral

We talk about being honest and open, but in practice there are many things that people do not want said.

I attended the funeral of a friend's father. I had only met the man - I'll call him Bill - once and that was on his death-bed a week before. Although he was then in an advanced stage of dementia and no meaningful conversation was possible I still felt that I had arrived at some sense of the man, so the funeral was not meaningless to me. It had seemed, however, that my friend and her father were very different people; one could have been forgiven for thinking that they belonged to different races, his angular features not matching her soft Celtic ones, his conventional and quiet life being different from her more adventurous and social one. "I'm more like my mother", she said.

The funeral took place at a crematorium. In addition to supporting my friend, who was naturally moved, and having my own lesser feelings about her father, I also had a professional interest in seeing how the Anglican clergyman did his duty. I was struck particularly that this Christian funeral seemed much more retrospective than a Buddhist one, more a backward look on the deceased than a gathering to see him on his way to a new life. There should not really be any reason for that to be so since Christianity revolves around ideas of entering into eternal life, but the references thereto seemed in some way more like fillers than the central significance of the event. The drama and interest lay in the eulogy rather than the committal. We all registered that Bill had a weakness for fruitcake and, even if we did not quite grasp what was supposed to be happening to him now, that he was dead.

A further oddity about this particular funeral was the complete absence of any reference to Bill having had a life before he married his second wife. This lacuna included the complete omission of any reference to my friend or her brother which seemed bizarre, given not only that a description of his having had children is certainly something to include in anybody's life story, but also that she was present at the funeral and was actually the closest blood relative there. It crossed my mind to wonder what would have happened if she had insisted on speaking, but we chose discretion. Presumably Bill's second wife wanted the funeral to publicise a certain version of his life and this, presumably, reflects feelings that she has had about their life together and the way they met.

All this left me pondering the difficulties of human communication. We talk about being honest and open, but in practice there are many things that people do not want said. Rather we want to establish a coherent story. Further, the injunction to be honest is tempered and at times completely over-thrown by the injunction to be sensitive. Indeed, when contemplating speech or action one is often in a cleft stick between these mutually antagonistic requirements. People who are critical of something, for instance, often want their criticism discussed in private because they would not want to be thought critical by third parties. How far should one cooperate or collude? We are two-faced in many ways and even assist each other in being so, and sometimes appropriately so, but the judgement can be a fine one. I even hesitate over whether to publish this piece of writing. Having participated in a funeral in which the story of the deceased has been misrepresented, does that bind me into keeping the secret? Since I am publishing this I clearly think that the answer in this case is negative, but I still do not feel entirely comfortable exposing the deceit in public. I am being insensitive to one party in order to be just to another.

This then raises a question at a higher level: is offence objective or is it just a matter of feelings? Kindness is often taken to mean sparing somebody's feelings. However, the same act may be offensive to one person, not to another. If one steals a thousand pounds from somebody who does not care about money, is that theft? One might say, yes, because there is an empirical loss to the victim. Whether he cares or not, he is still a thousand pounds worse off; but does that matter and if so why, if it does not matter to him? On the other hand, if it does all come down to feelings, then there really is no firm basis since feelings change very easily, cannot be relied upon and do change *post factum*. They depend, in particular, upon the sense that one makes of a situation. Change the way you construe it and you change the way you feel. A spiritual person may, in fact, be one who considers feelings, but does not allow this consideration to be overriding. A spiritual person has a wider range of tolerance, of things that they genuinely do not mind that others would protest at. Does that make it acceptable to treat spiritual people worse than others? One can hardly think so. The traditional Buddhist view is that the more holy the victim the worse the karma. Also, it is courageous to do what is right in a situation where this will upset or offend people, but is it necessarily wise? "Right", here, may be open to a short and long term significance, which may point in different directions, but, then again, who can predict even the short term, let alone the long?

In our religious order there are precepts. These precepts are of two different kinds muddled up together. Some are behaviourally specific, e.g. Do not carry weapons. Some, on the other hand, are exhortatory, e.g. Be generous. This muddle reflects the fact that what really matters is the spirit and the faith. The precepts are descriptive rather than prescriptive: they describe the life that we are attempting to live. When we find we have fallen short in some way, they provide a wake-up call and make us reflect. Sometimes we then regret what we did. Sometimes we can see clearly that what we did was appropriate even though it broke the letter of a precept because it was conducive to a better outcome in the long run. If the only way to get to somebody who needed help involved carrying a weapon, should one not? Surely one should, but should one then use it? Life is not simple.

After the funeral we went to a reception at the house of a relative. As at so many events of this kind a wide diversity of humanity were assembled. It was a pleasant gathering. Some old acquaintances were profitably renewed and new ones made. I had good conversation and made friends. It was a good event. At the same time, with such a diversity comes an ethical maze. Alcohol or no alcohol? Vegetarian or meat? And then the conversation: it is amazing what some people have spent their life making money from and here all sorts of right-livelihood issues arise. Is it one's place to approve or disapprove? Can one help oneself? Humans tend to sort themselves out into sub-communities in order to be able to live with people of similar habits and values. At the same time there is an important value in being able to mix, like Vimalakirti, and feel at ease anywhere. Often the best way to make money is to trade on other people's vices. The spiritual person prefers not to do so, but does that then lead to sourness and disapproval? In practice, whatever a person has done, one cannot actually know the condition of their soul. I spent a good bit of the time conversing with an international arms trader. I came away with some new friends and much to think about and I think Bill would have been happy with our good spirited little party.

Preliminary Thoughts about Spiritual Education

Spiritual education does not value self-esteem as such, but rather values the cultivation of esteem for the conditions of life, physical, social and spiritual.

Buddhism is, among other things, a system of education, incorporating a theory of epistemology, in which method and content are mutually consistent. As an education, Buddhism has character cultivation as a primary goal: a cultivation leading to liberation and enlightenment of the heart and mind. Underpinning this system are assumptions about karma, about conditioning and about freedom.

Foundational to these underpinnings is the belief that perceiving in terms of self is the commonest and most powerful form of distortion that the human mind employs. The world is as it is, but one tends to reconfigure one's perceptions as though the world existed for self alone, or for self primarily. In spiritual education, therefore, the cultivation of objectivity should have a high priority. It should be a special objectivity, since it extends further than the term's general usage in contemporary Western discourse. Special objectivity does not stand in contradistinction to subjectivity. Rather it means cultivating an objective attitude toward all matters that are commonly called subjective as well as to externals. In ancient Indian thinking the mind was regarded primarily as a sense organ. It is the organ through which we see spiritual reality.

The methodology of spiritual education thus relies upon training the attention. The mind is conditioned by its

228

objects. As the mind's diet so becomes the person. Attention is controlled both by inner direction and by available stimuli. Here, therefore, we are as much concerned with creating a conducive environment as with teaching inner control. The two mutually reinforce. In the ideal, a cultivated person has a mind so liberated that she can be immune even to the potentially most corrupting influences, but the ordinary (i.e. less totally educated) person is conditioned by environment, both the physical environment and the moral and psychological environment or ethos.

Spiritual education thus seeks to immerse a person in a wholesome environment governed by a wholesome ethos and therein to give them progressively graded responsibilities or studies in which to learn to exercise skills, knowledge and authority in ways that are non-self-centric. It thus extends to all aspects of life and is not limited to the academy.

Self-centredness (ipsocentricity) is a form of tension. It springs from self-centric perception (ipseity). We could coin a term and call this tension "ipsion". For the person who is highly ipsocentric, only an environment that does not threaten the self will induce a reduction of ipsion, whereas for the person who is already less ipsocentric in habit a wider range of situations can be coped with without heightening the level of ipsion. Buddhist Education aims to increase a person's skill in being able to reduce ipsion. To increase this skill requires practice. Practice means experience of being in situations that might normally increase the tension. For each person there is a "comfort zone", a mild discomfort zone and more extreme discomfort zones. Education requires the trainee to enter mild discomfort zones and learn to reconfigure their perception away from ipseity and thus reduce ipsion.

Spiritual education also involves facing certain key existential fundamentals. These include the observations that all conditions are impermanent; suffering is part and parcel of being alive; oneself is not the centre of the universe; ipseity is actually delusion; karmic consequence is inevitable; liberation (from ipsion) is possible. These teachings operate within a time-space framework of vast scope in which neither the beginning nor the end of time or space is conceivable. They are threads that run through the content of spiritual education as well as being considerations shaping its methodology. It is at least as much concerned to cultivate a character that can face eternity as to train a person to do a job. It does prepare people to fulfil roles, but those roles are themselves regarded as educational steps. Having a time perspective that extends to almost infinite lifetimes, it is able to regard a person's whole life opus as simply one more step in his long term cultivation.

So spiritual education is not just instrumental. It is education for its own sake, or for the sake of a bigger life, a broader mind, a more generous heart. There has been a trend in modern times toward utilitarianism such that in a university in Britain one is now more likely to find a course on catering than philosophy. Spirituality is not impractical but it is not narrowly utilitarian. Practical tasks and skills fall within higher values, rather than replacing them in importance.

Spiritual education should be critical. Spiritual movements generally begin as reform movements, critical of the social and religious *status quo*. Christianity,

Buddhism and Islam all share this feature. Criticism at best develops logical analysis, argument, rhetoric and critical thought. The injunction to test things for oneself is a core characteristic of Buddhist instruction. Spiritual education should encourage the individual to deploy doubt in a constructive way, understand logic, cultivate the ability to think divergently, and understand the potentiality for creativity.

At the same time, spiritual education recognises that the path to escape from ipseity can be pursued in a constructive or a deconstructive manner. The self can be deconstructed by analytic or meditative reflection. Alternatively, the self can be abandoned by investment in what is not self. Attention to otherness (alterity) is as important as self-criticism, and ultimately more important. Deconstruction has an inherent limit that alterity does not have. Alterity is the ultimate antidote to ipseity. Thus, though spiritual education often begins with what are called "self-power" (*svalbala*) methods, since the self cannot ultimately abandon itself, self-power has to give way to other-power (*para-bala*) eventually.

We thus have here a system that, on the one hand, cultivates *ekagata*, the ability to stand alone, think for oneself, be courageous and of strong character, yet, on the other hand doubts the existence and validity of the self and looks for special objectivity, other-concern, and other esteem rather than self-expression or self-indulgence. Spiritual education does not value self-esteem as such, but rather values the cultivation of esteem for the conditions of life, physical, social and spiritual. It is not education in the sense of "drawing out" so much as in the sense of liberating by dethroning the centrality of the self.

People carry out their lives within a matrix of conditions, commonly reifying those conditions to an unrealistic degree, and remaining, therefore, stuck in a much narrower range of thought and behaviour than is actually available to them. Many of these restrictions also operate in a demoralising fashion. Spiritual education should help a person break out of this narrowness by teaching the deconstructive analysis of conditions and by inculcating a larger more objective perspective with ever widening horizons.

An Approach to Ethics

The well-cultivated person does not claim personal merit, credit or ability, but lives in an ambient state of gratitude and appreciation.

The Buddha advocated moral cultivation, but not in a simplistic sense. His followers have an extensive corpus of writings on ethical instruction, but the ideal is less that the adept be able to recognise the good and discard the bad and more that she should have the capacity to perceive and to generate good even in bad situations. This is called transforming adverse circumstances into the path. While this approach respects values, ethics and injunctions that have a ring of eternal validity, it recognises that the practical ethical life is dynamic and situational and that it generally requires wisdom and compassion more fundamentally than knowledge to choose the most skilful course. Ethics is concerned with the reduction of suffering, but it should not be narrowly utilitarian. Or, to put the same thing differently, if we are considering the greatest good of the greatest number, we should not understand the term "good" as relating to the indulgence of individual wants, but to the potential to contribute to the spiritual liberation of all beings.

In this approach ethics are a function of intention, or we may say of the state of one's heart. Many Western discussions of ethics revolve around what a person "should" do, but this level of analysis is relatively superficial. A person who is not spiritually trained, not spiritually educated, would generally recognise that the spiritually cultivated person acts in an ethically correct way. They would see that such a person does not kill, steal, lie and so on. However, they might well not see what lies behind such behaviour. What lies behind it is a heart at peace, a spirit attuned to the needs of others, a mind big enough not to be disturbed by trivia. Furthermore, even these things are not fundamental. Behind them lies, on the one hand, a deep appreciation of impermanence, spiritual danger, and non-self, and, on the other hand, an all-encompassing awareness of wholeness.

However, while the cultivation of wise compassion can be regarded as a goal, there lies here also the danger of falling into the pursuit of an ideal self which is merely a deceptive chimera. Wisdom and compassion are the result of genuine concern for others, not of self-development. They are better regarded as by-products of walking the path than as goals. The well-cultivated person does not claim personal merit, credit or ability, but lives in an ambient state of gratitude and appreciation. The person of highest character has no character, merely an ecstasy of appreciation.

Buddhism relies upon a psychologically sophisticated theory of conditioning. Eighteen different modes of mental conditioning are recognised and their benign and pernicious effects considered. The basic notion of conditioning is non-deterministic. Conditions conduce but do not determine. Blindness to conditioning commonly results in inadvertent or unconscious abdication of responsibility. Recognition allows one to see that although the conditions are conducive to such and such a course of action, one remains free to reject it. Most truly moral acts require some such "standing against the current". In this way, insight can liberate.

However, while this approach cultivates clarity of thought, it is holistic in that it seeks to bring emotion, vision, intuition, intellect, attention, reasonable care for the body, and all other aspects of the person into balance. This may and often does mean remedying deficiencies. It is normal for humans to get by rather than to realise all their potential. It is not just insight that liberates. Everything that enables a person to abandon the defensive stance in relation to life and become open to possibilities helps.

A person is a karmic stream. Within are many potentials, a great proportion of which are obstacles. Buddhism does not see liberation as a matter of emptying the karmic reservoir: to do so would be impractical. Rather it is a matter of a "lateral leap": a sideways step that enables one to view one's situation with new eyes: a change of heart. Such change engages one's deepest emotions. It springs from convincing personal experience. Spiritual training is thus a process that has both a steady progressive aspect and also a sudden breakthrough possibility. These two paths - the sudden and the gradual - complement one another. Both, however, rest upon engagement with experience in as direct and deep a fashion as possible.

Soul Therapy

True therapy partakes of the ethos of the confessional. If a person cannot safely be honest and open in therapy then real therapy is barely possible.

I was trained as a psychotherapist many years ago. My original training was as a psychiatric social worker. My teachers Marigold McLarren and Anne Trembath were remarkably professional, skilled and insightful. They were certainly among my first gurus and it was from them that I learnt what it meant to be therapeutic. Later I received other trainings. In particular, I learnt a huge amount from my second wife, Jenny Biancardi, and from my psychodrama trainer Elaine Sachnoff. Then there was the time I spent with Carl Rogers and his close associates. Eventually for professional reasons I needed a qualification and studied with John McCloud at Keele University where I obtained my masters degree and doctorate. Looking back over it all, the things and the people that taught me most were quite randomly related to obtaining qualifications or certifications. What mattered really was that I learnt a greater realism about human life. Being a therapist is not at all unrelated to what it means to be a spiritual friend.

A therapist knows some techniques, but therapy is not technique. Therapy uses them, but no technique is therapy without the insight that the therapist brings. Again, a therapist is a citizen in society, but therapy is not a matter of holding a particular set of social attitudes; in fact, political correctness or ideas about justice, say, can be a real handicap to doing therapy. A therapist often works as part of an organisation, but therapy is only incidentally a matter of implementing organisational policy, even less so government policy. Therapy is a mode of working with a client that enables that person to encounter the truth of their life, expand the range of possibilities in their heart and mind, understand the constellation of conditions that are supporting their stories, sometimes change those conditions and those stories, and so arrive at an enhanced ability to navigate life's obstacles, optimise its opportunities and recover from its setbacks. A therapist helps a person learn from experience; helps them to grow emotionally, personally, socially and spiritually. Therapy does not aim to fit them into any mould. It enables them to find what it is that brings the fullness of life to them and enables them to play their part in life's larger meaning or spirit. Therapy is part of spiritual education.

If a person comes to me wondering if he should leave his marriage or his job, for instance, it is not my task as therapist to make that decision for him nor even, really, to help him to make that decision. Rather it is my job to work with him in such a way that whether he stays in the marriage or leaves it he does so in a more fulfilling and constructive manner; that he learn the lessons and profits from the experience and that, to quote Zen Master Dogen, he be enlightened by everything. To be enlightened by everything is to "forget the self" and to forget the self is to be a bigger hearted person.

When I look back over the period of my involvement in the therapy world I am appalled at how that domain has gone. When I was trained, therapy was a sacred space. Nowadays, if the therapist is employed - and an increasing proportion are - the degree to which therapists have to cope with managerial interference in their work is substantial. They also have to work within codes of "ethics" or organisational policies many of which require that what the client tells the therapist be reported to authorities if it reveals that the client has engaged in socially disapproved or illegal behaviours. In other words, if you have been bad, there is now no longer anywhere where you can go and talk about it safely. This, to me, undermines one of the main foundations of what therapy as I learnt it was supposed to be.

True therapy partakes of the ethos of the confessional. If a person cannot safely be honest and open in therapy then real therapy is barely possible. At best it is seriously handicapped. If the therapist has to report to a supervisor whose priority is organisational rather than therapeutic, again real therapy is seriously compromised.

Fortunately, thus far, there is no proposal for state registration of Buddhist priests. As a priest I can take a person's confession without feeling any pressure to divulge this information to the secular powers. Thanks be. Of course, with the development of the chaplaincy profession no doubt the state will eventually get its claws into at least that corner of the priestly function. The writing is already on the wall in that department.

Sometimes I feel I am a member of an endangered species. When a person comes before me I am concerned for the long term good of this person's karmic continuum - or "soul" if you prefer - and that only. The term client used to mean the person who was in charge. Gradually it has been eroded until it means a person who is in a dependent position. To me, however, the client remains the captain of her/his own karma. I am a consultant. A therapist is a consultant to souls, not a social policeman. I am not a director. I am certainly not an informer. I am not a manipulator of techniques. I do not regard my client as a mechanism and certainly not as a miscreant even if she has done lamentable things.

My client is doing the best he or she can within the light they have to find their way through this gloom that is sometimes mistakenly referred to as "the real world". Along the way they have many fantasies some of which they tell me about. They do many things, some honest, some not; they act or flinch, are conscientious or cut corners, and, like everyone else, have done things that were lethal, lascivious, and lax as well as other things noble, kind and loving. They have reasons for all the things they have done. Some of these are conscious, but many are not. Many spring from karmic promptings the roots of which are long lost. My job is not to judge or report or fix them. It is to understand and be a spiritual presence that respects them and trusts the deep source of love that holds us all: to trust the process.

In the Tao Te Ching the Taoist sage says, "Those who are of good faith I have faith in; those who are of bad faith I also have faith in; thus does faith grow." This is the basis of all true therapy, including all spiritual growth. It does not mean that I think that everything my client says is true; probably very little of it is perfectly valid, but that is normal. To have faith is what is important, not to know the unknowable.

I am so glad that, in the spiritual domain there remains a tiny enclave free from the depredations of secular social control. Long may it survive. Here lies the seed from which a restoration of true value may one day regerminate. In that seed lies the genetic material from which Buddhas are born, Buddhas who view all beings with the eyes of compassion free from condemnatory judgement or fantasies of control.

PART FOUR: BODHISATTVA PATH

The Republic of Sukhavati

If spiritual training does not make people into citizens of the world, concerned for all sentient beings, then it is missing something vital.

Sukhavati is the name of the land created by the Buddha Amida, also called Amitabha. It is a vision of a perfected world where there is no oppression, cruelty or prejudice, where it is easy to learn wholesome principles and to live a compassionate life. The vision of Sukhavati as a Pure Land of harmony provides Buddhists both with a sense of where they would like to be reborn in their next life and also what they would like this world to become. Buddhist training and practice is then conceptualised as a personal contribution to the process whereby Buddhas are trying to bring this transformation of society about for the benefit of all beings.

We have been discussing the foundations of a critical and socially engaged Buddhism. This has been partly a new look at the principles set out in my book *The New Buddhism* and partly a review of how practice has evolved within my approach to Buddhist practice and training. Practice refers to the expression of love, compassion, sympathy and equanimity through wise actions and skilful means. This is collective as well as individual. It is not so much that we train people in order that they individually will later use what they have learnt in order to be errant bodhisattvas following a path on their own as that we collectively shall engage in actions to resist oppression, assist the afflicted and demonstrate an alternative.

In our socially and culturally engaged work it has often been our approach to co-operate with other groups. The other groups may be such that our alliance with them is limited to one or two points of agreement, but even such alliances can bear fruit. Sometimes we also form relationships with groups that we have a lot in common with or that are guided by people who have a close affinity with our own approach. Our experience of working in partnership has generally been that it does not lead to the actualisation of what any of the partners originally envisaged, but it does always lead to something valuable, including a good deal of learning by all involved and, frequently, completely new developments that nobody could have foreseen.

Working in relationship, or in a team, is not just a way of getting things done that one could not do on one's own. It is also a way of learning important lessons about how ego-centric one is, how open to co-operation one is, how capable one is of taking initiatives that benefit the collective and not simply oneself. Thinking in collective terms is a different mind-set from looking after oneself.

The Amida approach is not that of importing and extending an Asian way of doing things. Nor is it a matter of imposing Western ideas upon Buddhism in order to make it more "relevant". Rather it is about applying basic Buddhist principles of ethics, faith and wisdom in a diversity of ways, both for the benefit of society and as a means of spiritual development of the people involved. The results are various. We do not replicate projects or services. We respond to particular concrete situations and develop something appropriate. Whatever has already been developed is seen as a potential springboard for something new. Thus the India project has gone through numerous transformations and will no doubt go through more in the future. If we were to start a second project in India, however, there is no reason why it should necessarily look anything like the existing one. It would be a new response to a new situation. For sure we would use what we have learnt from work in a wide range of settings, but there is no sense of having a final formula.

The matter of practice and training and the matter of developing an alternative society are complementary. Our idea of practice involves work to create an alternative: a society based on love and compassion. Our idea of training involves placing trainees in social situations where they will be challenged, will learn to relate to all manner of people, will acquire the ability to lead, to follow, to take individual initiative, to co-operate, to be imaginative and constructively critical, and always to have a sense of the greater good. If spiritual training does not make people into citizens of the world, concerned for all sentient beings, then it is missing something vital.

On the one hand, the alternative society needs such trainees and on the other hand such training needs the projects that are a part of the alternative. This also means that a variety of different initiatives can all form elements within the alternative and be part of the emergent Republic of Sukhavati. The Dharmic society does not just consist of Dharma practice centres and retreat houses. It also needs arts, health, education, food production, care for the dependent, production and distribution. It needs new forms of economic organisation. It needs groups that co-operate. It needs all kinds of synergism.

The synergistic principle is one key to this approach. In our Amida sangha we are unlikely to embark upon a new venture unless it has a synergistic effect. That means, unless it contributes in more than one way to things that are already happening. Assisting an alternative health project, say, may help the users of that project *and* provide an application of practice and training *and* create a placement opportunity for people learning counselling skills *and* bring on-stream new educational possibilities including courses in alternative forms of care *and* bring users of the project to an interest in other activities of the sangha, and so on. It is these kinds of synergism and feedback that make it possible for the sangha to do so much with so few resources, that cultivate co-operation, and that enable an organic approach to flourish. They are the creation of a culture. What we are talking about here is a culturally engaged spirituality, one that aims to foster the growth of a higher culture, not just among Buddhists or among religious people, but for everybody.

The organic idea is another important principle. The model for the alternative society is not social engineering, it is more that of jungle. By jungle we mean areas where a fully mature organic culture has developed. In tropical rain forest there are a vast number of different species all living together in an ever changing dynamic balance. In a jungle there is such a depth of fertility that every possible niche is quickly filled by some new life form, whereas when such forest is cleared and some kind of farming or monoculture is substituted 99% of the richness is lost. Much modern thinking about society is of this forest clearing type and, unfortunately, even many Buddhist groups are a kind of monoculture.

We shall go on discussing and applying these ideas and experimenting, and we hope thereby to increase the richness of spiritual life for individuals who choose to train and practise at the same time as we create at least pockets of the organic, synergistic, Dharmic alternative - pockets that influence the ambient society and that provide seedbeds for a revolution of values and the emergence of peace, co-operation and compassion as organising principles in society as a whole, a happy revolution.

Mendicant Life

Dharma does not actually take long to transmit. By a single exposure you can catch it.

From time to time I teach in South Korea, giving lectures on Buddhism and psychotherapy. Currently, my life is a series of travels and teachings and I learn a lot from the many wonderful people that I meet along the way. I go where I am invited rather than where I choose, as an apostle of the Dharma. People have been very kind to me. The mendicant life is one of accepting. Sometimes one is accepting poverty, sometimes riches. It is a life of saying yes. Last night somebody said "Could you just squeeze in one more lecture an hour before you catch your next plane?" and I said "Let's see if we can," but then another person in the group that is looking after me here said "Absolutely not!" so we let that one go. But the attitude of the Dharma-farer is always "Yes" and that does mean sometimes that we have to act to protect one another. When we love one another we do not have to be defending ourselves. I could, just about, have squeezed in the extra lecture, but it was also important to say "Yes" to the person who was giving the gift of protecting me.

I hope each of you finds as satisfying a life as this that I have fallen into, but this life does not come by looking for satisfaction. It is not by having "my idea", but simply by responding to need and call. We are all trying to give more thought and attention to the spirit and to the influence of the sages. Sometimes I travel alone and when possible I travel with somebody who is similarly on the

Dharma path. This is a kind of modern version of the life of Shakyamuni's earliest disciples. Though I am by no means as saintly and wise as they are depicted in the sutras, still it is an inspiration to know how they went forth all over the world that they knew of.

This is a work that is all-consuming. Dharma is caught rather than taught and one sometimes thinks would it not be better to stay in one place for longer, but the contagion of the Dharma does not actually take long to transmit. By a single exposure you can catch it. This is clear in the sutras. Being in the presence of the enlightened is the most wonderful thing - "it is good to see such sages" - to have it even once is transformative. To be in the presence of their messenger may not be quite the same, but it is something and it is what I can give people. Honen Shonin says about the nembutsu, do it as much as you can while knowing that once is enough. Every once is then precious.

I have had several important teachers in my life. I was not able to spend huge amounts of time with any of them; generally only odd months, or weeks, or even shorter times. Even when I was a Zen monk my teacher only came to the monastery from time to time as she had much work to do elsewhere. Still the encounters that we did have transformed my life and confirmed a power that did, does and will eternally work in me as a result. As my life has gone on it has gradually become more and more consumed by the Dharma of their love. What could be more wonderful?

Why Are We Here in India?

Close to the spirit of the original Dharma of Shakyamuni.

This seems as if it is a good question. However, if this really means "What is our aim?" there is really no very good answer. We do not have a plan. We simply go forth in faith.

We are wherever we are in order to enact the Dharma and benefit beings. We go where we are invited and teach those who ask us to teach and then one thing leads to another and, on this occasion, we find ourselves here. My own life is increasingly one of wandering in response to such calls. We follow the call out of faith. I came to India in the first instance a decade or more ago in response to a letter from Sakya Talukdar, a member of the Chakma tribe living in the North East who asked for help. Many Chakmas are refugees, displaced from their homeland in Bangladesh. Out of this friendship came others. Anomadharshi Bhikkhu, another Chakma, came to live with us in the UK for several years. He asked us to send somebody to teach English in Delhi, so, eventually, when we could, we did. That was the start of our operations in one of the poorer sectors of the Indian capital that have continued ever since. We taught English with no charge and an open door. We found, however, that the poorest were reluctant to come through that door and, as with so many things in India, it was often the well off who took what was on offer. It was suggested that we might offer classes out in the poorer areas, so we did, and still do even if it means working on rooftops or in the street.

Our style of Buddhism is as close to the spirit of the original Dharma of Shakyamuni as we can be in the modern world. I do not mean by this that we slavishly follow out of date forms and customs. I mean that we try to implement the spirit of what Gotama was saying and doing. He went forth for the good of the many to relieve suffering and we do the same. He taught that we should help one another and, in that spirit, we try to help people to help others. He taught that suffering and well-being both start in the mind. This does not mean that material conditions should be ignored. It means that one should act with a generous heart and use one's intelligence in constructive ways. Good heartedness and intelligence need expression through the conditions of the material world, and that is what we try to do.

Buddha taught faith and devotion and he taught mental cultivation. These are not two separate things. Our practice is to keep the Buddha always in mind. To help us do this we say his name on all occasions. The Buddha's name is our object of meditation and it is on our lips and in our heart all day long. This is the simplest practice and also the most profound one. For instance, in the Vissuddhi Magga, the most important Pali manual of meditation, the highest object of meditation is the Buddha. That is our practice too. In the Mahayana Buddhism of the Far East it is calling upon the Buddha that is the highest practice. If you have the Buddha always with you how can you do wrong? How can you lack inspiration? How can you fail to concentrate your mind? No obstacle can defeat you. It does not matter if your Buddha happens to be Francis of Assisi or Rumi or Abraham. To have in mind a great saintly, wise and compassionate spirit is a liberator.

We are in India and we are in many other places and all because we have the Sage in mind. We are, as yet, few, but we have far greater impact than our numbers would suggest possible and this is simply because it is not by our power that results come, but by our self-entrustment to an other power that goes with us and is always ahead of us. We follow the call of sentient beings in need and we have faith that things will unfold as they should. Everybody must do something with his or her life. What one does will be a function of what one holds most dear. If you hold the Dharma most dear you will end up with a life such as this; and a wonderful life it is!

Perhaps one day there will be many of us or perhaps we shall always be few, but even if we are few we can continue to bear witness to the possibility of such liberation, such inspiration and such joy and what could be better?

Great Beings Throughout the Three Times

We are continuing the work of Dr. Ambedkar. Dr. Ambedkar was continuing the work of Shakyamuni Buddha. Shakyamuni Buddha was continuing the work of Amida Buddha.

This piece was written in India where the work of Dr Bimrao Ambedkar is the inspiration of millions of the most disadvantaged citizens.

There is the past, the present and the future. Each exists in a different way for us and our life is a function of them. These are called the three times. In the three times there are many saints, sages, apostles and bodhisattvas, many great beings (*mahasattva*).

What is a Buddha? A Buddha is a fully enlightened being. In particular, a Buddha understands the past, present and future. A Buddha understands dependent origination. Dependent origination is the way in which the future emerges from the present and past, and the way that the present has emerged from the past and future. If we understood dependent origination we would not be conceited about ourselves: we would be full of awe and reverence for the wonder of existence. If we understood the three times we would have no motive to do bad things because we would be fully aware of the consequences. Buddhas see true advantage and true disadvantage without distortion. Buddhas help us to see more clearly.

What is a bodhisattva? A bodhisattva is somebody who does not think of himself, but thinks of the good of others. A bodhisattva is somebody who is on the way to becoming a Buddha. A bodhisattva is somebody who is beginning to be a great being. There are little bodhisattvas and there are great bodhisattvas. Dr. Ambedkar is a bodhisattva. Dr. Ambedkar began life in very disadvantaged conditions, but he became a saviour for many people. We continue to benefit from his work and inspiration. He helps us.

We are continuing the work of Dr. Ambedkar. Dr. Ambedkar was continuing the work of Shakyamuni Buddha. Shakyamuni Buddha was continuing the work of Amida Buddha. We shall continue the work in the future and we are little bodhisattvas. Some of us shall one day be Buddhas and great bodhisattvas.

How does one become a great being? There are two factors. The first is important, though it is the lesser of the two. This is the effort that one makes oneself. We have intelligence. We have life. If we also have a good heart we shall make the best we can of this life. Everybody should become educated and organise for the common good. Each person should make a personal vow. That is the first way.

The second way is that we are helped by our spiritual ancestors and we have to be willing to be helped. If we each insist on doing things our individual way nothing will be achieved. If I just want my own idea to prevail, I may achieve a small thing. If I want Dr Ambedkar's idea to prevail, if I want Shakyamuni's idea to prevail, if I want Amida's idea to prevail, then something much greater will be achieved.

We cannot change the whole world on our own, but the Buddhas and bodhisattvas can change it if we are willing to help them and be helped by them. This is why we have statues and pictures, so that we are always honouring these great beings, and so that we never forget. If we never forget the great beings then we shall not fall into conceitedness; we shall not become selfish or corrupt. Rather we shall be helped and we shall be part of a great work. Our lives will become meaningful and one day we too will be great beings.

All this comes through understanding the past, the present and the future.

Learning Patience in India - Journey to the East

So we were now completely cut off.

Life in India involves a great deal of patience. Although there is a vast amount of activity and bustle everywhere, it takes a remarkable amount of time to get things done. Getting a train ticket without resorting to bribery and corruption, for instance, cost us many hours over several days, much of it waiting in queues at different station windows and then getting the news that we needed to be in a different queue at a different station. Then we were on a waiting list. Finally getting to the head of another queue two hours before we were due to depart, we were told that our ticket was indeed confirmed. Then we very nearly missed the train by being on the wrong platform because our train did not appear on the station departures board. I asked the station master about it and was told, "I think it has gone; try platform one on the other side of the station." We actually jumped onto the train just as it was pulling out and then had to find our carriage and seats which takes some time as Indian trains are huge, a bit like taking a whole street on a journey.

In class 2a, which we were, there are seats that turn into bunks at night with a further bunk above. This arrangement is designed for four passengers per bay. Our two travel companions were charming, generous and helpful and this made our 40 hour train journey much pleasanter than it might have been. However, about half way the train filled up and we were joined by another four people which made things rather cosy for a while. Our companions told us that getting tickets is no easier for Indians. "Sometimes you pay double and still end up with no ticket."

Trains are invariably late arriving, often by several hours. The message "Inconvenience is deeply regretted" delivered by the public address system is ingrained on one's brain after a few hours of sitting on platforms. Whether on platforms or on the train watching India's interminable paddy fields, the art of meditation is immensely useful. With Amida Buddha in mind this too can be the Pure Land.

Along the corridor comes a continual stream of vendors and beggars. The vendors call their wares so there is quite a cacophony. They sell a variety of edibles, toys, bags, trinkets, and, most of all, liquids, which are essential, including what I initially heard as "Barley water" until I learnt that it was not barley but paani which is Hindi for water.

I enjoyed the whole experience. Waking the second morning I climbed down from my bunk to see a change of vegetation. As we approached Assam the greenery got thicker and included palms and banana trees. I started to feel even more emotional - nostalgia for past times in those parts and a clear feeling of home-coming. Assam has always somewhat reminded me of the Cyprus of my early years.

I was concerned that my mobile phone might run out of battery so used it quite sparingly en route as we would need to communicate with our contacts in Assam by phone as soon as we arrived. Eventually the train pulled into Guwahati and we got off, saying fond good-byes to the two fellows from Nagaland who had been with us since Delhi and now still had another eight or ten hours travel ahead of them. Once off the train I took out my phone and soon ascertained with a shock that we had no network in this part of the country, so we were now completely cut off. We decided to check into a hotel for the night. The first dozen we tried were all full. After all it was the day before Christmas. We were starting to think we might be looking out the traditional stable for the night when we found a lodging with one free room for one night and settled in. The shower was cold, the phone did not work, the bed was hard, but it was a clean room where we could unwind, wash out some clothes and take stock. Namo Amida Bu.

The Reality of India

Their hopes are all in the future: with the children and with Buddhism.

He has only one eye. This genetic trait he owes to membership of a caste group. Here in India exogamy is taboo and in-breeding often leads to handicaps that would be much rarer anywhere else.

He is 55. By English standards everybody in India except the privileged is old for their age. He peddles a rickshaw, which is heavy work for a man of his age. In the past he has held a variety of jobs and through one of them was fortunate enough to glean a smattering of English which makes it possible for me to communicate with him. In regard to the three commonly more lucrative areas of employment in contemporary India, however, he is excluded; he cannot get a government job because of his eye, his English is not good enough to work in a call centre, and his education is too poor to work in electronics, so he is reduced to finding a manual job and being a rickshaw man does offer a degree of independence.

He was born a Hindu but has become a Buddhist and refers to me with evident affection as "my guru", with some stress on the possessive adjective. Guru or not, I am considerably challenged by thinking about the difficulties that he and his family labour under.

The most pressing of these is that he has a sister who has three daughters nearing adulthood and recently her husband contracted a disease and died. Now in the West having a daughter may be a delight and a four woman household would be a quite viable unit, and furthermore their problems would not necessarily be an immediate or ultimate concern to the mother's brother. Here in India, however, daughters are an economic liability. They all have to be found husbands and dowries. If they manage to find Buddhist husbands a dowry might not be asked for, but this is not that easy to accomplish. My disciple is now, in effect, father to these young women. He refers to them as his daughters even though they are actually nieces. How will he provide for them?

He is not among the poorest of the poor. He is blessed with a one room house for his wife, himself and his son. It has a yard that floods when it rains and it is to be found round the corner at the bottom of a long side road that, when I traversed it, was eighty percent under water. Where does this water come from? It has not rained in ages. Well, it comes from a variety of sources, some of them unmentionable, but, one way or another, from the surrounding dwellings. Along this street wade buffalo, innumerable children play, vendors ply their various wares and life goes on. The road is so deluged that he cannot actually get his rickshaw to his home and has to park it at a garage on the "main road" some half kilometre away.

His son is studying. The lad proudly showed me his stack of textbooks. How does he manage to study in these cramped conditions? He certainly has my admiration. There is only one electric light bulb in the house and this gives a feeble light being run off a neighbour's generator. Cooking is on two gas rings on the floor. Water is fetched in buckets from a standpipe some distance from the house.

The woman of the house is a quiet woman, silently bearing the family difficulties. They married because according to the restrictions imposed by caste and astrology they had almost no other choices available. Nonetheless this does give every appearance of being a strong marriage: he speaks of her with evident care and she regards him with kindness in her eyes. Their hopes are all in the future: with the children and with Buddhism. They hope that Ambedkar's vision of a casteless society will one day be realised and that the Buddha's teaching of honesty and kindness will bring this about.

For myself I would love to help this family - and so many others - to realise these dreams. My work here does contribute something to spreading the change of consciousness that it needs and, where one can, one injects items of material aid in such a way as to encourage the process of mutual aid. In the end it is not going to be achieved by aid, but by education and organisation, but resources are still needed. Nor does one have confidence that just making India more like Britain or America is the answer. If this family lived in the UK they would have better housing, better medical care and better public hygiene and their present worries would not have foundation, but they would have other stresses and, probably, fewer friends, less hope and less sense of purpose. Here the education system may be poorer, but people are keen to learn; conditions are poor, but economic development is going on apace; there is a future and what is at stake is what system will shape it: capitalism, naxalite communism, militant Hindu castism, Ambedkarism? Here the Buddhist vision is not just about inner calm or personal psychology. It is about community co-operation, social liberation, education and building a new world. How much of the traditional Indian way will this new world encompass? How much will it be driven by the greed of commercialism? How much will the old prejudices and cruelties of caste persist? How successful will we be in bringing the Buddhist vision to actualisation? And what part will my rickshaw man and his family play in all this? A lot is at stake.

Time to Revive the Alternative Society?

When something is unleashed in the world there is no telling where it will end.

Our world is changing. There is austerity. There are rising prices. There is anger. Where will it lead? What will people do? They may over-throw governments in the hope that new ones will do better - but the new ones will have the same problems as the old ones and less experience. They may persecute minorities; this is quite likely. There may be wars, though this is increasingly difficult in the contemporary world of weapons of mass destruction because there are no real winners any more. There may be civil disorder and civil war is possible in some places. Governments are likely to retrench and extensive systems of social control such as have proliferated in recent decades may strengthen further or may become impractical. This creates conditions favourable to new movements. Discontent can be turned negatively into hate and strife or it can be turned positively into new construction and values.

In the nineteen fifties, sixties and early seventies there was the idea of the Alternative Society. This was an ideal of greater liberation and greater togetherness that took many forms. There were many associated sub-movements - beatnik poets, hippies, communes, etc - and various periodicals sprang up. It generated much popular music which celebrated the sense of hope. Some of the manifestations - the free love and the drug culture - now appear to have been aberrations, but they were all manifestations of a spirit of hope and freedom, both social and psychological.

At that time, knowledge of Buddhism was in its infancy in the West. Buddhism was, in many ways, at that time, a sub-movement within the Alternative Society. I myself lived in a Buddhist commune. The population there was from several kinds of Buddhism. There was a sense that meditation achieved what drugs were supposed to achieve, only more effectively and enduringly and without the unwanted side effects.

Since then, Buddhism has become more institutionalised and is now in danger of stagnation, which will, I fear, be its fate unless it can indeed rediscover that spirit of liberation and become the focus of hope for young people. Most Buddhist groups in Europe at least now have ageing congregations. A renewal is already needed and it needs to be a renewal that reanimates idealism about all aspects of human life. Buddhism is not just "a practice" or, even worse, "one's own practice", that isolates a person from the corrupt world. Buddhism is a light for the world itself and a light does not just illuminate the light-house.

This, however, is not just a Buddhist movement. The new spiritual age may take on a myriad forms and associations. We should think of ourselves not as "the answer" but as a rich contribution. If we have a real sense of our own bombu position, then we can contribute to a renaissance of hope in society at large. The ideals of liberation and of the Alternative Society can be a beacon. When something is unleashed in the world there is no telling where it will end. We are entering such times.

Thinking of the Common Good

Each person in the choir should be as capable of performing a solo as of blending in.

Our Amidist spiritual Order came about as a natural result of the attempt to actually carry out socially engaged activity. If you send people forth, then they need a framework to go forth in and they need confidence that there is somewhere and someone to come back to. The fraternity that supports a person who goes forth needs to be as loyal and committed to the overall venture as the person who actually does the going forth. Just as mountaineers need a base camp, so we discovered that there need to be committed people backing up as well as similarly committed people willing to go forth.

More broadly, evolution is not so much the survival of the fittest as of the best connected. Humans need one another. The modern person has attained a degree of apparent social independence only by the existence of large scale universal systems that provide him or her with what they need. Formerly, and in many parts of the world still, they would have to rely upon neighbours for food, shelter and security. Now we rely upon an abstraction called the state. The emergence of the state has made many of the old functions of community, including the religions that made communities meaningful, redundant. We all know that this is a gain and a loss. The modern person exists in a kind of artificial vacuum, effectively worshipping a human made system, the ideal of which is to be as impersonal and impartial as possible. This brings social benefits, but is not an optimal environment for the soul. However, the modern world has also brought new media of communication and transport that make it possible to create entirely new forms of community, to have friends in all parts of the world, to pilgrimage not just once in a lifetime, to defy the parochialism of immigration control systems and assert both the possibility of spiritual communities that transcend social barriers and of values that are more truly international and universal than has been possible heretofore.

While many people may be lulled by modern mass facilities into living a life that is tied down by routines more or less empty of meaning, feeling compelled to work most of their waking hours in an instrumental employment to earn the money to support the lifestyle that one has to have in order to be in a position to keep an employment of that kind, a closed loop that in total does not mean very much, we can, if we have the courage for it, become an altogether new kind of person living the liberation not just of the soul but also of thought, vision and lifestyle.

Right livelihood has never been so challenging, but never had such a high possibility. What Shakyamuni Buddha or Francis of Assisi advocated can come alive in today's circumstances if people will go forth in faith and grasp the opportunity that is now unfolding. To do so, however, they have to let go of the worship of money.

Modern people have grown very used to living in a system of working for pay. This wage system has become very widespread and ultimately grew out of the serf system of feudalism. In England, William the Conqueror abolished slavery and substituted a system in which serfs had certain rights. It took numerous centuries for this rights-in-return-for-labour system to evolve into what we have today.

Even though they are actually paid servants, the fact that people have "free time" makes them think they are independent. The idea of letting that go fills most people with great anxiety. They have become highly conditioned to the wage system. The wage system, however, also reduces people's sense of commitment to what they do. Where the position of the serf was originally a personal bond to a particular lord and a particular community, the waged or salaried worker in a modern bureaucracy or commercial corporation is more alienated from what he or she spends their life doing with all the consequences highlighted by Marxists on the one hand and Existentialists on the other.

Many great religious founders and reformers have preferred to establish a system based not on earning, but on sharing, at least for the most committed. We have emulated this pattern in our own sangha to a degree. We do not practice a formal communism of giving up all possessions, but by living in community within an ethos in which substantial private accumulation makes no sense, we do, in fact, practice a high level of sharing. This has a number of beneficial consequences. It makes our communal life less materialistic and, in many ways, lighter on the planet and upon ourselves. Most importantly, however, it socialises participants into a different way of thinking that is not concerned with personal entitlement, but with collective good.

This shift of outlook from personal profit to collective good is a very important part of spiritual training. It is not likely to work in society at large because the people there are not in such training and do not have this kind of spiritual bond with one another. Spirituality practised by a group, however, does give rise to an alternative society.

Modern people commonly want to be as independent as possible, but public opinion and opinion within social groups is now so strong, given the power of modern media, that most modern people are much less individual than their forebears were. In the sangha it is the other way round. We are aware of our spiritual independence and so are individual, but we are not independent socially: we co-operate together and help one another. As individuals, we encourage critical thought and discussion and each person is helped to develop to the full and think for him or herself. Some may ask how it is possible for people to think for themselves and also have a common set of values. The doctrinal framework of our sangha is, however, very simple. It provides enough commonality for us to function as a community, but it is far from being a straight-jacket and there is no doubt that we are a gathering of characters who are more distinct for being part of this. We aim to be a commonwealth of individuals, whereas the society around us aims to be, rather, a regiment of independents. This is a significant difference.

Our core practice is chanting. Singing is an essentially collective activity. It is practice in harmonising. Each person has a unique voice, but the practice involves one in using one's unique voice as part of a whole. In that whole, mostly the separate person disappears, but from time to time there may also be solo parts. As a sangha we

266

are a choir. Ideally, each person in the choir should be as capable of performing a solo as of blending in and vice versa.

The Zen Master Lin Chi (Rinzai) said that the true Zen practitioner was "a person of no rank" (i.e. neither high nor low nor in-between). They transfer merit rather than taking credit. "Be a light to the world by making the Dharma your light" was the nub of Buddha's message expressed in his final words. Many people have misunderstood this. A fully individuated person has no need to boast, but gets satisfaction from making a contribution. That contribution will have unique qualities – a unique voice - because each person is unique. There is a world of difference between a person who is truly individual that can be trusted to see what is needed and contribute in their own special way, and one who seeks only to make him/herself stand out as a special case with special demands and special needs.

We say that spiritual training is about overcoming the ego. In practice this means that one important aspect of it is learning leadership, teamwork and responsibility. One of the most potent areas where ego appears is in relationships with co-workers. To be able to work with others harmoniously, whether one is in authority, subordinate, or in a peer position, and to be able to be in any of these three positions with equal ease and grace is immensely valuable and only possible in as much as personal conceit has been set aside. Having people who can do so makes it possible to have effective flexible teamwork. We found that we needed to develop the ability to work in situations where members must frequently substitute for one another. Members of such a sangha are loyal, reliable, and relatively free from petty rivalries and resentments. All this is a challenge to the ego that wants its independence and covets narcissistic resources. Of course, we are not perfect: this process of sangha development is constantly unfolding. We are all in a process of learning just what it does mean in particular situations. Frequently we fail and lapse into old habits. We lose sight of the Dharma light and drown in self-pity, envy or lose our composure in the dynamics of inter-personal situations. However, we do understand that the more fully people enter into the sangha spirit the more the sangha is able to do in the world for the benefit of sentient beings and the more satisfying and enriching the life becomes for all of us involved in it.

Trikaya

3 Bodies of Budha

1) Dharmakaya – truth body

2) Sambhogakaya – body of mutual enjoymet (bliss)

3) Nirmanakaya – created body

Being a Sangha Member

The goal is to be able to live a fully human life in a noble manner.

What does sangha membership imply? A sangha is a spiritual community. It has a core of spiritual teachings. A member accepts the framework of spiritual teachings of their community. In our case these are the trikaya nature of Buddha, the bombu nature of the adherent, and nembutsu as primary spiritual practice. All sangha communities have some basic points of principle and it is better if these are clear. At the same time, these merely provide a frame within which discussion takes place. A sangha member is expected to take an active and intelligent approach and to use the teachings in ways that are helpful to practice. All teachings are koans. They provide focus and bring an "edge" to the practitioner's spiritual enquiry. They help the practitioner to enquire more deeply.

A sangha member holds practice dear. Each spiritual community has practice. In our sangha this is calling and contemplating and various auxiliary practices. The auxiliaries are less important than the core practice, but a positive attitude to practice is necessary. This does not necessarily mean that a sangha member has to do a certain number of hours practice per day or per week. For some people such regularity is a good idea. For others it is not. Different people have different needs and the same person has different needs at different stages.

A sangha member is a disciple, looks to more experienced members for advice and guidance, and will have one or more mentors. Discipleship is a relationship. It implies an attitude of actively seeking teachings and valuing being in the presence of those for whom the teachings are more completely internalized. Being a disciple is not a matter of becoming a clone or of imitation of the teacher. One might in some ways model oneself on one's teacher, but maturity on the path goes beyond this stage. The teaching does not lie in the form of what the teacher does, but in the spirit in which she or he does it. The disciple is not learning to do what the teacher does, so much as learning how the teacher would approach a situation. Buddhism is a heart to heart transmission. The closer a disciple comes to the teacher the more the teacher will share their humanness with the disciple because the goal is not to become inhuman, but to be able to live a fully human life in a noble manner.

A sangha member values, celebrates and contributes to the life of the sangha. This may mean living with other sangha members or being an active member of a local group or congregation. It may mean travelling. It may mean functioning as a local representative of the sangha and carrying out roles in the local community. A sangha member contributes to the life of the sangha with time and energy. Their contribution may be financial, intellectual, practical, and/or social and will often be all of these. A sangha member co-operates with other members in commonly agreed activities that spread the word and do good work. He or she contributes to consultations about the life and future of the sangha. A sangha member participates in gatherings, services, ceremonies and rites of passage that celebrate the collective life.

The Pleasure of Complaining

It does enhance happiness to drop the habit altogether.

I have been asked to say something about complaining. Humans complain. Of course, people do get something from moaning. It is not all bad. Most people's greatest sense of intimacy comes when they share with another what they feel they could not say directly. If A feels hurt by X, A might not want to confront X and might, indeed, feel that doing so would makes matters worse, but A still feels discomfort at keeping the hurt to himself. He therefore shares it with B. In this way he relieves himself and also gives B the message that if he has anything that he wants to unburden himself of, then this is a space where that might be possible. We only tell our secrets to our intimates and so sharing secrets is a way of communicating and enhancing intimacy. Complaining, therefore, is not all bad and the immediate reward it produces can readily create a self-sustaining cycle so that, in no time, it is a habit that we are hardly conscious of any more. While it does enhance happiness to drop the habit altogether (which is true of many addictive behaviours) if you are going to do it it is nicer (and safer) to do it socially than in secret. Ideally, of course, one's friend takes it for no more than what it is - a tension reducing pastime - and does not take it over-seriously.

The complaining habit has a lot in common with other addictive behaviours - like consuming alcohol, say. Shakyamuni did not say that such behaviours are without gain - he simply pointed out that the drawbacks outweigh the advantages. The basis of most Buddhist behaviour training revolves around "seeing the disadvantage". If one really sees the disadvantage then one may be able to kick the habit, rather as people kick smoking when they realise their lungs are diseased. Better to have stopped earlier. The correct view of such behaviour is, therefore, not puritanical - there are gains and one can have fellow-feeling - but if we have the faith to face life fully then we can see the balance and choose the healthier course.

In regard to complaining particularly, the Mahayana Precepts include the injunction "Do not be proud of yourself and devalue others". This is a high level koan for most of us and certainly an interesting exercise to have a go at and see if one can keep for, say, a day, or maybe an hour is more realistic. We advocate sympathy and fellow-feeling. We are all foolish beings. Let's do the best we can to be understanding toward one another. As faith and sympathy grows, the taste for complaint may fade; indeed it may start to feel sour in the mouth. Then one may be able to kick it without immediately falling into self-righteousness. What a mess a human is! But it can be a fertile mess.

Practical Wisdom

One should not try to turn a family home into a monastery. The important thing is to live the spirit of the teaching in a way appropriate to the circumstances.

We have a spiritual exercise that we call Nei Quan in which we review what we have received: we count our blessings. Blessings may be physical, such as food, clothing, transport and so on, social, as in the support that we receive from the presence and goodwill of friends, or spiritual in that we have the Dharma and the example, presence and assistance of the spiritual ancestors. The spiritual help is what can carry us through times when other circumstances are adverse. If one has the Sage in mind then one can cope even if physical or social conditions are unconducive. In the ideal state one would be like Kshitigarbha, who is able to maintain his spiritual resolve even though he spends most of his time in the hells where he goes to rescue other beings. However, most of us are not as spiritually advanced as that. We are ordinary and the presence of conducive conditions is very important to us. In nei quan we cultivate gratitude for whatever such conditions we have.

In this respect there is an interaction. The more a person spends time in and appreciates spiritually conducive conditions the more acclimatised to them that person becomes and the more they value them. Such a person is then more likely to reproduce such conditions when they have the opportunity. When we go to the city there are many temptations and inducements to depart from the life of simplicity that characterises the spiritual person. Depending upon the habits we have developed we shall be more or less susceptible. When people go to a Dharma centre they dwell for a while in good conditions, but then they must go home again. A person who has been inspired by the experience of living in the Dharma community will want to reproduce some of its features in their own life back at home. It is not possible to completely reproduce the atmosphere of a Dharma community, perhaps, but one can do some little things that eliminate spiritual obstacles and add reminders of the holy life. One can simplify. At the same time, one cannot and should not try to turn a family home into a monastery. The important thing is to live the spirit of the teaching in a way appropriate to the circumstances.

One can help to provide good conditions for others. Exactly what these will be will vary with the case; I am not talking about trying to force others into the straight-jacket of our ideals. Nonetheless, we can all help by the conditions that we create for each other and avoid colluding in creating bad karma for others and to contribute to circumstances conducive to good. This is partly a matter of having an eye to the longer term. It implies, for instance, that it is not always correct to simply go along with what others want. Parents have to make many decisions in respect of their children that have the long term well-being of the child in view even though they are not what the child wants in the immediate situation. Although we do not stand in the position of parent toward other adults, we still need a degree of 'parental mind' whenever we are in a position to influence conditions that will affect others. The current norms of self-determination may sometimes blind us to what is best in this respect. Just because a person has a right to be self-determining it does not follow that one should always be that person's accomplice.

Through nei quan we gradually understand through our own experience how interactive our inner and outer conditions are, and we learn some skill in the art of adapting to circumstance. For instance, there are times when giving a person a gift will touch their heart and influence their whole life in a wonderful way. There are other times when giving a person a gift will make them think that you are a soft touch and encourage them to exploit you, thus making you an accomplice in their accumulation of bad karma. There are times when assisting a person in doing something, even though it is something that one would not normally do oneself and might even have scruples against, will move that person and cement a wholesome relationship leading to many good outcomes. There are other times when it is important not to budge from one's principles. All this is what we call skilful means (*upaya*) and it calls for a kind of practical wisdom.

Through nei quan we discover a great deal through reflection upon our own case. 'One's own case' is what in Zen is called the koan. Nei quan is a reflection upon the koan that arises naturally in daily life. How simple everything would be if we could just learn a few fixed principles and then apply them rigidly throughout the day. Alas, such an approach commonly leads to shipwreck. Life is complex. Compassion needs practical wisdom and discernment that rest upon experience and investigation. All of this is the development of what we call secondary faculties. It is not the core of our faith, but it is still an important element in the spiritual life that makes for satisfaction and constructive living.

No Distance in Dharma

Faith operates at an unconscious as much as a conscious level.

Buddha created a sangha by inviting people to the spiritual life. Members of the sangha are scattered all around the world, but we are all part of one family. There is a bond of love here even between people who have never met face to face. This is something quite remarkable. Each member and each group contributes in a unique manner. Each shows their faith and love by whatever means they can. We are not just local groupings. We are all part of something that is growing simultaneously in many places with a common energy that is somehow organic. This organic aspect (*bija-niyama*) is very important in creating synergisms that gradually become more and more creative. We are carried by a faith that operates at an unconscious (*chitta-niyama*) as much as a conscious (*karma-niyama*) level.

Also, it is quite characteristic of our sangha that people drawn to it are often those who already have a good deal of experience of the spiritual path in one or more other spiritual traditions. They find here something particularly valuable that might be more difficult for the less experienced to appreciate. This also means that not only individuals but also some of the groups that affiliate have an existing history of spiritual engagement and this in turn means that the sangha as a whole gains and grows by these in-flowing currents. Of course, it also brings along difficulties of orientation and acclimatization, but in general this is experienced as a welcome enrichment rather than a problem. Confluence of different experience expressed through a common framework leads to creativity and spiritual maturity for us all.

Thus the people and groups that constitute the sangha make up a distinctive kind of society, less standardized and more creative, in which each contributes to the whole rather than just to their own immediate locality or sub-set. This is sometimes an ideal and sometimes a reality, but it certainly provides a useful way for us to think as the sangha expands into new areas and domains. Not so much, "what do we have to do to follow the correct spiritual path?" more, "what can we contribute to the international movement for spiritual awakening?" In our case, we contribute our active spiritual lives, lived with the frame of the bombu paradigm, the practice of calling, and relating to the source of spiritual refuge as embodiment of ultimate truth. Within this broad frame we are all culturally engaged spiritual practitioners acting as a leaven in our world in as many different ways as our imaginations will stretch to. Each is part of the whole wherever they are and whatever their means of staying in touch.

In the scripture in which Dharmakara follows the bodhisattva path and makes great vows these include vows to serve all awakened beings in all their different modes of operation. The Great Path is extremely broad. Whatever teachers have been awakened and liberated spiritually are objects of refuge. We need to get away from the idea that the spiritual path is a "club". We might need a club ourselves to help us and support us and give us courage, but it is not membership of that club that constitutes the path. Other clubs may serve a similar purpose. The path itself transcends such affiliations. Calling, in its essence, can be practised anywhere and the Dharma life can enrich all nations.

Different Kinds of Love

Intimate relationship can be a demanding spiritual path.

The spiritually awakened teach us to live in the "unconditioned". What is the unconditioned? The unconditioned, also called nirvana, is love. There are different ways of practising love. There is the love of the renunciant who loves all equally, but with detachment, and there is the love of the *bhakti* practitioner who loves passionately and devotedly. There is love for the Holy One and love for one another.

The problem for a great many Western practitioners, however, is the question of whether the ordinary love of lovers and family members has any place in spiritual life or whether it is just a distraction from it. Does being spiritual mean detaching oneself from one's nearest and dearest? Is it a matter of avoiding grief by never caring sufficiently about one person to be vulnerable? Undoubtedly some people do interpret spirituality that way.

However, intimate relationship can also be a demanding spiritual path. In the midst of a close intimate relationship one is likely to be challenged at a greater psychological depth than in almost any other situation. Issues of power, commitment, willingness, self and selflessness, vulnerability, the management of emotional vicissitudes, the translation of sentiment into action, the challenges of conflicting loyalties, in fact all the stuff of real life, appears here often in magnified form. In an intimate relationship one's habitual scripts and old karmic patterns are exposed. One's bluff is called. One goes through a process that changes one deeply and goes on being an ever unfolding mysterious process of discovery.

Sometimes people choose the religious life in order to escape from all this and to do so is a quite understandable life strategy. However, the religious life is subject to the same dynamics and dilemmas. There are spiritual "games" that one can play in order to hold onto an ideal that provides apparent stability and while failing to grasp the deep meaning of the saying that the bodhisattva has no ground on which to stand. The celibate life can be liberation but can also be deeply challenging or become a rut that one gets stuck in. To practice the path of love, in whatever modality, always means to remain vibrantly alive.

In a spiritual community, too, there will be people on different paths in this respect. Can we all respect each other's different ways? Can we be supportive to one another when, in this respect at least, paths are different? It seems that we can, though one should not ignore the difficulties. In fact, the key to peace in the world is not in the domain of finding common ground, or all being the same, it is in finding ways to appreciate and cherish what is other and different. To do so is love. This appreciation of the other is assisted by the knowledge that the other is also held in love by all the Holy Ones, just as one is oneself. Sometimes we have difficulty believing that I myself am loved and sometimes we have difficulty believing that others, or a certain other, is lovable, but it is in this area that much of our most penetrating spiritual practice occurs.

Further, the most important thing in relationships is not so much understanding as kindness. I have heard various people teach that love comes out of understanding, and there are certainly schools of spirituality that put wisdom in a superior position to compassion, but in a relationship it is kindness that is of supreme importance. If a person understands his or her partner, but is not kind to them the relationship will be poor, but if they are kind even though much about the other person remains a mystery, the relationship may still be a good one. We are all lacking in wisdom, but this does not preclude our being kind to one another.

T.N
Hahn

Missionless Mission

Trusting in Other Power means having a sense that all will be well.

I'd like to say a little about the vision that we hold here in our sangha. When one looks around the current spiritual scene one sees a number of organisations that have carved out a particular niche. Some run retreats of a particular kind. Some have created a particular kind of centre and aim to have as many of them around the world as possible. Some offer a particular service and want to replicate that service to as many examples of the client group as they can identify. In other words, there are many examples of groups that have found a workable formula. They then look for people to apply the formula to. In worldly terms this can be a successful approach. Is that, however, the spirit of awakening and does having as many such-and-such groups as possible really constitute a noble goal?

I suggest, therefore, that generally it is better not aim to replicate a formulaic procedure. Do not even aspire to evolve one. Our understanding of awakening is a bit different. The awake person knows that they do not know what comes next. The person who thinks they know is dreaming.

We hope, rather, to be always specific, always distinctive, always unique to the particular set of conditions that we encounter. This is because the only dogmas in this approach are the bombu, the trikaya and the nembutsu – nothing else.

284

At the core of what we are doing, in fact, lies a method of training people to have faith in such an alive approach; people who can offer leadership, who can think creatively, who value each particular person and each particular situation, and who, so trusting, can act as a team. They can act as a team not just in delivering a preplanned solution to a single situation, but in being sensitively responsive to a wide range of situations. This is the ideal of the errant apostle who has no particular ground to stand on, but who is willing to go anywhere amongst all manner of people for the benefit of all manner of beings. The spiritual path is to support and cultivate such people.

Of course, this may well mean that one gives up becoming a large institution. Worldly success may well come more readily to a more standardized, packaged approach. The sangha nonetheless grows slowly but surely. As we have more people we do more. We do not make new replicas of things we have done before, we do new things that respond appropriately to new situations. Sometimes we start something on our own. Sometimes we establish a new organisation in order to do something, as we did with a community support project in the Midlands of England. Sometimes we act in partnership with another group, as we did when we started our India project. Sometimes we support another agency. Sometimes our support goes to an organisation, but it is more common for it to go to individual people, supporting them to do something worthwhile. Sometimes we send one or more of our number to assist within another organisation or institution. Sometimes we just arrive in a situation and find out what is possible.

All this means that we are a sangha. We are not really focussed upon being an organisation. Sometimes organisation is what is needed to do a job, but it is a means not an end and it is important to guard against it becoming an end. Once one is organised there is a tendency for the preservation of the organisation to become the goal, but an organisation is only a medium. So long as what it is a medium for remains healthy, preserving and fostering the organisation remains a good thing, but only to that extent.

We are focussed upon the spiritual training of persons who are within or related to our core team and with friendship and love toward persons who are outside of that circle. Some of the latter may be people who have particular needs, but we are not primarily a social work agency. Our approach is friendship. If our friends have needs we will try to help them, but it is always a two way street. Nobody is only needy; everybody also has something to offer. The sangha supported Amrita Dhammika and she used that support to develop the Tithandizane Project in Africa. Tithandizane means "we help each other". Amrita's way of helping others was to help them to find ways to help other people. That is the right spirit.

This also means that our primary concern is with a certain quality of relating; a quality that is full of faith in the power of love. Quality matters more than quantity. Sometimes one is relating to one person, sometimes to hundreds. This one person might turn out to be the saviour of the future age. How would one know? Certainly one should aim to give them the kind of attention that incorporates that possibility. It is good to spread the Dharma and to make it available to many, many people, but one should not become overly concerned about numbers. One does not know in what way things are going to grow or spread. One has more control over what one is spreading. A little faith and love can go a long way.

The sangha is building a wholesome community. In this community there is individual responsibility as well as deep mutual concern. Here people learn to take responsibility for their particular areas of concern at the same time as learning to listen deeply to one another. This is a profound training. There is nothing superficial or flaky there.

Sometimes people mistakenly think that relying upon Other Power means that one should become passive and do nothing. Nothing could be further from the truth. Relying upon Other Power gives one the confidence to act and do more. While we rely upon self-power we are much more likely to dither or retire because it often leaves us anxious to avoid making a wrong move. Trusting in Other Power means, like Julian of Norwich, having a sense that all will be well. Go forward in faith. Faith, as one of our Order members memorably once said, "turns the traffic lights from amber to green".

This is a very important point. If one has faith one does not hesitate so long. One does not need a formula or a guarantee. One does not confine oneself to what has worked in the past. One is willing to do what is new and creative. One is not overly caught in regulation. Others with less faith can come along and regulate later. Faith makes one a pioneer; a trailblazer.

The genius of this approach lies in its potential to generate a community of trailblazers; a team; a matrix of teams even. Commonly things fall between extremes. One extreme is the person of initiative who cannot co-operate with anybody else. The other extreme is the person who can do as they are told but not hold authority. Liberation implies learning to do both and aiming for the point where the two are perfectly balanced, so that we can be creative and still be a team. Not only can we be one team, we can make many teams that form and reform according to the needs of the situation. Finally, the "team" or community spirit that is generated may be the greatest gift of all, superseding the apparent aims for which the team was formed.

This approach is intelligent and alive. We do not know exactly what we might undertake next. We do not know exactly what our existing projects may be doing next year. We do know that they will be alive, vibrant, interesting and meaningful. We do know that we shall all be learning from them and growing as persons and, in particular, as persons of spirit. No two sangha groups are the same. If you learn the ways of a spiritual community and you go from one group or centre to another you will usually know the form. However, this is less true in our Amida sangha. Some things you will recognise, but the form of each group also owes much to local conditions. In all groups you are likely to find bombu people calling and the presence of the Tathagata. How that works out in practical terms, however, is a function of local chemistry.

What then is our mission? In a sense, it is to not have a mission, but rather to be open to possibilities. Or, our mission is to be loving and stay alive, to proceed in faith and encounter every situation with freshly awakened eyes. Our mission is to wake up again and again so that the world is ever fresh and the spirit of love, compassion, joy and equanimity lives.

Intimacy & Its Dilemmas

Love provides the motive for understanding rather than being a result of it.

The subject of intimate relationships is challenging and complex. Such relationships are one manner of practising a spiritual life. To walk the path together requires overcoming selfishness and practising generosity, give and take, sharing, thoughtfulness, enthusiasm, patience, wisdom, calm and many other excellent qualities, which is, perhaps, why relationships so often do not come up to scratch. We are, after all, human. However, whether a relationship continues forever or not, it may still play an important part in the spiritual evolution of the person. Some steps forward are best mediated by solitude and some by encounter. The idea of rebirth also adds a sense of relationships being something that continues not just for a part of this lifetime, but through many lives. From this perspective, the reason we are unaccountably drawn to this or that person is that there is a karmic bond from a previous life, and with it unfinished business and opportunity. The Buddha often told stories about people's past lives, showing how the constellation of relationships in this life was a natural consequence of past encounters. Whether one believes in past lives or not, this kind of account imparts a sense that the relationships that we are living now each have a significance in the greater scheme of things that transcends this immediate situation and that there is a longer term spiritual goal being served by our encounter.

Some people see an antithesis between relationship and spiritual practice and this has given rise to the idea of celibacy as an ideal. My own belief is that celibacy is, indeed, one ideal, but not the only one. Both being celibate and being in a relationship can be excellent ways to advance one's spiritual life if one takes them on in a positive spirit. At the core of all human activity is love and this is especially true of relationships. However, love is difficult. It challenges our ego.

Love is not a function of conditions. Love is not a dependent variable, it is an end in itself. However, love does not generally persist a long time when it is unrequited. Many modern relationships come to grief because they are infiltrated by ideas that are essentially political or social rather than intimate. Love, for instance, has nothing to do with equality or any other political or economic ideal. Modern people live lives in which the intimate space is reduced to a minimum, and public scrutiny intrudes more than ever before. The presence of the television and other mass media, the fact of both sexes working in careers, of families being smaller, more mobile and more isolated from kith and kin, and the widespread prevalence of democratic ideals are all good things in themselves, but they can all also erode the conditions that underpin good relationships.

Thus, while ideas of equality are immensely important factors in politics, when a couple starts discussing trying to achieve equality it can very quickly degenerate into a hopeless wrangle because there is no possible standard of objectivity for weighing one person's feelings and standardising them against those of the other person. The reason that this kind of discussion often gets quickly bogged down is that it is based on each person trying to get what they want rather than thinking about the other person or about what they can contribute. Love is a generosity. It does not care whether it gets due recompense. For a relationship to function well, both partners have to put in more than they try to take out. The surplus thus generated keeps the relationship healthy and avoids the necessity to keep count. Good relationships are not about measurement of relative benefit. Of course, if the balance of benefits is persistently highly one sided, the relationship will probably fail or be dysfunctional, though, of course, there are many relationships in which one partner is handicapped in some way so that inequality is built in and this does not harm the relationship necessarily. The basic point, however, is that love is something quite different from profit.

There is a sutta in which Buddha delivers a discourse to Sujata, the daughter in law of Anatapindika. This discourse is, in some respects, a rebuke because it is prompted by the Buddha hearing Sujata up-braiding the family servants in a harsh manner. Buddha says that there are seven types of wives:

- The trouble-maker is neglectful and contemptuous of her husband.
- The thievish wife squanders the family wealth, is dishonest and cannot be trusted.
- The domineering wife is lazy, shrewish, rude and tyrannous.
- The motherly wife treats her husband as if one of her children.

- The deferential wife treats her husband as if he were an older sibling. She is biddable but does not take responsibility readily.
- The intimate friend wife loves her husband as her best friend in the world and is devoted to him.
- The submissive wife is calm, patient and obedient.

There are, no doubt, an equivalent seven types of husbands.

When I look at this list I can see that modern thought might well agree that this is a list in ascending scale of desirability up to, but not including, the last. This is interesting. The ideal in the text is complete submission and in the modern context this then runs aground on the rocks of issues of gender equality. However, the ideal of complete submission can cut both ways. The ideal of unconditional love would actually make both partners slaves of the union with neither giving a thought to rights and interests. This, however, is a very high ideal and beyond the reach of most, so that the highest that we aspire to in practice is the state of husband and wife as intimate friends devoted to one another. Even this is rare. It is commonly pretended to, but seldom realised.

Relationships at the level of grades 3,4 and 5 all suffer from dynamics of varying severity around power and responsibility and many "games" get played out in couples around this with one or other partner domineering or avoiding responsibility or both. Broadly we can say that insofar as love is missing, to that extent power issues fill the gap and these are fuelled by and fuel selfishness. Attachment to power is a substitute for love and springs from fear, whereas love springs from faith and trust which is the antidote to fear.

It is commonly said these days that partners should settle their differences by talking to one another. Now there is some sense in this and it is certainly good to practise empathy toward one another, but there are also inherent pitfalls. We are used to talking as a form of negotiation, but the spirit of negotiation is not love and too frequent recourse to such negotiation can soon undermine the ethos of a relationship substituting contractual relations for ones rooted in open hearted generosity. Again, it is said that love grows out of understanding. This again is at best only half true. A growing understanding of the other does provide an increased range of ways in which love may be effectively expressed, but love itself is not dependent upon understanding and may be a living force whether understanding is there or not. Love provides the motive for understanding rather than being a result of it, though, of course, when an act based on understanding demonstrates the attentive care of the other person this can touch the heart deeply. This is because in this case the understanding demonstrated gives evidence of the love behind it. What is most obstructive to love is non-requital. When one's love is not received or is unwanted one experiences turmoil. One might then be patient and spend longer trying to win the heart of the beloved, but eventually the love may become exhausted.

What makes all this complicated and difficult is that a great deal of our communication with one another about these matters is anything but straightforward. Not only do we not tell the other person the truth, but we often do not know what it is ourselves. On top of which there are innumerable social conventions and personal fears that conspire to induce or coerce us into pretending to have feelings that we do not really have or to hide feelings that are actually burning holes in our heart. Nor does analysis and unscrambling of all this always work either, since there are good reasons for such self and mutual deception. It is certainly not the case that the person who makes their wishes and objectives clear to all and sundry is the person most likely to obtain them, even if they do know what they are. Life is a process of discovery. Sometimes we discover that we have loved somebody for some time without realising it. Sometimes we find that we have not loved somebody whom we are going through the motions of loving on a regular basis, or that they do not really love us. Again, in relation to the tokens of love, in terms of behaviour, different people speak very different languages. "She must love me because she...." "She cannot possibly love me acting like that toward me," thoughts of this nature may be completely incongruent with processes going on in the heart or mind of the other and it may be very difficult to find out what the other person really does mean by what they do.

It follows that there is an essential element of mystery in every relationship and love, if it is to thrive, has to accept and go on transcending this. One has to proceed in faith in many situations. One has to respect the other as they are and love them for it, not require them to be something different that more closely approximates to one's personal profile of what one believes to be loveable. Unfortunately, in many relationships, an initial attraction and early stage of shared bliss soon gives way to a more practical, less intoxicated phase in which characteristics in the other that were initially seen as curious and fascinating suddenly transform into irritating features that one longs to remove and reform. Just as in the life of groups, relationships tend to go through phases of forming, storming, norming, performing and mourning. The storming is clearly the most difficult and it requires a depth of true love to pass through this difficult time without either, on the one hand, doing so much emotional damage to one another that the relationship is eternally scarred or, on the other hand, suppressing so much of one's true feelings that trouble is stored up for a much later date.

Personally, I can claim to have quite a lot of experience and a modicum of learning but am still far from having mastered the art, yet I retain clarity that it is the fullness of love that matters, whether the relationship be long lasting or short, voluble or quiet, compatible and comfortable or exciting and challenging, and at every stage.

Marriage and the Spiritual Path

Fortunate indeed are those who are loved through thick and thin by people who support and understand.

Marriage is a fulfilment of a karmic connection. The general sense is that when two people are strongly drawn together while it could be something completely new it is much more likely to be the result of a connection that stretches back through many previous lives and will probably continue long into the future. These two people have some special significance for one another and, correspondingly, something to do together or for one another. These two karmic streams are each meaningful and the relationship between their respective meanings is both a resource and a challenge each for the other. There is more to marriage than just happiness and strife: there is purpose. The people in question do not necessarily know, however, what that purpose is until afterwards.

The fact that marriage is due to karmic connection means that it is never perfect. It is born as much from our lack and limitation as from our positive qualities. Subjectively, we have the sense of needing one another and being fulfilled by one another. This can, of course, flip and leave us asking ourselves why we are together if we have so little in common. The sense of being the same and wanting the same thing sometimes seems powerful and at other times completely lacking and the vicissitudes of mood and emotion that accompany these tides are by no means always comfortable or charming. They are, however, always an evidence that something bigger than our own will is in play, since, in many cases, we would not will them if we had the choice, even though we do seem to will to put ourselves into the situation where they happen. Humans are drawn to put themselves into the hands of greater power. This is why surfing on ocean waves is so exhilarating. People do not always seek safety.

Not only marriage is a function of karmic connection; this applies also to other close relationships such as parent and child, friends, or even teacher and disciple. Each has something to learn and the universe has purpose in putting these two people together.

Shakyamuni Buddha's mother gave birth to him and then died. What is the meaning of this? Is it just a useless tragedy? I have written elsewhere that it may well have been this circumstance of having been the cause of his mother's death that made Siddhartha Gotama ready for his remarkable later insights that made him the great sage. He was brought up by his mother's sister Pajapati. She performed the role of mother for him, but then later became the first woman of Buddhism.

It is not just blood relationships that change as they gradually reveal their deeper meaning. Siddhartha took a wife. Actually he won her in an archery competition - the ways of the world are often mysterious. Later he left her with his clan family as he went out on his spiritual quest. Modern people who live in nuclear families often struggle with this bit of the story because the modern vision of marriage is totally different from that which pertains in a patriarchal society of extended families. However, at a later stage we see Yasodhara reappearing as a leading disciple and carrying forward the vision of enlightenment herself.

Although the fact of attraction and association is karmic, the actual form of marriage is something that is socially relative; or, to put this a different way, something that belongs to the karma of the society rather than the karma of the individuals. There have been Buddhist societies that are monogamous, polygamous and polyandrous, some more patriarchal, some more matriarchal. There is no dogma in Buddhism about what marriage is or should be.

Further, Buddhism teaches impermanence and expects things to change. We meet somebody and we know that there is chemistry; we sense the karmic connection but we do not understand it. In fact it is the mystery that both compels our involvement and also tells us that there is something here that needs to be done, or, at least, needs to be known. We do not yet know what that something is, but we may be confident that all will be well in the end one way or another in spiritual terms whether the relationship prospers in a worldly sense or not. Something is happening and we do not know what it is, though we might gradually find out. However, learning is not always conscious. It is not always the case that we know as conscious knowledge what it is that we have learnt on the spiritual path. If there is an exam at the end of the course, then that exam is not cognitive, it is life itself. The "learning" that we do spiritually makes us more mature. It might also make us more knowledgeable, but if so that is incidental.

If people are growing and developing there will be changes in their relationships and in the roles that they perform for one another. These changes will not necessarily come entirely out of the unfolding of the interpersonal dynamic, they will also be a function of the impact of other karmic connections. If the people involved are advancing spiritually then these changes, whatever implications they have in the social world, will leave them wiser, kinder, and able to function more effectively in the service of others. They will help us to grow up.

Such changes may not always be comfortable. Being bombu we do not always understand what is going on at the time, nor do we act perfectly. 'Why am I with this person?' is an important question. What are we meant to do together? What am I supposed to learn? How am I supposed to help? The formative factors may be opaque to us at the time and it may only be when we have the perspective that comes from the passage of time that we are able to look back and see what-that-was-all-about. However, in the day-to-day practice of a relationship it is not finding the meaning that is important; it is kindness that is important. Too much questioning into the meaning may actually be destructive. Wisdom comes in its own way in its own good time and cannot be forced. It comes out of the practice of kindness, not out of straining to be clever in one's conceptual understanding of what is going on.

Nothing is predetermined, yet we feel constrained. Everything is meaningful, but we do not know what that meaning is. This is why the path begins with faith and, when lost, resumes with a return to faith. If we live with a good heart, the meaning will often become apparent, but, even if it doesn't, it will still unfold. The unfolding meaning will involve change. Some of those changes will be pleasant and some difficult. Sometimes we might feel that we have to "move heaven and earth" to change a situation in order to bring it into line with what now feels to be the emergent karmic reality. Sometimes things may flow smoothly like an old river. There needs to be both determination and acceptance, affirmation and willingness, but it is neither passive nor wilful. Always we are in the grip of meanings that are bigger than ourselves and that we sense, but do not fully understand or control. Our meanings evolve in relation to a greater meaning that we only vaguely sense. The important thing is to keep faith with the bigger picture even though one only actually has a small corner of it accessible to one's own perception.

Relationship can teach us about surrendering to a process bigger than ourselves. The most compellingly wonderful times in a relationship are times when this is most apparent. When a baby is born or when somebody is dying, for instance, we are overwhelmed by the sense of participating in something miraculous; something that has its own energy and reflects a cosmic power that is bigger and stronger than ourselves and we do not experience this as a defeat, even though the ego is at such times more or less redundant, but as what C. G. Jung called a "participation mystique". It is exactly these times that we know as most wonderful.

Each relationship - friendship, family bond, romance, business partnership, or whatever - is a spiritual practice and is part of the bigger picture of one's karmic stream. By means of spiritual practice we modify or even escape from that stream. This is true whether the relationship is harmonious or not. We cannot see the bigger picture directly. Looking back one may see that even a "failed" relationship taught one about kindness, or forced one to reconsider one's principles, or forced one to accept some of the realities of this limited world. One may be able to look back and bow to people that at the time one struggled to understand, or even wanted to get away from. One might be able to recognise, even, that none of all this is ultimately for oneself. One's children are not one's possessions. The projects that one develops are for the benefit of all beings, or they are nothing. Even the skills and abilities that one develops, the wisdom and experience, are only such inasmuch as they benefit others. At one level one thinks about what one has gained, but really one gains nothing. The universe gains. We are just media within which these things happen. Whether one has such insight or respect or not, one can be sure that whatever unfinished business remains will live on as a karmic association into the distant future. We shall meet again and try again somewhere in the fullness of time.

We shall, of course, be most fortunate if when we meet that person with whom we have that special chemistry we do so in circumstances where something at least approximating to a Pure Land prevails. Marriage, whether carnal or of minds alone, is rarely if ever really just a two person matter as it takes place in a social context. The capacity of the surrounding community to be welcoming, supportive, understanding, facilitative, kind and warm is of enormous importance. The reason that people celebrate their connections through various forms of ceremonial is substantially to invoke the assistance of their sangha, both the living sangha around them and the spiritual tradition to which they belong. Fortunate indeed are those who are loved through thick and thin by people who support and understand.

Getting Real as a Sangha

We imperfect beings are trying to create a community that goes a quantum leap further in honesty than is normal.

In the Pasadika Sutta in the Pali Cannon the Buddha expresses his pleasure that his disciples are proficient in the true Dharma, and that among the sangha there are experienced, trained and skilled teachers who are liberated and able to proclaim the Dharma and refute wrong ways, that there are middle ranking disciples who are experienced and trained, that there are novices and lay followers, that there are males and females, celibate and non-celibate. In this way the perfect life flourishes. It is clear from this passage that Buddha drew huge satisfaction from the existence of this community that he had brought together. This was his boast. He had created a wholesome community; one in which there would not be major quarrelling or trouble and which had a capacity to be of benefit to people far and wide. We would be mistaken to think that the Buddhist path is something just for individuals or that the Buddha would have been satisfied with a situation where each individual had their practice that they got on with in their own way in their own space. He certainly did tailor his injunctions to the needs and temperament of individuals, but the life that he led them toward was one in which there was a whole and wholesome community with all its constituent parts playing their respective roles, each complementing the others.

When we start a major ceremony in the sangha we ask, "Is there harmony in the community?" A harmonious community is the basis for right action by the sangha. It is important for us to ask, therefore, what such harmony and completeness in the sangha really means. It is, after all, possible to create an impression of harmony in a community or society by repression. Autocratic regimes do this as a matter of course. If dissent is suppressed there is harmony of a kind. However, this is not real harmony and it does not last. Spiritual and religious groups are vulnerable to pressure to appear more holy than they actually are and individuals within such groups may strive to appear to fit the ideal irrespective of the reality of what goes on hidden inside them. Buddha, however, wanted to create a community with real and enduring harmony, a sangha that would endure for hundreds or thousands of years and go on doing real good for humankind forever. He was remarkably successful. To be a real community that does real spiritual good, however, is quite different from being a gathering of people each concerned about their own standing and appearance of virtue.

The kind of harmony that we need is not one in which people sweep difficulties under the carpet or pretend to be good. To really join the sangha one has to:

a) face up to and admit one's bombu nature - and feel the relief of doing so;
b) start to think of the collective good rather than merely individual interest;
c) take refuge; and
d) do the practice.

Implicit here is a greater degree of personal honesty and openness than is common. Facing the truth about ourselves (*sange*) is the beginning and end of the matter. Between that beginning and that end lie a huge number of learning experiences, most of them coming about through our encounters with one another. Sensei Gisho Saiko used to say that one of the most important things to attain is realism about human nature. We say "just as you are" meaning that Buddhas accept and love us and shine their light upon us without first demanding that we achieve a particular standard of virtue. This is a wonderful relief and reassurance. Even we are accepted! Spirituality thus ceases to be a competition in sanctimoniousness. At the same time "just as you are" is an amazing demand. Can I dare to be just as I am? Can I afford not to pretend? Will I not be rejected by everybody if they see how I actually am with my mistakes, half-truths, short-cuts, envies, defensiveness and so on? These are legitimate fears. In human groups survival may depend upon dissimulation. A sangha is a group that aims to be otherwise, a community in which truth is not taboo, but this is a tall order.

A sangha should therefore have psychological sensitivity. We know that superficial appearances are deceptive. We therefore try to listen to one another carefully. We facilitate. We encounter. We do not just gloss over feelings, smoothing them with pious generalisations or ideals. Creating an ambiance in which people can say what is in their hearts and expect to be received is quite a challenge. None of us behaves perfectly; none thinks faultlessly; none speaks a stream of wondrous utterances unremittingly. We are human. We imperfect beings are trying to create a community that goes a quantum leap further in honesty than is normal. Often we fail, but then, we would, wouldn't we? We ordinary human beings are the raw material. Those who can only tolerate totally reformed characters find this impossible, but such have not actually faced themselves, which is the first step.

We shall go on refining the art of spiritual encounter, seeking honesty and cleanness in our relations with one another and doing our best to create a holding space of kindly mutual concern. Those who are trained are skilled in the ability to facilitate others and those who are experienced are able to communicate their own light and shadow and to be moved by others doing similarly. We have recently had a number of meetings in which I have been heartened to see a growing willingness of members to be real. Here enlightenment is not a matter of waking up to one's Buddha nature so much as to one's bombu nature; that is actually far more important and consequential and is what makes real community possible. Here a liberated teacher is one who is familiar with his or her own nature and so not shocked when others speak openly of theirs. Where people dare not look into the shadows in their heart the foundations of spiritual life are weaker.

The awakened sages ask us to do our best to care for one another, act with kindness, be honest, and, in particular, build a resilient and wholesome community for the weal and welfare of many beings for a long time to come. When such a community is evidently in existence with both experienced and inexperienced, male and female, old and young, and all varieties of truly human beings each playing their part and being real with one another, Buddha is happy. Our task is to create such a community. For the individual to advance spiritually is good, but what it means is not to advance self, but to advance beyond self, in other words to advance in and through community. A healthy community needs people who take initiative on its behalf, who think of its good, and who are not precious about themselves. To refute wrong ways in Buddhism substantially means to avoid falling into self-conceit and to take refuge in Buddha, Dharma and Sangha. Such loyalty liberates.

Celibacy or Relationship

When varied elements conspire together the scope for creativity and mutual aid expands exponentially.

We are practising Buddhism with a human (sometimes very human) face. It is a generic spiritual path for ordinary people. In Japan the vast majority of Buddhist priests are married. They conduct the religious life of the community in a similar manner to Protestant clergy in the West. By contrast, Buddhism in the West has generally developed around the monastic lifestyle and has a rather puritan ideal even though, in practice, very few Western Buddhist communities have managed to sustain this discipline in practice.

Many Western people, surprisingly, seem to feel more at home with that kind of austerity even when it is practised by denominations that also practise sexual discrimination, authoritarian organisation and ethnic bias. I find this a bit odd. Perhaps, to attract a following, groups have to present themselves as morally superior and that translates for many people as meaning non-sexual.

Here at Amida we are not so austere. We have both a celibate and a non-celibate track. We revere as founders both Honen Shonin, who was celibate, and Shinran Shonin who was not. To paraphrase Honen, our attitude is that if being in a relationship would impede your practice of nembutsu, then be celibate; if being celibate would impede your practice, then enter a relationship.

At the present time our sangha is clearly going through a developmental change. Several people are entering into new relationships and having children. Personally, I feel that this is much to be welcomed. It is in keeping with the norm in Japan and it tends to make our sangha one that ordinary people in society can more easily relate to. It means that some members of the sangha will have a partner who can be a support and help them to carry out their role in the spiritual community. At the same time some other people prefer to remain celibate. This is also excellent. The celibate path is a very special one that provides the opportunity for people to dedicate themselves to practice and to have an openness to others that is universal. Both paths are important and it has always been my intention that ours would be a sangha in which both tracks are available and work together in harmony and co-operation.

I was ordained in 1977. Since then I have seen a lot of changes in the Buddhist world. The order in which I originally ordained did in due course give up on having married priests and now only has a celibate track. I thought, and still think, that this was regrettable. As the leader of a sangha myself it has always been my wish that in our own sangha both tracks should be available and treated with honour. Furthermore, I do not see any reason why people should not move from one track to the other in either direction so long as this is accompanied by serious reflection, commitment and decorum. A lot of this is simply a respect for naturalness. It is natural that people sometimes fall in love. It is natural that sometimes relationships end and it should be quite acceptable for people to choose to enter or not to enter into a new one. The training that people receive in the sangha equips them very well for both styles of life. After several years of celibate training people sometimes then feel ready for a married life and are much more mature in their approach to it. Similarly, after experience of relationship some people come to realise that their spiritual life will actually be a lot richer and their capacity to help others stronger if they are independent of relationship ties. Respect for this diversity should be a hallmark of our approach.

In the early days we maintained these principles by having an amitarya track that had restrictive relationship rules and a ministry track that did not. This dispensation served us well at that time. However, it gradually became apparent that the essential difference between being an amitarya and being a minister was not the factor of openness or not to relationship, but rather to do with mobility and sense of community. Pressure grew to change the system. Initially I was resistant to changing. However, as so often, not only was I wrong, but once the changes came in I was one of the first to avail myself of them and I now see how the new situation that has emerged is preferable with all four options (celibate and non-celibate amitaryas, and celibate and non-celibate ministers) catered for.

When people are on different tracks there is, of course, always a risk that polarisation occurs or factions form. We are human, after all. There may be the feeling that "our group is gaining" or "our group is losing" when somebody changes from one track to another. When we stand back from the situation we soon see that such feelings, while understandable, are misplaced. A sangha develops. From the inside this can seem erratic, but there is generally a higher wisdom in play, unseen by the participants. I have learnt to trust this.

Sometimes there are more women and sometimes more men, sometimes more elderly people and sometimes more young ones. There are any number of criteria upon which we could create factions. The essence of sangha, however, lies in our ability to transcend such sentiments and adhere to what is more fundamentally true. We are all together in our refuge in the Three Jewels and in this light all such polarisation seems trivial.

An intimate relationship provides certain advantages and poses certain problems. Being celibate and independent also provides certain advantages and also poses some problems. Whether the advantages outweigh the drawbacks depends essentially upon the amount of goodwill. There is an obvious hazard when members of a religious community have spouses. The spouses arrive with a different culture. Will this be a cause of friction? Will the outside world culture thus imported undermine the distinctive culture that the community have so carefully nurtured over many years? Undoubtedly there will be some effects of this kind. However, if the community is mature there is also great gain through the additional creativity that results.

The success and excellence of the sangha community often rests on its exploitation of synergism. When varied elements conspire together the scope for creativity and mutual aid expands exponentially. Applying this principle to the phenomenon of community members taking outside partners one can assume that in the long run there will be an overall gain for the community. In some couples there will be not enough goodwill and those couples will eventually part company with the community or with one another. In other couples there will be sufficient goodwill for the gain to work in favour of the community and the partnership. Overall the gain will be greater than the losses. This principle applies to a wide range of activity. It is why our community has so often seemed to be facing a difficulty and then invariably emerged stronger. There seems to be a difficulty when the difference factor is in focus, but when one can stand back and take a wider perspective one sees the synergistic gain.

In order to gain from synergism it is immensely important that we listen to one another and discuss things in a spirit of goodwill. Gatherings in which we share our spiritual life in an atmosphere of deep mutual respect are a hallmark of our way - our "sacrament", one Order member has called them. Currently, as a direct consequence of the recent changes that I am referring to here, we are seeing a deepening and an opening in these gatherings. People feel freer to share their emotional inner process than formerly. I certainly do. This has benefited us all and is an immediate gain for everybody involved. Some Buddhist communities restrict such frankness out of a mistaken concern for the formalities of "right speech", but here we believe that truly right speech is not speech artificially stripped of all challenging content, but genuine sharing from the heart in which we all become vulnerable, in which we acknowledge bombu nature, care for one another and trust in an Other Power to take care of the emergence of collective wisdom. This is where miracles do occur. During periods of change in the community such gatherings are particularly important and it has been deeply moving to see some of the sharing and extraordinarily touching encounters that have occurred. Let us not be afraid to be "just as we are". This is an amazing opportunity. Learning to drop our masks in trustworthy company is a vital part of spiritual training.

Our own sangha has now lived through and digested a huge amount of collective experience in a relatively short number of years and this has made it an intensely interesting and exciting adventure to be part of. We have evolved a strong and unique culture. We are not particularly trying to imitate other groups or approaches or to replicate Japan in England. We are unique. I am entirely confident that the changes that are going on at the moment will enrich that unique and amazing culture and there is ample opportunity for all the people currently involved - younger and older, celibate and in relationship, lay and ordained, men and women - to contribute now even more than before to this increasing richness and the synergistic developments that it makes possible. Where else can one have such an opportunity than in spiritual groups of this kind?

Restoring Tribal Consciousness

A sangha is a place that people go forth from and come back to, an oasis for the heart and a nursery for bodhisattvas.

Sangha is spiritual tribe. It is not an institution ruled by rational principles: it rests on faith and family feeling. It is not somewhere where everybody is signed up to an identical social philosophy; its dogmas are few. It is not necessarily efficiently organised; efficiency is not a bad thing, but it is not a supreme or primary value in itself. A sangha is a natural, growing thing and exhibits the redundancy that all living things exhibit; just look at a tropical forest. It is a place where real depth of relationship is found with true spiritual friends who care about one another and respect one another's differences as well as fostering and appreciating co-operation when it is possible, but it is not a place where people regard their ego and its sensitivities as sacred. It is a place where people put themselves out for one another, listen to one another, care to see others successful, and dare to understand what it is to be an ordinary, doubt-filled, nervous, sometimes thoughtless, human being falteringly seeking the deeper satisfaction of one's heart.

The sense of tribe is supported by appropriate ritual, though this does not have to be according to a rigid formula or under tight central control for ritual should be a collective enjoyment and celebration. In any case, living ritual is a language in which many things can be expressed, including new things. Ritual is like the language of bees, pronounced in dance.

A tribe is an ever evolving network in which there are numerous over-lapping sub-groups that are each partly functional and partly amicable, organically self and mutually organising. The sense of tribe is supported by an organic style of relating and working together where it is possible for new synergisms and ideas to emerge naturally. It is somewhere where people gradually work out their respective relationships, duty toward and need of one another within a reliable sense of being-there-for-one-another.

A tribe may, but does not necessarily, have a land. It may find expression through places, ultimately through the creation of Buddha lands, but it is essentially the culture that grows in, but is not limited to such places that matters. Culture binds together and also provides a medium. Everything that happens within a culture is conditioned by that culture, yet also modifies it, be it ever so slightly. Culture is not uniform, but it involves a family or clan style of relationship. Through it our loves and longings take form in a myriad ways. In our sangha we draw on Japanese culture, Western culture, traditional and modern Buddhist culture, the ancient shamanic ways of early peoples, many sources, but essentially we are seeing a new unique culture emerge around a few central values: the bombu paradigm, the light of wisdom and compassion, cultural engagement, a gentle but not puritan ethos, in which friendship plays a key role. Even our socially engaged activities grow out of friendship rather than a blue-print for service delivery.

Modern society is founded on rationality, but rationality is not community. Rationality relies on treating things as similar when they are in fact diverse, as interchangeable when they are not, on justice rather than mercy. The rational ordering of society is necessary, but within society there needs to be room for community and the adoption of social values is tending to squeeze out community values, thus producing efficiency at the cost of alienation. Participation in rational forms of organisation provides utilitarian benefit and functional satisfactions, but people need more than that to be fully human.

In our sangha, we do not deliver services as though service could be organised on an industrial model; we serve one another with respect for the humanity of everybody involved. We do not set goals and achieve them so much as simply apply ourselves in worthwhile ways, trusting that good will unfold from it.

A tribe is not created by a contract or a committee. It is a trust. It is a trust between the people of the present and the spiritual ancestors and it is also a trust between ourselves and those who are to come after. In Buddhism we call this transmission. It has a long-term assumption built into it. We are here not just for ourselves or for the present moment but for those who are to come.

A tribe is always changing, but slowly. There is nothing in it that will remain the same forever and yet there is an enduring familiarity about it. Things do not change willy-nilly. New forms emerge gradually. New relationships develop step by step. What is good from the past is carried forward into the future. It is a community in which learning is always going on, most of it through people observing and listening to one another. Ideally, everyone wants the best for everybody else knowing that this will generate the best for all. This is the opposite of the principle of rational society in which the best for all supposedly comes from each person pursuing their personal interest.

A tribe is a place where there are many different roles and different degrees of experience, and where these are respected. A tribe is not simple: it takes time to become a part of it. It is a place where there are traditions, many of them idiosyncratic, related to a particular history and folk-lore. It is also a place where different ideas can co-exist. There is no need to expunge all differences. When a tribe extends to more than one locale there is no need for each to be run in identical fashion. If the spirit is there it will be recognisable and will adapt to local conditions and personal characters. It will not need to be enshrined in standardised procedures. Does this mean that there will be no "rules"? - not at all. Any community is littered with precedents and mores, ways of doing things that each have a history and constitute a kind of collective benign set of prejudices that give everybody a sense of belonging without ever becoming immutable or exclusive of exceptions.

A spiritual tribe can be a place of safety where people can make mistakes without being pilloried; where emotions can be felt and expressed; where people fall out but not too grievously and make up again; where it is possible to change one's mind; where sentiments are touched and hearts moved; where people grow toward maturity rather than solipsism. As a place of love, all the relationships within it are particular and each is unique. Although they are aided by some degree of formalisation of reciprocal roles, the human element is always as important as the formal one. For this reason, a spiritual community cannot be more than a certain size without sub-dividing in some way.

A sangha is a place that people go forth from and come back to, an oasis for the heart and a nursery for bodhisattvas.

GLOSSARY

All words are in English or Sanskrit unless otherwise stated.

adhisthana: spiritual support, power or ground.

advaita: non-dual.

akunin (Japanese): evil person.

Ambedkar, Bimrao: author of the Indian constitution, leader of the untouchables who converted to Buddhism near to the end of his life thereby starting a large scale movement of conversion.

Amida: measureless, the name in the orient of Amitabha or Amitayus Buddha.

Amitabha: Buddha of measureless light.

Amitayus: Buddha of measureless life-span.

anamnesia: (Greek) un-forgetting, remembrance of things previously forgotten.

anatma: non-self, other.

anitya: impermanence.

Anshin: (Japanese) peaceful heart, settled faith.

arhat: one who has gained insight into the true nature of existence, overcome greed, hate and delusion, and achieved nirvana (q.v); a fully liberated person.

Asekha: (Pali) the state of being beyond training, enlightenment, the condition of an arhat (q.v.).

atma: self, ego (see: anatma).

avidya: a-vidya, non-seeing, ignorance, spiritual blindness, inability to see the greater whole or ultimate truth.

bhakti: devotion, religious practices that are ecstatic in nature, love and worship of the yidam (q.v.).

bija: seed.

bodhi: enlightened vision.

bodhisattva: a person who has the courage of their enlightened vision, the Buddha before his enlightenment, an angel embodying a particular enlightened quality (bodhisattva of compassion, etc), a person who has vowed to keep returning to this world lifetime after lifetime in order to help all sentient beings.

Bombu: (Japanese) ordinary being of wayward passions, vulnerable, fallible, and imperfect.

Buddha: Siddhartha Gotama, the founder of the Buddhist religion. Any fully spiritually awakened being.

chih quan: (Chinese) contemplation in silence and stillness, letting go (see also: sammatha).

chitta: mind, heart.

Denkoroku: (Japanese) text recording the transmission of the light, a record of the koans passed by each of the great historical masters of the Zen tradition.

Dharma: real things, truth, especially spiritual truth. Probably from a root word meaning to hold, as a mother holds a child.

dhi: vision (see: samadhi).

dhyana: meditation, contemplative absorption, the term from which the Japanese word Zen (q.v.) derives.

Dogen (1200-1253): Japanese Zen master who established Soto Zen in Japan and wrote important works.

dukkha: affliction, situations of spiritual darkness or danger, the first truth for noble ones.

dukkha-samudaya: the spiritual-emotional energy and states of craving that arise in dependence upon the occurrence of dukkha (see: dukkha, samudaya).

dukkha-samudaya-nirodha: the mastery or channeling of the energies that arise in dependence upon dukkha, (see: dukkha-samudaya, nirodha).

Dzogchen: (Tibetan) an approach to Buddhism in Tibet, especially in the Nyingma School, that is similar to Zen (q.v.).

eka: one, singular.

ekagata: independence, singularity, the state of being free from compulsive relationships with internalised others.

eko: (Japanese) to turn over, turn round or transfer. Often refers to transition from one spiritual realm to another, as passing to the Pure Lands at death or returning therefrom in a new birth.

eko-hotsu-gan-shin: (Japanese) the intention to transfer merit so that all may enjoy rebirth in the Pure Land (see also jodo, gan, shin).

gan: (Japanese) prayer, vow.

guru: teacher.

guru yoga: spiritual discipline of devotion to the guru; in many spiritual paths the primary method is to imbibe the mind of the guru.

hijiri: (Japanese) wandering sage or holy man (see sadhu).

Honen (1133-1212): Japanese sage who popularised Pureland Buddhism.

ishtadevata: altar god, a rupa used for worship, especially in tantric (q.v.) practice.

jara: decay, degeneration.

jaramarana: jara-mara-na, degenerate-deathli-ness, spiritual failure or abasement.

jing tu: (Chinese) Land of Harmony (see: jodo).

jiriki: (Japanese) self-power, the belief that one has the power within oneself to achieve spiritual liberation by one's own practice (cf. tariki, svabala).

jnana: clear awareness.

jodo: (Japanese) Pure Land, a realm where one can be with a Buddha and therefore the ideal condition for enlightenment.

Jodo: (Japanese) School of Pureland Buddhism deriving from the teachings of Honen Shonin.

Jodoshin: (Japanese) School of Pureland Buddhism deriving from the teachings of Shinran Shonin, a disciple of Honen Shonin.

Kami: (Japanese) god or spirit, often associated with an elemental or natural phenomenon.

karma: drama, intentional action and its consequence.

kaya: a body, incorporation or manifestation.

Ko: (Japanese) light.

Koan: (Japanese) a universal spiritual barrier occurring in unique form in a particular life.

Kshitigarbha: bodhisattva that protects children and travellers and rescues beings from the hells.

Lin Chi Yi-Sen (810-866): Chinese Buddhist master, founder of the Rinzai school of Zen.

Madhyamaka: middle path, the name of a philosophical school of Buddhism prevalent in Tibet.

mahasattva: great being, collective term for saints, bodhisattvas, Buddhas, apostles, avatars etc. (see also: sattva).

Mahayana: great vehicle, the approach to Buddhism that emphasises the bodhisattva ideal and is found in Tibet, China and across east Asia, in contradistinction to Theravada (q.v.).

maitri: loving kindness.

Manjushri: bodhisattva (q.v.) of wisdom.

mara: death, often personified as Mara.

marana: deathliness, abasement of spirit, lack of vitality. (see jara, jaramarana).

marga: track, the spiritual path, especially the eightfold path of wholehearted view, wholehearted thought, wholehearted speech, wholehearted action, wholehearted livelihood, wholehearted effort, wholehearted mindfulness, and wholehearted samadhi.

metta: (Pali) see: maître.

mon: (Japanese) gate, question.

myokonin: (Japanese) a greatly shining person, the ideal of a person of simple faith, a genre of holy persons in Japanese history (see also hijiri).

muni: sage.

Nagarjuna: second century Buddhist philosopher and sage who developed a dialectical approach showing the limitations of conceptual knowledge and gave important teachings on faith and ethics.

nama: name, bearing in mind the principle that names have power.

nama-rupa: concepts and objects that frame or control our life, the things and concepts that our life revolves around - job, car, house, country and, pre-eminently, our own body.

namo: I call upon, I rely upon, so, by extension, I take refuge in.

Namo Amida Bu: short for Namo Amida Buddha, I take refuge in Amida, a key prayer in oriental spirituality. Has slight variations in different countries, such as Namo Omito Fo in China, Namo Adida Phat in Vietnam etc.

nei quan: (Chinese) investigation inward, meditation upon the evidence of one's life and its dependent nature, related to vipassana (q.v.).

nembutsu: (Japanese) mental impulse or thought toward Buddha.

nirodha: confinement (see: dukkha-samudaya-nirodha).

nirvana: the extinction of greed, hatred, and avidya (q.v.).

niyama: order, law.

Nyingma: (Tibetan) the name of the earliest school of Tibetan Buddhism.

Nyorai: (Japanese) tathagata (q.v.) in the sense of tatha-agata.

Pajapati: the Buddha's mother's sister who became his step-mother and later disciple and leader of the Buddhist nuns.

parabala: power from beyond one's own, other-power, help from the Buddhas, the idea that one does not have the capacity to enlighten oneself and so needs spiritual help and needs a refuge; realisation of parabala is closely linked to prasada (shinjin) and the sudden awakening of faith.

param: beyond.

paramita: other shore, ultimacy, the viewpoint of an enlightened being.

prasada: clear faith; the realisation of one's own need for refuge (see shinjin).

pratyutpanna samadhi: the samadhi of perceiving Buddhas everywhere.

quan: (Chinese) investigation, meditation, looking into (see nei quan, chih quan).

rimpoche: (Tibetan) precious jewel, a title used for a Tibetan Dharma teacher.

Rinzai: (Japanese) school of Zen that emphasises the use of formal koans (see also: Soto)

rupa: originally, object of worship, hence any object or form that has a power over our emotion or perception, things that draw or hold attention. Things as they appear rather than as they are (in contradistinction to dharma q.v.).

sadhu: holy man, sage, teacher, generally itinerant, one who has renounced the world.

samadhi: consummate vision, concentration on spiritually wholesome objects.

samjna: trance, entrancement, being hooked by something, ordinary consciousness that skips from one tantalizing or repelling object to another blindly.

sammatha: calm meditation, tranquil abiding, stopping in silence and stillness (see also chih quan).

samsara: going round in meaningless circles, the un-free condition of the deluded person.

samskara: mental formation, attitude, psychological complex. The unnecessary complications that we generate that impede our own lives.

samudaya: co-arising. (see: dukkha-samudaya).

sange: (Japanese) contrition.

sangha: the spiritual community, contemporary or ancestral, the spirit of community.

sarva: all.

sati :(Pali) see: smriti.

satipatthana: (Pali): setting up of mindfulness.

Satori: (Japanese) spiritual awakening that enables one to transcend a koan and enter the spiritual path.

Sekha: (Pali) spiritual training.

Shakya: the tribe that Siddhartha Gotama was born into.

Shakyamuni: an epithet of Buddha, sage of the Shakyas.

Shan Tao (613-681): Chinese sage who taught Pureland Buddhism.

Shan Tao's Commentary: text commentary upon the Contemplation Sutra that interprets the text as indicating that spiritual salvation is available to all.

shin: (Japanese) faith.

shin: (Japanese) true.

shinjin :(Japanese) true faith, the experience of awakening to faith (cf satori, anjin).

Shinran Shonin (1173-1263): disciple of Honen Shonin, commonly treated as the founder of the Jodoshin denomination.

shunyata: emptiness, especially absence of self-centred distortion (cf nirvana), absence of dependence or impermanence.

Siddhartha Gotama: the Buddha.

skanda: aggregate, elements that accumulate into a (deluded) personality (see rupa, vedana, samjn, samskara, vijnana).

smriti: mindfulness, remembrance, equated here with Plato's anamnesia.

Soto: (Japanese) School of Zen Buddhism that emphasizes serene reflection and sees the koan as arising naturally in daily life (see also: Rinzai).

sukha: sweet.

sukhavati: the sweet realm, the Pure Land, a realm created by an enlightened being.

sutra: thread, spiritual text (thread of teaching).

sutta: (Pali) see: sutra.

svabala: self-power (see: jiriki), the idea that one can become enlightened by dint of a capacity within oneself or by practices, disciplines or trainings carried out by oneself.

ta-li: (Chinese) other power (see: tariki, parabala).

tantra: spiritual practice of transforming ordinary passions into spiritual energies, sublimation.

tariki: (Japanese) other power, originally a term for dependent origination, developed into a term for dependence upon the saving power of Buddhas. The belief that one does not have the power within oneself to attain spiritual liberation by one's own efforts, that such liberation comes as a grace (cf. jiriki, parabala).

tatha: thus, such.

tathata: thus-ness, just-so-ness, reality, positive acceptance.

tathagata: as tatha-gata, one who has gone to thusness, a spiritual leader and exemplar; as tatha-agata, one who comes from thusness, a spiritual saviour, friend or helper.

Theravada: The way of the elders, the form of Buddhism found in south Asia that emphasises the arhat (q.v.) ideal.

tri-: three, threefold.

vedana: knowingness, recognition, the feeling that arises with recognition which either attracts, repels or disinterests us.

Tao: (Chinese) way, term for spiritual power at work in the world.

Tao Te Ching: Chinese book of wisdom attributed to Lao Tzu, an older contemporary of Buddha, Confucius and Socrates.

te: (Chinese) virtue.

trikaya: the principle of a trinity of manifestations of spiritual truth. [see: kaya].

upaya: skilful means.

vidya: clarity, radiance, understanding.

vijnana: unconscious mind, mentality, the collection of taken for granted attitudes that control intention and attention (see jnana).

Vimalakirti: central character in the Vimalakirti Sutra, he is an enlightened layman who carries out his spiritual practice in the midst of worldly situations and who defeats other disciples of Buddha in debate.

vipassana: insight meditation (see also: samatha, nei quan).

Vissuddhi Magga (Pali): the way of purity, an important manual of meditation method and doctrine in the Theravada tradition.

Yasodhara: the Buddha's wife.

yidam:(Tibetan) see: ishtadevata.

yoga: spiritual discipline, uniting the relative and ultimate.

Zen: (Japanese) meditation, the name of a tendency in Buddhism that emphasises meditation practice and sudden awakening (see: dhyana).

zazen: sitting meditation, just sitting.

APPENDIX

THOUGHTS ON CREATING A BUDDHIST ICON

Maitrisimha Kouwenhoven

Nembutsu Triptych

Thoughts on Creating a Buddhist Icon

Maitrisimha explains the process behind creating the nembutsu triptych, the middle section of which forms the cover for this book.

When I created the triptych (left), I tried to make something that mirrored the feelings and emotions I experienced when walking the path of Buddhist faith.

I began walking the path of Nien Fo (keeping the Buddha in mind) when I moved into a religious community whose central practice was not only Buddhist, but deeply devotional.

I was shocked to see the subject of faith entering my life again. Buddhism had first attracted me not only because of its techniques for evoking higher states of consciousness, but because I thought it wasn't religious – I thought it was just a deep philosophy of life. This non-religious Buddhism fitted me comfortably – it provided a toothless, soothing notion of wellbeing whilst in reality my life was grinding to a halt.

Pureland Buddhism taught me the meaning of seeking refuge: there is nowhere else to go but the Dharma. Later I learnt about Sange (contrition) or Metanoia, as Tanabe called it. Tanabe himself, a Dean of the Kyoto school of Buddhism, was inspired by Shinran (the founder of the Shin school of Pureland Buddhism) as well as the works of Pascal and other Western philosophers and mystics. Sange/Metanoia is the fundamental change of heart that comes through repentance.

I found myself inspired by Tanabe's thinking. His theory helped me to understand the dual path of Sange and Liberation of Amida Buddhism. The path of Metanoia is a path of action, faith and witness: learning to act in good faith, and to bear witness to the faith one rests in. This witnessing happens not only in one's inner religious life (witnessing one's own settled faith), but also naturally in one's daily life with others.

My art/craft is an attempt to witness or to express some powerful insights that I have experienced on the path of Nien Fo, Sange and Metanoia. The cover image is taken from a triptych which is an example of this approach.

This triptych represents the three minds concept of the Pureland tradition.

Just as one can say the trinity of Faith, Hope and Love is one of the core concepts in Christianity, the theory of the three minds is one of the core doctrines of Pureland Buddhism.

The three minds are the sincere mind, the deep mind, and the mind that transfers merit to others, or as I call them, the sincere soul, the deep soul and the soul that transfers merit to all others, or to Amida. Shinran calls this last mind 'the serene mind'.

The triptych shows this core doctrine, and shows how this doctrine describes the way of devotion, Sange and Metanoia. I gave myself some artistic license in this, so do not look for doctrinal purity in how I talk about and paint these ideas.

Soul is the radio-telescope or the receiving station for Divine Love. A pure soul is empty in the sense that it can appreciate the ethereal beauty of a soap bubble dancing on a breeze, a pure soul can appreciate its vulnerability and its playfulness, instead of getting caught up in the self-world. This experience of emptiness contrasts with the dense red colours I used for my triptych. The soul, a feather on God's breath, stands in opposition to the density of one's samsaric life of dukkha (a life of suffering).

To me, sincere faith is faith and hope. It is a world of training and (self) discipline. It is the hope that walking the eightfold path and leading a preceptual life would bring me peace. In this place of hope I see a door, a golden gate, the promise of an entrance to the Civitatis Dei (the Kingdom of Heaven) and to Sukhavati (the Pureland). From this place of hope I am inspired and empowered to endure the hardships of training, because it is all for a good cause.

Sincere faith is the faith of my past, the faith in the path of purification, of meditation and following the precepts. It leads step by step up a mountain until I am standing alone, looking into my dark soul. Here I am at the door to deep faith.

This road of purification helped with some aspects of my spiritual training, but at the end of the path I was presented with my fundamental failure. I could not practice the eightfold path deeply enough, or keep the precepts well enough.

Deep faith is the faith of my present.

In the first part of this deep faith I am completely confronted with my own failure and deeply ashamed about my failure to live a noble or preceptual life.

My deep faith then has to be strong enough for the confrontation with my feelings of "ought" that come with my experience of sincere faith.

This deep faith is not my own faith; it is the faith that is given to me, streaming from a source that is totally and absolutely outside my power to comprehend.

I was overwhelmed when I heard my teacher, Dharmavidya, say, "We are broken people, but the light of Amida shines through the cracks."

That is precisely what I tried to express in the middle of the triptych, the section that forms the cover to this book.

My experience of deep faith is deepened by the path of Sange, looking into my own heart with the courage that is given to me by the mercy of Amida, by the continuous support of the sangha and, above all, by Shakyamuni's own example.

Held by deep faith I can become a witness, or a bearer of evidence, for the work of Other Power.

If the soul is the receiving station of Divine Love, with deep faith I am sometimes able to see very deeply into this love. My mind is quiet and I am overcome by an unbearable gratitude for living. I cannot do anything else but declare myself a tool for Amida.

In this moment I want to transfer merit to all others, and this is the last type of faith. The faith of my future.

I call it serene because in this faith it is possible for me to lay down my self-defences and illusory judges. Deep down there is an enduring and unmistakeable feeling of peace.

This feeling is disrupted over and over again by daily compulsions and habits, the same habits I sought to overcome by walking this path. But with serene faith I can look at these habits with merciful irony and with a smile... Until I am overtaken by them again. Then I confess that I have failed, but I know that Amida, my sangha, my family and my friends love me anyway.

Serene faith is the faith that associates with (Divine) Love. It is the faith of the future, Maitreya Buddha coming towards us.

This path of faith is also the challenge, and the honour, that my Buddhist name (Maitrisimha) offers me: to be a loving lion. A lion that tries to be a witness to the wonderful working of the Dharma, and to the vow of Amida Buddha. A lion that tries to be a witness to love, the love of Maitreya, the universal love that helps us to live, to enjoy life, to live as if performing a dance of gratitude whilst singing a lament for the suffering of all beings.

The natural expression of love is compassion, and it is in this spirit that I offer my art to the world.

Namo Amida Bu.

Maitrisimha Kouwenhoven

April 2013

About David Brazier

David Brazier, whose Buddhist name 'Dharmavidya' means "clear perception of what is fundamental", is a travelling Buddhist teacher, authority on Buddhist psychology, President of the Instituto Terapia Zen Internacional, Head of the Order of Amida Buddha, Spiritual Guide of the Eleusis Centre, Patron of the Tathagata Trust, scholar, doctor of philosophy (PhD), Buddhist priest, author of eight previous books, psychotherapist, social worker, published poet ("Her Mother's Eyes & Other Poems"), inventor of pandramatics, the other centred approach and Zen Therapy, founder of spiritual communities, international traveller, inspirational lecturer and philanthropist. He was fortunate to encounter leading Buddhist teachers at the beginning of his adult life and their teachings spoke to his condition. He travels widely and has been the creator of aid, education and social work projects in Europe, India and elsewhere and of training programmes in Buddhist psychology, Zen Therapy and Buddhist ministry. His books include works on psychotherapy and on Buddhism and commentary on the relationship between spirituality, art, myth and culture. He has three adult children, five grandchildren, likes gardening, walking and photography and lives in Belgium.

It is
Not about —
  gaining / getting
but <u>letting go</u> of that
  which no longer serve:

- Critisism
- Control / Force
- Judgement
- Own agenda
- Insecurity
- Doubt
- Self hate / judgement
- Defensiveness

Be:
sensitive
considerate
listen
curious

what is happening?

Have

faith in your own
goodness /soul — love
and grace is enough

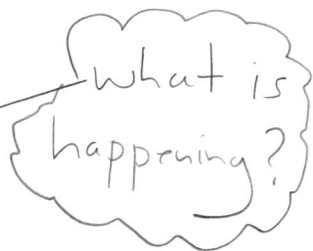

Natalie Goldberg
Writing down the bones

—

David Schneider
Street Zen

⌐

david_schneider@
shambhala-europe.org

—

The cloud of unknowing

Lightning Source UK Ltd.
Milton Keynes UK
UKOW051213280413

209890UK00006B/113/P